Feminism and 'The Schooling Scandal'

NUT Info. Unit / Library

00007638

N.U.T.

371.
822
SKE

LIBRARY & INFO. UNIT

WITHDRAWN

This tremendous book offers a definitive overview of the development of feminist thinking in and on education in Britain from the 1970s right up to the present day. It is therefore of major importance both to those new to gender and education and to those like myself who have lived through the ups and downs of the period. For the newcomer it offers an accessible, insightful, finely-tuned and information-rich analysis of the development of feminist ideas about education and the context in which they emerged. It is thus an important corrective to the often crude and shallow claims of policy-makers, media commentators and 'specialist consultants'. In particular, it offers an impressive and comprehensive grounding and analysis of key areas of gender and education such as the overt and 'hidden' curriculum, the inter-relationship of social class, ethnicity and gender, sexuality and sexual harassment, teaching and learning, and the 'boy' as well as the 'girl' problem.

The authors, Christine Skelton and Becky Francis, are acutely sensitive in their careful historical analysis of the differences and continuities between second-wave feminist ideas emerging in the 1970s and 1980s and third-wave feminist ideas of the 1990s onwards; and, at the same time, the book is bang up-to-date, presenting and commenting on research just published. For older generations of educational professionals who were active in second-wave feminism and its attempt to 'de-gender' education, the book offers a marvellous opportunity to recollect, reanalyse and reconceptualise; and to recognise and appreciate what third wave feminism has to offer us, and to education as a whole.

Professor Gaby Weiner
University of Edinburgh

Feminism and 'The Schooling Scandal' brings together feminist contributions of two generations of educational researchers, evaluating and celebrating the field of gender and education. A retrospective on the key concepts emerging from second-wave feminist research in education, this book provides an analysis of the ways in which these concepts have been developed and reworked in the contemporary field, seeking to answer the question: 'To what extent have experiences and opportunities in schools changed in the period since second-wave feminism began in the UK?'

D0162106

The focus throughout is on the years of compulsory schooling, examining key concepts in gender and education identified and developed by international thinkers in educational feminism. Topics covered include:

- Social class, ethnicity and sexuality in relation to experiences in school
- Theories and methodologies for understanding gender
- Pedagogy and practice in education
- The direction of educational policy and the 'problem of boys'.

Providing a comprehensive overview of contemporary research and theory emerging out of second-wave feminism and assessing their impact on pupils and teachers in today's schools and classrooms, this book is essential reading for anyone studying gender and education.

Christine Skelton is Professor of Gender Equality in Education, University of Birmingham.

Becky Francis is Professor of Education, Roehampton University.

Feminism and 'The Schooling Scandal'

Christine Skelton and Becky Francis

LONDON AND NEW YORK

First published 2009
by Routledge
2 Park Square, Milton Park, Abingdon, Oxon, OX14 4RN

Simultaneously published in the USA and Canada
by Routledge
270 Madison Ave, New York, NY 10016

*Routledge is an imprint of the Taylor & Francis Group,
an informa business*

© 2009 Christine Skelton and Becky Francis

Typeset in Times New Roman by Keyword Group Ltd
Printed and bound in Great Britain by CPI Antony Rowe,
Chippenham, Wiltshire

All rights reserved. No part of this book may be reprinted or reproduced or
utilised in any form or by any electronic, mechanical, or other means, now
known or hereafter invented, including photocopying and recording, or in
any information storage or retrieval system, without permission in writing
from the publishers.

British Library Cataloguing in Publication Data
A catalogue record for this book is available from the British Library

Library of Congress Cataloging in Publication Data
Skelton, Christine.
Feminism and the schooling scandal/Christine Skelton and Becky Francis.
  p. cm.
  1. Feminism and education—Great Britain. 2. Sexism in education—
Great Britain. 3. Women—Education—Great Britain. I. Francis,
Becky. II. Title.
LC197.S54 2009
370.82—dc22   2008028828

ISBN 10: 0-415-45509-X (hbk)
ISBN 10: 0-415-45510-3 (pbk)
ISBN 10: 0-203-88433-7 (ebk)

ISBN 13: 978-0-415-45509-1 (hbk)
ISBN 13: 978-0-415-45510-7 (pbk)
ISBN 13: 978-0-203-88433-1 (ebk)

Contents

Tables

Acknowledgements

We would like to thank Uvanney Maylor for her comments on Chapter 4, and Carole Leathwood for her feedback on Chapter 5. Becky and Christine would like to thank their friends and family (for Becky especially Dan, Ben and Louis) for keeping them sane.

1   Introduction

Those of you familiar with the first flurry of books on girls' education that came out of the women's movement of the 1970s might recognise the phrase *'the Schooling Scandal'*. It was the sub-title used by Dale Spender for her 1982 book *Invisible Women* in which she argued that it was men's knowledge and understandings of the world that were taught in schools and it was male interests that dominated the curriculum and the classroom. Spender's book was one of many that caught the consciousness of myriad, mainly women, teachers and academics, working in schools and universities at that time. A glance at our own bookshelves offers up an array of contributions on girls and schooling that began to appear in the 1970s. Feminists across the western world started to raise the issues that formed the 'gender agenda' for the coming years; in Britain, the majority of these followed the passing of the Sex Discrimination Act in 1975.[1] Of course, feminist concerns with education were not unique to the UK and some of the earliest writings on girls' schooling came from the USA[2] (see, for example, *Sexism and Schooling and Society* by Frazier and Sadker, 1973; *And Jill Came Tumbling After: Sexism in Education* by Stacey, Bereaud and Daniels, 1974).

Several decades have passed and several hundred books on gender and education have been written since the publication of these early texts. Although some of these UK academics have put together retrospectives of their work (see Arnot, 2000; David, 2003) there is no one book that brings together the ideas generated by these key feminist thinkers in education and follows them through to the present day. Furthermore, this book provides an opportunity to recognise and pay tribute to the work of those UK educational feminists who have contributed so much to our knowledge and understanding of gender and education and who are now reaching retirement age.

Our aim in writing this book is to provide an overview for those new to gender and education of the developments in feminist thinking on, and approaches to, gender and schooling in the context of the UK educational system. We have chosen to focus predominantly on the research studies undertaken and written from a UK perspective for two reasons. First, the intention is to track the debates in the specific context of the UK; and second, as we have said, the book is to recognise specifically UK feminists from 1978 to date. In so doing we have had to skim over the contributions of the many feminists located in other countries who have added substantially to our knowledge and understanding. A further point relates to our attention to the compulsory educational sector. This focus reflects the initial interests of second-wave feminists from which the themes of this book derive; as well as our own recognition that it is impossible to cover everything in a single book. We realise that this means we are not attending to the substantial bodies of feminist work that have emerged in early years, Further and Higher Education, Special Needs education, and other extra-compulsory aspects of education. It also needs to be said here that, even within our sector of focus, we recognise that we cannot address *all* the work that has been done, for example on particular curriculum areas; and in any book like this in which one aim is to 'celebrate' feminist work, there is always the risk that we have missed many important contributions. We do not mean to exclude, and hope that, rather, any feminist researcher readers will take the book for its aims (to provide an overview), and excuse any omissions!

We decided to include the phrase 'the Schooling Scandal' in the book title for a particular reason. It has been thirty years since Spender and her colleagues showed that the 'scandal' of schooling lay in the ways girls were treated as though they were of less consequence than boys. For example, curriculum text books centred around boys' interests (e.g. history books focused on political and military events); school and classroom organisation emphasised difference and status (e.g. registers separating boys' names and girls' names with boys coming first, separate playgrounds for 'girls and infants' and 'boys' football games'); teachers' perceptions of boys as more active and able learners than girls with the consequence they received more time and attention than girls and their work assessed more positively than girls. Doubtless, in the intervening decades there have been changes in teaching practice, social expectation and legislation regarding gender and schooling. Yet, the reason for retaining the phrase 'the Schooling Scandal' is to highlight how two of the central concerns of early second-wave feminists are as prevalent (and relevant) in the present day as they were over thirty years ago, namely: 'achievement' and 'gendered experiences in schools'.

In the literature on gender and schooling in the late 1970s and early 1980s, the discussions focused on the take-up and underachievement of girls in maths and sciences in comparison to the successes of boys in these areas (Fennema and Sherman, 1977; Harding, 1980). However, feminists researching education also commented on how boys were underachieving in literacy. For example:

> Boys and girls might learn to read and write together, but it is clear that they pick up very different messages about reading. Girls seem likely to bring more suitable experience to the printed page than boys do … We're not offering the same opportunities to the boys – they are missing out!
>
> (Lee, 1980: 126)

> Boys, far more often than girls, are referred for 'learning disabilities' typically involving problems in reading and/or writing.
>
> (Serbin, 1983: 24)

Understandings about the 'school pupil' in research and literature on education and schooling had largely been based on boys and their experiences (see for example, the discussions on 'pupil' pro- and anti-school subcultures based on Hargreaves [1967] and Lacey [1970] research on two boys' schools [Meighan, 1981]). In order to redress this imbalance and lack of representation of female experiences, second-wave feminists focused their attention on the particular issues for girls, and the gendered implications of boys' underachievement in literacy were not, at this time, pursued. At the same time, whilst girls' underachievement in the maths/sciences areas of the curriculum were thoroughly researched and some interventions introduced into schools to tackle this problem (see Chapter 6), it remains the case today that girls continue to avoid these subjects, thus limiting future career opportunities. Of course, what the intervening years of research into gender has shown is that it is far too simplistic to compare 'boys' with 'girls' as if all boys and all girls liked the same subjects, achieved or underachieved in the same ways. To gain a more accurate understanding of gender differences requires that we consider how a range of factors impact upon pupils' experiences and educational opportunities, including such variables as ethnicity, social class and sexuality.

In this book we trace the debates and discussions from 'The Schooling Scandal' of the 1970s to 'The Schooling Scandal' of today. Indeed, the present day 'schooling scandals' (the ways in which girls' experiences of schooling have changed little over the past decades, the gendered underachievement of boys in literacy, and the underpinning of gender inequities by social class and ethnicity) are attributable to the same two themes identified by early second-wave feminists: achievement and experience. What has changed is the broader social and economic context. The neoliberal market which placed schools in competition with each other magnified the focus on 'achievement' whilst simultaneously playing down the effects of 'experience' on the construction of learning identities.

As we have observed, the discussion in the book will be concentrated mainly on the situation in the UK – however, where appropriate, reference will be made to the debates as they emerged in the USA, Canada, Australia and Europe. The main themes emerging from the early texts that have continued through to the current day are: sex roles and schooling (gender identities in today's idiom), social class, 'race', sexual harassment and sexualities, curriculum and subject choice, the education and schooling of boys and teacher gender. Where we draw out statistics to illustrate our discussion of achievement, we use Key Stage 2 data (the exams in England at the end of primary schooling, age 10–11). This is the mid-point of compulsory education, marking the transition between primary and secondary schooling.

Before starting out on our exploration of those issues, which have shaped the debates about gender, schooling and education from 1978 to the present day, we spend some time on the findings of feminist historians of education such as June Purvis, Anna Davin and Carol Dyhouse, whose analysis of the social, cultural and political agendas around girls' and women's experiences in schooling provides a backcloth for what follows in this book. In particular, the work of feminist historians showed how significant social class was (and is) in shaping the opportunities and experiences of girls and women.

Girls' and boys' education: an historical context

In England the Education Act 1870 (known as The Forster Act) introduced the system of mass state schooling for girls and boys aged between the ages of 5 and 10.[3] However, it was not until 1880 that schooling became compulsory and it was only in 1891 that it became free (Purvis, 1995). Some form of schooling was available prior to state education. In England there were a range of offerings from the prestigious public schools for upper-class boys through to, for example, Dame Schools, Ragged Schools and Factory Schools.

Many parents could not afford the ninepence per week fee charged by some school boards between 1870, when state schooling was introduced, and 1891 when it became free. As a result, the education that working-class girls and boys received tended to be rather haphazard. When working-class parents did have the money it was more likely that it would be spent on educating their sons rather than their daughters. And, middle- and upper-class parents either employed tutors or sent their sons to public schools.

Feminist historians have commented on how the very question of whether girls should be educated at all was highly contentious. Victorian society in the mid- to late-nineteenth century was evidently and obviously gendered and classed, and there were distinct differences in expectations of males and females with women occupying a clearly subordinate role in relation to men. Pauline Marks (1976) and Dale Spender (1987), in researching the history of girls' schooling, have shown that education was regarded as physiologically undesirable as it might interfere with the female reproductive system. There is some evidence to suggest that this concern was not solely because of fears that education might 'weaken' the physical constitution of girls (Measor and Sikes, 1992) but also because it might encourage more middle-class women to become 'bluestockings'; intellectual women who, on principle, rejected marriage and motherhood (Jackson, 1989; Purvis, 1991). However, girls were included in the move towards mass state schooling, but as the system was heavily inscribed by patriarchal relations then both middle- and working-class girls were to be educated for their future domestic roles (Davin, 1978; Delamont and Duffin, 1978; Dyhouse, 1981; Purvis, 1991).

The different forms of domestic curriculum received by middle- and working-class girls were in accordance with dominant versions of 'respectable' ladies and women. As June Purvis (1987) has said:

> What was considered appropriate, relevant and attainable for middle-class women was inappropriate, irrelevant and unattainable for working-class women. (p. 255)

The cultural ideal of the working-class female was conceptualised in the 'good woman', whilst for the middle-classes the model was the 'ladylike homemaker'

(Purvis, 1991). The 'good woman' was one who demonstrated her practical abilities and skills as housekeeper, wife and mother. In contrast, the 'ladylike homemaker' was achieved by middle-class women using their organisational skills to provide a stable, 'tastefully elegant', supportive, domestic environment. The forms of curriculum offered by the schools catering for the different social classes were then in accordance with these 'ideals'.

Elementary schools taught working-class girls domestic skills which they could employ in the home and with their families. In the early 1870s, girls would spend as much as one-fifth of their time in school doing needlework (Sharpe, 1994). What subjects were to be taught was largely a matter of what grants the Education Department gave out; for example, domestic economy was made a compulsory subject for girls in 1878, followed by cookery in 1882 and laundry work in 1890. The emphasis placed on domestic subjects has been explained by considering wider societal and economic factors. First, a constant supply of army recruits was needed for Britain to maintain its empire but the poor health of many working-class males made them ineligible. This was seen to be the result of inadequate knowledge of nutrition and hygiene amongst working-class women (Davin, 1978; Turnbull, 1980), and schools were given responsibility for addressing this problem. Second, training working-class girls in domestic subjects would equip them with the skills needed to enter domestic service (Dyhouse, 1981; Purvis, 1995). A third explanation has been put forward by Lisa Picard (2006) who says that philanthropists, such as Angela Burdett-Coutts, were so dismayed by the children who arrived at the Ragged Schools wearing, literally, rags, they insisted that the education these children needed was, first and foremost, those skills that would enable them to survive. This included the ability to make clothes and keep themselves fed; given the gendered expectations of the time these domestic skills were taught to the girls.

For middle-class girls the situation was different. To begin with, between 1870 and 1914, girls of the more prosperous middle-classes were still educated mainly at home by governesses and their family, although in the early part of the twentieth century there was an increasing number attending the prestigious private schools such as Roedean. For a majority of middle-class girls, schooling, if it did take place, occurred mainly in the private sector and in secondary rather than primary schools (Purvis, 1991). The curriculum offered by the private schools to middle-class girls varied according to whether the headteacher could be classified as a 'separatist' or an 'uncompromiser' (Delamont, 1978). 'Separatists', such as Dorothea Beale of Cheltenham Ladies College, wanted better standards of education for girls but this did not mean they were expected to study the same subjects as boys. The curriculum would, then, include subjects like deportment, drawing and callisthenics (Cobbe, 1894). The curriculum offered by 'uncompromisers', such as Frances Buss of North London Collegiate School, was similar to that of equivalent boys' public schools but, nevertheless, still 'aimed to prove that educated women and girls could still be feminine by insisting on respectable womanly dress, deportment and behaviour' (Measor and Sikes, 1992: 39). Unlike elementary schools, the curriculum offered by these private girls' schools was not subject to any official government educational policy.

The evidence of domesticity so prevalent in the curriculum for working-class elementary schoolgirls did influence the curriculum of the girls' high schools but in a rather different form. Rather than emphasising the practical skills of housekeeping the stress was on the 'scientific principles' underlying domestic management. In 1900, Sara Burstall, the head of Manchester High School, introduced a housewifery course. The content actually covered a much wider range of subjects than those offered to working-class girls; that is, it included English, history, French, specialised household arithmetic, science, cookery, laundry work, hygiene, household management and needlework (Burstall, 1933). The place of science in the curriculum is worth noting here. In her book *The Science Education of American Girls*, Tolley (2003) comments on how, in the US, in the early part of the nineteenth century, science was taught *only* to girls in the form of astronomy, natural philosophy (physics), chemistry and botany. At this time, the prestigious curriculum subjects were the Classics and these were regarded as the preserve of boys. Such information sheds light on how subjects are culturally constructed, and is something discussed in more detail in Chapter 6.

The granting of the vote to women of 30 and above in 1918 and developments in technology leading to an increased demand for typists, telephonists and clerical labour, forced changes to the curriculum of schools (Weiner, 1994). However, whilst the Elementary School Code of 1904 did recommend that the curriculum be widened to include a broader range of subjects, a Board of Education Report in 1923 criticised schools of both sexes for offering too academic a curriculum to their (working-class) pupils. At the same time, this report retained the notion of an education based on 'natural' differences:

> ... equality does not demand identity but is compatible with, and even depends upon, a system of differentiation which either sex seeks to multiply at a rich interest its own peculiar talents.
>
> (Board of Education Report, 1923, reported in Weiner, 1994: 36)

This idea of 'appropriate' and different forms of schooling for boys and girls was one which continued throughout the early part of the twentieth century, even where there was an emphasis in educational policy on the concept of 'equality'. An example of this can be found in the Butler Education Act of 1944, which was intended to redress inequalities experienced by working-class children by directing them towards different types of school, specifically grammar, technical and secondary modern schools. The decision as to which school a child attended was based on their measured intelligence, that is how they performed in the 11-plus examination (David, 1993). Although the tri-partite system of grammar, technical and secondary modern schools was not intended as socially divisive, inevitably it was the academic grammar schools which were seen as having higher status and it was places for girls in the grammar schools that were at a premium. As Rosemary Deem (1981) noted, this was achieved through various sleights of hand, e.g. having fewer grammar school places for girls than for boys and then weighting the results differently. Goldstein (1986: 3) explains:

> What was happening was that, because girls obtained higher average scores than boys but then had their scores adjusted downwards to equalise the sex distributions, some girls were being refused admission to grammar school despite having higher raw sores than some boys who had been selected. The reason for this differential treatment was the assumption that, although boys were 'manifesting less potential at the time, they actually have more potential for the future than do girls'
>
> (cited in Gipps and Murphy, 1994: 8)

Dean (1995) has also pointed to the way in which education from the 1940s was shaped by the need to ensure that men who had served in the military services during the war could be re-employed and one means to achieve this was to encourage the view that both middle-class and working-class girls' futures lay in domesticity:

> At the close of the war the major concern was that a rapidly demobilizing military machine, predominantly male, should find employment in peacetime Britain ... The immediate task was to lure women back from the workplace to the home. What seemed to be required was a mixture of persuasion, education, rewards and warnings. (p. 19)

A consideration of the wording of the Education Act 1944 and subsequent education reports demonstrates that Dean's argument is not unsubstantiated. For example, one section of the act calls for schools to:

> ... afford for all pupils opportunities for education offering such variety of instruction and training as may be desirable in view of their *different* ages, *abilities* and *aptitudes* (para. 8[b], our emphasis)

One possible interpretation of pupils' 'different abilities and aptitudes' is that boys and girls should continue to follow different curriculum subjects, with the former receiving instruction in those subjects which would possibly lead on to higher education and a professional career or, at least, as a member of the mass labour force, whilst the latter undertook subjects suitable for homemaking. Also, Wolpe's (1977) analysis of two other major post-war reports (Crowther Report 1959; Newsom Report 1963) demonstrates that, although intended to be reformist, they were inscribed with ideological assumptions which perpetuated proscribed futures for young women (and men) that were classed as well as gendered. For example, young middle-class women were presumed to have a 'dual career', part of that 'dual career' meaning their job as wives and mothers in the home!

As can be seen from the dates, the Crowther and Newsom reports were amongst the last ones to appear in the UK prior to the advent of second-wave feminism. Wolpe's analysis of these documents brought the historical picture up to the point at which feminists were able to challenge policy and practice as it was being enacted. The work of feminist historians in identifying the numerous ways in which education and schooling had always been deeply gendered both for pupils and teachers has, and continues to provide, fundamental insights into how women have been able to challenge political agendas on schooling (Martin, 1999; Martin and Goodman, 2004).

To sum up, what we have found in tracing the debates and discussions from their inception to the present day is partly how deep seated and resilient (if not resistant!) traditional notions of gender are in educational policy and practice. Of course, we are aware that there is a 'commonsense' idea amongst the general population that 'feminism has had its day' and that it is no longer of relevance to today's young women (Volman and TenDam, 1998; McRobbie, 2004). This can be seen in a poll for the charity 'Womankind', carried out in 2006, which found that 71 per cent of women did not consider themselves to be feminist (although one may wonder what proportion of women have ever actively positioned themselves as feminist). Christina Scharff's (2007) review of the literature lists the various reasons why feminism appears irrelevant or distasteful to many young women, including the idea that it is all about White, middle-class and middle-aged, heterosexual women's worries and concerns; that equality has been achieved and there is nothing else to argue for; and feminism is presented by the media as something unattractive, appealing only to angry, repellent women. However, as we show in this book, it is the socio-economic climate that has had a dramatic impact on the perceived relevance (or irrelevance) of feminism. In a neoliberal policy environment where individuals of both genders are expected to sell their labour in a global market place, and are positioned as responsible for their own success or failure therein, liberal feminist concerns of opening up the market to women may be read as having largely been addressed.[4] More radical feminist agendas, opposed to the neoliberal status quo, tend to go unrecognised in the mass media and policy circles. These tensions will be unpacked further in later sections of the book.

The book comprises eight chapters. This first chapter has provided a context for the themes that were to emerge through second-wave feminist agendas on education. These themes form the basis of the following seven chapters.

Chapter 2, *Sex Roles and Schooling*, is concerned with theories and perspectives which have informed how we consider gender and education since second-wave feminism emerged. Historically, the debates were around 'nature' versus 'nurture' and feminists such as Ann Oakley (UK) and Barbara Licht and Carol Dweck (US feminist psychologists) succeeded in driving forward the ideas of gender as socially constructed, whilst 'sex roles' were located in physiology and embodiment. Following this line of argument through to today we reach the postmodern stance adopted by third-wave feminists whereby embodiment is itself seen as socially constructed (Butler, 1990, 1997; Halberstam, 1998). Thus, ideas around gender as relational, diversity, and identities are discussed.

The third chapter explores *Social Class in Schooling*. The different experiences of middle- and working-class girls in school have informed second-wave feminist research from the beginning. The chapter draws on qualitative research on girls, social class and education and also presents current statistics on achievement to demonstrate how socio-economic status influences opportunities.

Chapter 4 on *Ethnicity, Gender and Education* shows how the work of Black feminists drew attention to a number of 'commonsense' (pathologising) presumptions about the experiences and potential of different cultural groups. Furthermore, Black girls' achievements were subsumed by concerns over Black boys' underachievement; and, indeed, continue to be under-represented in debates on children's educational experiences. In a similar style to that of Chapter 3, both qualitative and quantitative research are used to detail the ways in which feminist educationalists have presented, critiqued and analysed this field of enquiry.

In Chapter 5 on *Sexualities and Sexual Harassment in Schools*, we examine the major themes in relation to issues of sexuality in education: sexual harassment, sex education, sexual cultures and subjectivities. Here we show how the more recent theorising in the research and literature on sexuality, gender and education are brought together and intersect.

Chapter 6, *Curriculum, Knowledge and Schooling* begins by considering feminist research and writing on two 'types' of school curriculum: that relating to the official curriculum subjects – their content, the resources used to deliver them, whether they are 'masculine' or 'feminine' subjects and subject choice. Then there is what was termed in early second-wave feminist work as the 'hidden' curriculum. This referred to the structure and organisation of school processes and practices, e.g. patterns of interaction, the way children were treated and classroom management strategies Since the initial forays into examining links between gender and curriculum, feminists and pro-feminists have moved on to provide insights into how girls and boys locate themselves in relation to specific subjects as a means of constructing their identities, e.g. being good at and enjoying English is discursively constructed as 'doing femininity'. Here we also discuss how recent research has shown the same situation pertains to teachers' engagement with pupils whereby their expectations of pupils' abilities, motivations and interests for a subject are related to their own knowledge and understanding of, and training in, that subject.

The focus in Chapter 7 is on *Schools and Boys* which, strictly speaking, was not an evident key theme for early second-wave feminists. The decision to include such a chapter was made on the basis that it is the challenging of the taken-for-grantedness of male knowledge, power and experiences that has been a main aim of feminism. In education, feminists have shown how boys' and girls' experiences of schooling and education differ. Furthermore, the more recent government and media attention on boys – particularly in relation to achievement – has prompted a substantial feminist response which requires consideration.

The final and concluding Chapter 8 is *Gender and Teaching*. There has been substantial feminist research and writing on women and teaching, not least because a career as a teacher, either in mainstream or higher education, was the starting point for a majority of key feminist educational thinkers in the UK. As such, trying to cover the all the issues that had been discussed and debated over the years would be unfeasible. Instead, the chapter concentrates on the two themes which are pursued through the book: achievement, and gender experiences. In so doing, the themes to be discussed are: the gendered nature of teachers and teaching; and the implications of new managerialism for gender and teachers' careers.

2 Sex roles and schooling

For some students it comes as a surprise to find that the course on gender and education they signed up for is based on feminism and feminist theorising. This may be because it is common for newspapers, the media and government agencies to talk about 'boys and girls' and the differences in their behaviours or academic abilities but rarer to find discussions of these differences based on anything more than physiological or 'natural' differences. As we show in Chapter 7, much of the current concern about boys' underachievement is based on the idea that boys' physiology explains the differences in their abilities and performance at school. Another example would be how many of the statistics analysing academic achievement distinguish between 'boys' and 'girls' as taken for granted categories. What feminism offers is more nuanced understandings of gender and a political account of apparent inequalities therein. The aim of this chapter is to set the scene for the discussion and analysis in the rest of the book. We focus here on those theories and perspectives which have informed how feminism has contributed to how we consider gender and education. Historically, the debates were around 'nature' versus 'nurture' and feminists such as Ann Oakley (UK) and Barbara Licht and Carol Dweck (US feminist psychologists) succeeded in driving forward the ideas of gender as socially constructed whilst 'sex roles' were located in physiology. Following this line of argument through to today we reach the postmodern stance adopted by third-wave feminists[1] whereby 'sex' is itself seen as socially constructed (Butler, 1990, 1997; Halberstam, 1998). Thus ideas around gender as relational, diversity and identities will be discussed. We start by looking at the debates at the beginning of second-wave feminism.

Second-wave feminism and gender and education

In the year 1978 when Eileen Byrne's *Women and Education* and Rosemary Deem's *Women and Schooling* were published, one of us began an Open University degree. 'The division of labour by gender', written by Ann Oakley (1981a), was one of the course units we studied and the accompanying booklet included a seven page section on 'Formal Education'. To say this short introduction on gender inequalities in education and schooling was an 'eye opener' would be an underestimation of the impact it had. As a primary school teacher, with no prior awareness of 'gender issues', it was astonishing and salutary to read of how we (teachers) were actively contributing to divisive and inegalitarian practices in the classroom. These ranged from using curriculum books and resources which placed emphasis on male experiences, adopting management styles to both motivate and control boys, and organisational practices that marginalised girls and privileged boys (see Chapters 6 and 7 for details of these). What was of particular interest in this Open University unit on gender was the explanations for the existence of these gender differences. The main question asked was that frequently echoed today in relation to boys' underachievement; that is, does the answer lie in 'biological' or 'sociological' explanations?

Early second-wave feminists put forward strong arguments supporting sociological explanations. A body of work on the relationship between sex attribution and gender expectations, led by researchers such as Kessler and McKenna (1978) and Lake (1975), showed how people behaved very differently with infants depending on what they perceived the baby's sex to be. For example, in one frequently repeated study mothers were handed the same baby at different times but told 'this is Adam' or 'this is Beth'. When the mothers believed they were dealing with a girl they were far more likely to call them 'sweet', to handle them and smile at them more (Lake, 1975; Smith and Lloyd, 1978; Whyte, 1983). Others pointed to anthropological studies showing that other cultures organise gender differently. For example, the women in Carol Hoffer's (1974: 173) study of the Mende area of Sierra Leone were not seen as vulnerable or economically unproductive because they bore children but rather as 'strong and active agents in a society, capable of holding political office'. The idea that gender was a cultural construction and not a biological one was further refined by feminists through discussions of different social groups. That is, the different expectations and attitudes towards gender which were informed by social class and ethnicity (see Chapters 3 and 4 for discussion).

Whilst setting out to illustrate that gender was a cultural construction and not a biological one a majority of feminists did not, as was later claimed by anti-feminists in the boys' underachievement debate (e.g. Moir and Moir, 1999), reject the place of biology in explanations of gender. Ann Oakley (1981b: 53) wrote about the 'relative importance of biology' but noted the interrelationship of how 'nurture affects nature' (p. 61). Licht and Dweck (1983: 84) observed in their discussion of sex differences in mathematics achievement that they did not 'wish to discount the possible contribution of biological factors'; and Measor and Sikes (1992: 7), reflecting back in their book on *Gender and Schools* observed, 'What is clear is that there is a continuous process of interaction between social and biological factors'. However, it was gender as a socio-cultural construction that was the preferred explanation for second-wave feminists in understanding gender differences in education (Stacey *et al.*, 1974; Byrne, 1978).

As might be gleaned from the above discussion, whilst feminists writing about education were united in their conceptualising of gender as a cultural rather than a biological construction, there were differences in how they theorised these cultural constructions. For many teachers who were studying courses on gender equality and education at the time (including one of the authors), trying to 'match up' the standpoints of those feminists writing the books with the various theoretical perspectives seemed worth a degree in itself! Of the feminist authors we were reading, some clearly aligned themselves to one perspective, others seemed to draw on various perspectives but few expressly articulated their position. Christine Skelton remembers after one afternoon in the library of a local polytechnic with a colleague on the same course, sitting down in despair to compare notes on 'What kind of feminist am I? A Liberal, Socialist, Marxist, Marxist-socialist or Radical feminist?' What follows is a brief retrospective, at the risk of some oversimplification, of where early second-wave feminist researchers of education located themselves theoretically (for a more thorough account of feminisms in education up to the early 1990s, see Weiner 1994).

Feminist perspectives in education – circa 1970s/1980s

Liberal Feminism, Radical Feminism, Marxist-socialist Feminism and, later, Black Feminism, were by the mid-1980s the key perspectives used by western feminists to explain gender inequalities in education (Acker, 1987; Arnot and Weiner, 1987).[2] What was important to teachers in schools was that the different perspectives were used to, not only argue what was the underpinning cause of gender inequalities, but from there to generate 'solutions' – the point being that the perceived cause indicated the direction that should be taken in resolving the problem.

These feminist perspectives can be considered 'global feminisms' in that what united them in relation to education was the idea that 'girls' as a global group (albeit Black girls in the case of Black Feminism; or girls of different social classes within Marxist Feminism) were bound together by their common experiences of marginalisation and oppression. Furthermore, these various feminist perspectives were united in the shared perception of feminism as a political and practical movement; and consequently all the feminist perspectives above subscribed to the notion that the goals were,

Political: a means of action, not simply theorising
Critical: not to accept that all knowledge is objective – because it was/is manufactured by those who were educated and had access to writing, reading, and publishing their ideas (i.e. White men from the middle and upper classes).
Praxis-oriented: to change the way we did things. Not least the way in which we researched problems and acknowledged the importance of subjectivity in that process.

This 'globalism' can be particularly applied to the notion of 'Patriarchy', adopted predominantly by Radical Feminism. Patriarchy (meaning literally 'rule by the father') formed one of the central tenets of second-wave feminism: it was seen as oppressing *all* women (irrespective of 'race' and class). Where feminists might accept, modify or reject this explanation according to their theoretical position (e.g. is Patriarchy, Capitalism, White Supremacy, or a combination of these primarily responsible for oppression?), questions around power and control were key issues for most feminists. In terms of education, this was particularly about 'institutional sexism' where the superiority and power of maleness was unquestionably assumed (see Chapters 6 and 7) as well as personal issues over male power and control (e.g. sexual harassment of girls and women teachers by boys; or, the staffing structures of schools whereby men teachers were disproportionately more likely to occupy senior management positions).

What then did each of the feminist perspectives see as the source of girls' oppression in schools? Ironically, but not surprisingly, the perspective that was the most influential in that it was taken up by the government in its guidance to schools (see, for example, the Equal Opportunities Commission publication *Do You Provide Equal Opportunities* [1984]), which did not refer to 'oppression' or in effect include any analysis of power inequalities. This was Liberal Feminism. For Liberal Feminism the onus was on the individual – in this case schoolgirls and women teachers – who needed to be enabled to cast off the shackles of sex role stereotyping; and on the law and social institutions which needed to be altered to facilitate girls' and women's right to equality. Liberal Feminism is probably the 'oldest' of the feminist theoretical perspectives, having been first prominently expressed in Mary Wollstonecraft's book the 'Vindication of the Rights of Women' written in 1792. Wollstonecraft argued that women have as much potential as men but are prevented from fulfilling it because they are reared to fit an image of weakness and femininity, and degraded by having always to please men. The aim of Liberal Feminism at the start of second-wave feminism was to secure equal opportunities for girls and women teachers – if education is thought of as a cake, then the demand was for equal shares of that cake. To achieve this position legislation needed to be put into place that removed barriers to girls' and women teachers' progress and school resources, management and organisational practices had to be scrutinised to ensure that both genders had the same *access* to the same educational experiences and opportunities. The major themes of Liberal Feminism were then a focus on socialisation and sex stereotyping; equal opportunities; and sex discrimination legislation (see later section discussion on socialisation/sex role stereotyping).

The key to understanding the main difference between early versions of Liberal Feminism that set it aside from Radical, Marxist-socialist and Black Feminisms was the way in which power differentials were largely unheeded. Liberal feminists did not seek to change the foundations or epistemological bases of current systems (be these the broader socio-economic arrangements, or the nature of the education system), but rather to allow girls and women equality of opportunity within these existing systems. The writing of feminists on girls' schooling could be seen to hinge upon three elements: *access to, treatment in and outcomes of* educational experiences. For Liberal Feminism, the emphasis on 'equal opportunities' meant that the concern was centred exclusively on girls' and women teachers' access to the same kind of education and educational careers as boys and men. Here 'equal opportunities' meant 'the same', even though, as feminists writing from other perspectives pointed out, having the same choices may produce unequal outcomes. For example, one of the strategies for encouraging more girls to take up the science subjects (and for boys to take up cookery/domestic science) was to ensure these curriculum topics did not clash on the timetable. Those girls and boys who did take the opportunity to take up non-traditional subjects frequently found themselves in the opposite gendered world where the resources, tasks, assignments all presumed a specific gendered pupil. For example, Groves and Mansfield's (1981) analysis of chemistry textbooks found few illustrations of women, and Walford's (1980: 225) examination of physics textbooks revealed how these included demeaning images of women, showing them looking 'amazed or frightened or simply women doing "silly" things'. Liberal Feminist approaches to education included interventions to aid girls' access and achievement at traditionally 'masculine' subjects (notable contributions include the Girls Into Science and Technology (GIST) project and Women Into Science and Engineering (see Chapter 6), as well as those aiming to eliminate discriminatory materials and attitudes that might impede girls.

At a later stage, those researching and writing from a Liberal Feminist perspective did take up issues of power in contributing to gender discrimination in schooling (see Myers, 2000), but certainly, in the 1970s and 1980s, other feminists critiqued the stance adopted by this 'weak' approach towards equity in education (Weiner, cited by Arnot, 1985). In wider debates amongst feminists, Marxist-socialist feminists argued that Liberal Feminism, because of its emphasis on establishing legal rights to equality, did not take into account how poverty prevented many girls and women from taking up opportunities (Eisenstein, 1984). Black Feminists argued that Liberal Feminism was a middle-class, white movement which was only relevant to an elite group of women and ignored the obstacles encountered by women from other ethnic groups (Lown, 1995). Radical Feminists made the point that Liberal Feminism positioned men as fellow victims of sex role conditioning and failed to recognise the power that men held over women in a partriarchal society (Whelehan, 1995). At the same time, Black Feminism, Radical Feminism and Marxist-socialist Feminism were not in total accord either.

Those UK feminists in gender and education whose early writing was clearly informed by Marxist-socialist perspectives included Madeleine Arnot, Miriam David, Rosemary Deem, Diane Leonard and Ann-Marie Wolpe (see Middleton, 1987 for full discussion). Marxist and Socialist feminist perspectives differed in the extent to which they accepted the principles of Marxism. Whilst Marxist feminists identified capitalism as the root cause of women's oppression, Socialist Feminists argued that it was a combination of capitalism and patriarchy (Hartmann, 1981). A fusion of these perspectives, Marxist-socialist, was used to illustrate how, through a variety of mechanisms, schooling reproduces class and gender divisions. It drew attention to the importance of social class in sustaining patterns of inequality. For example, working-class girls were argued to be particularly disadvantaged in schools as, not only do they experience the same forms of social class inequalities experienced by their male peers, but they also received messages about their subordination to men in general. Furthermore, schools delivered a range of messages about appropriate roles and activities to girls and, as such, they (schools) occupied a central place in the reproduction of the division of labour (Arnot, 1983; Deem, 1983). Marxist-socialist Feminist writings tended to focus mainly on theoretical arguments, historical research and policy analysis (but there were exceptions, see, for example, Anyon, 1983; Weis, 1989). In contrast, Radical Feminists favoured empirical studies of classrooms to illuminate the ways in which gender-power dynamics informed day-to-day practices.

Sara Delamont's (1980) *Sex Roles and the School,* Dale Spender's (1982) *Invisible Women* and Pat Mahony's (1985) *Schools For The Boys*, are just three of the books that illustrate the perspective of Radical Feminists writing on gender and education in the context of the UK. The two major concerns of Radical Feminist research into schooling was, first, the male monopolization of culture and knowledge (as reflected in the curriculum) and, second, the sexual politics of everyday life. The shared view of Radical Feminists was that, like society as a whole, the education system reflected and elevated male values, and systematically demeaned and marginalised girls and women. Hence schools reproduce male domination of women by not only denying girls and women full access to existing knowledge and resources, but failing to recognise female contributions to these. Furthermore, school organisational structures and procedures ignored (and hence were complicit in) the daily harassment of girls and women teachers by boys and men teachers. What this research by Radical Feminists demonstrated was how boys dominated teachers' time and attention, how they monopolised the classroom in terms of space and securing resources, how their interests dictated the curriculum, and how they sexually harassed girls. In short, Radical Feminists saw schools as a key institution working to perpetuate patriarchy. In common with Marxist-socialist Feminism and Black Feminism, Radical Feminism sought change through positive action whereby the focus was on girls' *treatment in* and *outcome of* education which differed from Liberal Feminism's concern with access to educational facilities. The positive action sought by Radical Feminists was to place girls and women at the centre of any initiatives which meant giving value and a place to their perspectives. For example, Liberal Feminism might argue for strategies which encouraged girls to take up science and technology subjects (which was the aim of the GIST project) whilst the more activist feminisms would want to implement girl-centred approaches such as identifying the contribution girls and women had made to science and technology, how and why this contribution had been ignored, and why women have traditionally been marginalised from the field (Weiner, 1985). One of the criticisms of Radical Feminism was that it did not consider the influence of social class or ethnicity in shaping girls' and women teachers' educational experiences, however, this is not strictly accurate (see, for example, the work of Spender and Sarah, 1980; Jones and Mahony, 1989; Mahony and Zmorczek, 1997, which

Table 2.1 Feminist perspectives and gender and education

	Liberal Feminism	*Radical Feminism*	*Marxist-socialist Feminism*	*Black Feminism*
Key beliefs in the cause of women's oppression	Legislative gender stereotyping and individual differences	Patriarchy	Capitalism	'Race'
Research data collected and analysed on the basis of:	stereotypical differences	male-female power inequalities	social class and gender power inequalities	'race' and gender power inequalities

included analysis of social class). What Radical Feminism did do was centralise gender and relations of power; and it is this emphasis given to gender-power dynamics in the classroom that identifies those writing from a Radical Feminist perspective.

There was further criticism of Liberal, Radical and Marxist-socialist Feminism by Black Feminists, who have argued that the majority of studies on gender and education have failed to address 'race' issues (Carby, 1982; Bryan, Dadzie and Scafe, 1985) (see Chapter 4 for more detailed discussion). For example, in response to the writing on the experiences of women teachers, Black Feminists pointed out that what was of particular concern to them was how they were seen as 'Black' first and a 'teacher' second (Blair and Maylor, 1993). Some teachers noted how they felt they were recruited solely because they were part of local and national drives to increase the quota of Black teachers (Bangar and McDermott, 1989) and expected to lead on initiatives that promoted 'multicultural education' or in combating racism. These strategies did little to address the real problems that Black women teachers were facing whereby they were marginalised in relation to teaching in that they were expected to smoothly operate 'within the confines of White social practices, norms and structures' (Siraj Blatchford, 1993: 32).

Whilst the various feminisms in education saw the reasons for girls' and women teachers' marginalisation and discrimination in schools as stemming from different sources, the explanations of how gender was constructed developed over a longer period of time. The predominant explanation represented in the 1970s and early 1980s was that of sex role and socialisation (Frazier and Sadker, 1973; Delamont, 1980). Whilst theoretical frameworks based on the ways in which power shaped social and psychic investments in gender were in evidence in the early 1980s (Walden and Walkerdine, 1985), these took longer to become established within the field of education.

Sex roles and socialisation

Sex role socialisation, the notion that girls and boys absorb social messages about their appropriate gender roles, had a pivotal place in educational equal opportunities strategies during the late 1970s and 1980s (Lobban, 1978; Delamont, 1980; Jacklin, 1983). Sex role theories were felt by many second-wave feminists to be helpful, because they showed the ways in which gender differences were socially developed rather than being due to innate biological differences (Sutherland, 1981; Serbin, 1983). This was very much a 'top down' model which assumed that children observed and soaked up social information like sponges, emulating the behaviour of adults in the family, media and local community. For females it meant learning and internalising such traits as caring, nurturing and selflessness, whilst males demonstrated characteristics such as aggression, independence and competitiveness (Oakley, 1972; Seidler, 1989). There was no allowance in sex role socialisation theory for anything 'other' than being stereotypically 'male' or 'female', nor was it considered that children were active contributors in the construction of their gender identities.

There were evident benefits for feminist educationalists in adopting the sex role/socialisation explanation of gender identity construction as it offered the possibility of change. The strategies based on sex role theory for changing children's stereotypical views underpinned the majority of 'equal opportunities' programmes in schools (Myers, 2000). If children learned their gender identities through role modelling then it was thought all that was needed was to present them with non-stereotypical models and images. Reading books were vetted to ensure they provided girls (and boys) with a range of adult models; the 'Wendy House' became the 'Home Corner', teachers checked their language to avoid stereotypical allusions to, for example, 'tidy girls' and 'tough boys', and classroom practices that retained boys versus girls forms of organisation were abandoned (Skelton, 1989; Measor and Sikes, 1992).

Although sex role/socialisation theories were believed to provide possibilities for change they also presented problems. The implication of sex role/socialisation perspectives was that a self-fulfilling prophesy was in operation – the processes of schooling undermined girls' confidence, which resulted in them having lower expectations and not prioritising exam success but seeing their futures primarily as wives and mothers. The nature of sex role theory, with its locus in the psyche, meant that initiatives were focused on the 'individual' and it was up to them to take the opportunities offered and develop less stereotyped behaviours and attitudes. Furthermore, that individual was always a girl (that is, the expectation was on girls to change rather than boys). As Madeleine Arnot (1991: 453) argued:

> Sex role socialisation, which held together a multitude of projects as diverse as changing school texts, and establishing gender fair teaching styles, non-traditional role models, unbiased careers' advice and girl-friendly schools was seen to have a lot to answer for. … The simplicity of its portrayal of the processes of learning and of gender identity formation, its assumptions about the nature of stereotyping, its somewhat negative view of girls as victims had all contributed to the creation of particular school-based strategies. These strategies, although designed to widen girls' and boys' horizons, and give

them more opportunities in life were somewhat idealistic in intention and naive in approach.

When, in the 1990s, patterns of gender and achievement in schools began to change, with boys being upheld as 'victims' of girls' educational successes, the proffered explanations of sex role theories were brought into question. After all, how could girls' achievement be explained when studies continued to show boys' domination of the co-educational classroom (Sadker and Sadker, 1994; Kenway and Willis, 1996)? It was those theories which located power relations at the centre which were found to be more relevant in understanding gender identity construction.

Gender as a social construction

Numerous studies throughout the 1980s showed how important it was to girls and boys throughout their school lives to be publicly recognised and accepted as a 'proper girl' (co-operative, friendly, fashionable, attractive) or a 'proper boy' (independent, 'having a laugh', naturally adept at sport) (Davies, 1984; Paley, 1984; Lees, 1986; Stanley, 1989). Sex role theory, which draws heavily on psychological understandings, was used to explain why children at around the age of 5–6 years were particularly likely to resist non-traditional gender behaviours in themselves and others. Janet Hough (1985) describes how an infant girl's disconcertment at the sight of one of the boys dressing up in the home corner in a spangled evening dress saw her behaviour escalate from disapproval to actually stripping the dress off him. Whilst sex role theory might explain the girl's reaction it did not explain why the young boy wanted, and was happy, to dress up in female attire in front of his classmates. Nor could it explain why pre-schoolers in Serbin's (1983) observational laboratory study would cheerfully take up non-traditional toys when they were alone but as soon as another child entered the room the behaviour changed. Serbin notes how, when children were taken individually to a room which contained a variety of male and female stereotyped toys, they would initially, when alone, choose toys which were gender appropriate. After a time, the children began to play with toys usually seen as 'suitable' for the opposite sex such as a boy playing with the dishes and a doll, and a girl throwing aeroplanes around the room. However, no such occurrences were recorded when another child was in or entered the room. Such differentiated behaviours and the fluidity of 'gender roles' were increasingly recognised by feminist educational researchers, and theorised as 'accommodation and resistance' by researchers such as Anyon (1983) and Riddell (1989). The fixity of gender roles and of the humanist view of the individual evoked by the sex role theory's notions of reproduction of roles grew increasingly problematic for feminists working in education.

Hence, in the latter part of the 1980s, more fluid social constructionist accounts of gender began to be developed. These accounts, critical of sex role theory for the reasons provided above, were often particularly interested in the active part that young people themselves played in the construction of their gender identities and the ways in which such constructions were achieved during interaction in educational environments. One of the key contributors was R.W. Connell, who offered a strong analysis of gender and power, and famously drew on Gramsci's notion of hegemony to theorise how different constructions of gender (masculinity) are imbued with varying levels of social status (Connell, 1987, 1995). This position was highly influential from the late 1980s on, triggering the trend toward a plural terminology for gender ('masculinities' and 'femininities'), and underpinning some of the key studies of masculinity in education. Simultaneously, social constructionist social psychologists furthered the exploration of the child's active participation in the construction of her/his gender identity with examination of how the age of the child contributed to their 'performance' of their gender identities. Research studies with young children suggests that it is around the age of 5–6 when they acquire the notion that gender is 'fixed' rather than fluid (Short and Carrington 1989; Lloyd and Duveen 1992). From an early age children are aware of their biological sex but the understanding that this is socially expected to result in different behaviours and preferences takes longer to develop, and does so via a process of bodily inscription, the 'trying out' of the language, attitudes and behaviours associative of the two genders.

Post-structuralist accounts of gender

For some, the limitations of sex role theory could be addressed by post-structuralist perspectives, which only began to emerge in the education field in the latter part of the 1980s. The contribution of writers such as Chris Weedon (1987), who introduced post-structuralist theory to a feminist educationalist audience, is significant, but for many of us it was the empirical work of researchers like Bronwyn Davies and Valerie Walkerdine that illuminated the powerful potential of post-structuralist accounts in gender and education. Bronwyn Davies' (1989) study, in which she read various feminist fairy tales to young children, has shown how 4–5 year olds employed 'category-maintenance work' to ensure they, and others, acted out the 'correct' gender. This was demonstrated by the children labelling those characters who were acting alternative ways of behaving, such as the assertive princess and the boy who attended a dance school, as 'deviant' and so deserving of punishment by others. Davies also showed how these practices of gender category maintenance were perpetuated between children in the classroom and playground, and the resulting impact on children's (gendered) power positions. Valerie Walkerdine's work (e.g. 1988, 1989, 1990; Walkerdine and Lucey, 1989) drew on both post-structuralist deconstructive and psychoanalytic accounts to reveal the ways in which girls are positioned in education policy and pedagogic discourses as lacking, attending to the gender discourses at work in social institutions.

Post-structuralist theory offered an alternative position which addressed some of the limitations of social learning and sex role theories. It provided a radical critique of humanist views of subjecthood, as such appearing to many feminists to offer new understandings with which to enhance gender theory. As one of us has argued elsewhere (Francis, 1999, 2007) there were five key elements contributing to post-structuralism's appeal to feminists:

1 *Scepticism toward enlightenment concepts of objectivity and reason.* Post-structuralists shared feminist scepticism toward 'scientific' enlightenment discourses that maintain a rational approach and the possibility of analytical objectivity, and a separating of the reasoning mind (constructed as male), from the emotions and body (constructed as female). The critique of such 'masculinised' constructions of epistemology had been a key feminist contribution (see e.g. the work of Carole Gilligan [1982] and Sandra Harding [1986, 1990]), and post-structuralist positions appeared to support these endeavours.

2 *An alternative view of the self.* Post-structuralism sees the self as produced by text, and as fluid and fragmented rather than fixed and rational. According to Foucault, the self is positioned and positions others in discourses, shifting in construction depending on the discursive context. This perspective offered an explanation of the simultaneous resistance to and accommodation of traditional gender constructions, and the contradictions within these constructions, which proved so problematic for sex role theory. According to Foucault (1980), wherever there is discourse there is resistance: different discourses themselves jostle for hegemony, and within this a self may be positioned as powerless by one discourse, and then powerful via an alternative discourse.

3 *Discourse and power.* This post-structuralist discourse analytic position offered a new account of power and power relations. In doing so it facilitated explanation for some of the complexities challenging feminism during the 1980s: for example, the ways in which power is constituted between women (and between men), as well as between men and women.[3] Foucault's (1980) account of power as operated via discourse rather than existing as the possession of particular groups or individuals was able to address this theoretical problem. In this perspective, individuals are constantly both undergoing and exercising power, via discourse.

4 *Deconstruction of sex/gender.* This view of selfhood as constructed through ever shifting and competing discourses offered a new understanding of gender. The gendered nature of society, and gendered selves, are hence explained as constituted by discourses which position all people as male or female, and present these categories as relational. This position challenges gender essentialism and, as we shall see, allows an uncoupling of 'sex' from 'gender' as well as deconstruction of both categories.

5 *The emancipatory potential of discourse analysis.* The notion that we are not only positioned in discourse but also active in positioning others has been embraced by some feminists as potentially beneficial to the feminist cause. For instance, Davies (1989, 1997) argues that the analysis of gender discourse will provide better understanding of the way in which power is constituted, and the ways in which we are positioned within that discourse. She and others maintain

that this raises the possibility of our creating *new* gender discourses, and thus reconstituting ourselves through discourse. (Such interpretations have however been contested by those stressing the deterministic aspects of post-structuralism.)

On the other hand, this deconstruction of the humanist self, and of the modernist 'grand narratives' and 'truth claims', to which the postmodern movement (including post-structuralism) was opposed, raised challenging theoretical problems for feminism. As we have seen, the feminist movement was born from enlightenment, humanist premises of 'rights' and so on, and embraced what could be seen as a 'grand narrative' of emancipation and human betterment. As such, many feminists were concerned that post-structuralist deconstruction undermined the feminist political project (for examples of feminist scepticism about post-structuralism, see Balbus, 1987, or Hartsock, 1990). Many theorists, feminist and otherwise, have been critical of postmodernism's tendency to deconstruct, criticise and even ridicule political/ideological 'grand narratives', without suggesting anything with which to replace these in order to address continuing social inequalities. As such, some have even accused postmodernism (and post-structuralist theory within this) of reactionary conservatism (Hartsock, 1990; Eagleton, 1996).

As a consequence, both the impact of post-structuralism on feminist theory, and of critical reactions to this, contrasting theoretical strands are represented in contemporary feminist educational research. On the one hand, there is the continuing application and development of post-structuralist ideas: we shall look at these first, before turning to alternative positions currently represented in the literature. The mid-1990s saw emergent sociological notions of masculine 'crisis', combined with policy and media concerns regarding 'boys' under-achievement', spark a new focus on masculinity within educational research. A plethora of studies and books on masculinity in educational settings and on addressing boys' achievement were produced in this period (see Chapter 7 for elaboration). Debate raged concerning the political perspectives of some of the authors concerned, and indeed at the apparent focus on boys to the exclusion of girls (Skelton, 1998; Lingard 2003). As we have seen, the work of R.W. Connell in theorising masculinity as multiple was highly influential, and these ideas (though sometimes oversimplified) underpinned many of the sociological educational studies in this period. However, Connell's notion of different versions of masculinity has been criticised for an underlying essentialism, because masculinity is positioned as always expressed by males. Various educational researchers in the late 1990s commented that these different 'sorts' of masculinity ('subjugated/complicit/hegemonic' in Connell's conception; or different 'types' in the accounts of some educational studies) appeared highly diverse and yet often overlapping, with no criteria offered by which to distinguish them – as certain commentators mischievously observed, it was difficult not to conclude that all that these different 'masculinities' held in common (to identify them as masculine rather than feminine) was the possession of a penis (Hood-Williams, 1998; MacInnes, 1998). This conflation between sex and gender (whereby men always express masculinity and women femininity) indicated a problematic essentialism, and as critics asked, if gender is always directly related to the sexed body, what is the point of the concept of 'gender' at all – why not just talk sex (Hood-Williams, 1998; MacInnes, 1998)?

Offering a radical alternative to such positions was the work of Judith Butler. Her early book, '*Gender Trouble*' (1990) drew on key post-structuralist theorists to provide a post-structuralist account of sex/gender, arguing that in contrast to those who see sex representing the 'real' and gender as the performance of this sex distinction, sex as well as gender is a socially constructed distinction. In this sense Butler's own work represents an aspect of an identifiable thread of feminist work since second-wave feminist research to contemporary times; as researchers such as Garfinkel (1967) and Kessler and McKenna (1978) had similarly illustrated the social construction of dualistic perceptions of sex. Butler's work goes further in extending discussion of discursive dualisms to sexuality, and by providing an account of sex/gender as *performative* – constructed, normalised and maintained via the continual repetition of gendered acts which produce gender. These ideas, in combination with the impact of post-structuralist feminist studies in education toward the end of the 1980s such as those of Davies and Walkerdine, continue to influence post-structuralist studies in education today. Further, they are currently contributing theoretical tools by which to address the limitations of the 'multiple masculinities' approach discussed above.

Taking up Butler's ideas about sex and gender as purely performative, Judith Halberstam (1998) undertook analyses of *Female Masculinity* – as her subheading has it, 'Masculinity Without Men'. Here Halberstam's celebratory analysis of 'Drag King' masculinities challenges the body of research that continues to link gender to sex (the 'base/superstructure' model, as Hawkesworth [1997] terms it). Hence she applies Butler's theoretical position to the study of gender (masculinity) as produced in non-gender traditional bodies (bodies socially ascribed female), taking the understanding of sex/gender as socially constructed to its logical conclusion. In addition, her ideas have been applied in educational studies, both looking at 'female' performances of masculinity – for example Renold's (2007) examination of performances of 'TomBoyism' in the classroom; and Mendick's (2005) exploration of the constructions of excellence at maths – and 'male' teachers' performances of femininity (Francis, 2008). Yet, in severing the link between biological sex and gender performance, Halberstam's analysis also precipitates a range of theoretical problems; how to analyse power inequalities (based on gender), and how to categorise masculinity and femininity for analytical purposes, if not via the sexed body?

Hence these theoretical trajectories facilitated by post-structuralist positions offer novel accounts of the phenomenon of gender, and fruitful avenues of analysis in educational research. Post-structuralist perspectives have contributed an understanding of the different gender discourses represented in educational policy and settings, and the consequent multiple power positionings therein. Yet the challenges of maintaining a forceful account of power that can adequately recognise wider, resilient patterns of gender inequality – and of other forms of inequality – remain. There has been, and continues to be, tension between structuralist and post-structuralist positions on power and in/equality; between understandings of subjectivity as constituted by language or by the material world; and between emancipatory/activist and deconstructive post-structuralist approaches. As we have seen, many feminists remain sceptical of post-structuralism's ability to offer constructive accounts of inequality, and have turned instead to alternative theoretical positions.

Other contemporary theoretical positions in gender and education

Feminists demanding what they consider to be a more hard-hitting, coherent account of inequality have sometimes turned back to structuralist theorists (or redefined, developed manifestations of key theorists' work), as the theoretical underpinning of their work. Neo-Marxist positions remain represented (see e.g. Mojab, 2006), but, in particular, feminist educational researchers working in the field of social class and gender have often turned to Bourdieu's work to theorise their findings regarding social class inequality in education. This turn to Bourdieu in gender and education may arguably be seen in the UK to have been spearheaded by the prolific and powerful work of Diane Reay (e.g. 1998, 2001, 2002), although Bourdieu's work has also be rediscovered in the US and elsewhere (e.g. Luttrell, 1997). This has coincided with cross-fertilisation of ideas between such work and cultural analyses of social class distinction in sociology and cultural studies (e.g the work of Skeggs, 1997, 2004), which also draws on Bourdieu. Hence, in work on gender and education, researchers have drawn on Bourdieu's concepts of capitals, habitus and distinction to analyse the production of class inequality in educational policy and settings, and the intersections of social class with gender and ethnicity. This work, then, builds on the early concerns of feminists' writing on social class and gender in the 1980s.

Some feminists have found both post-structural and structural positions inadequate for explaining how inequalities and life experiences are not solely dependent on factors such as gender, class, ethnicity and so on. For example, that even people sharing the same family and educational backgrounds may experience life very differently. Further, some see semiotic and post-structuralist accounts of experiences as constituted purely discursively (via language) as inadequate to explain such differences, or indeed to explain emotional experience more broadly. Such concerns have increasingly resulted in a turn to psychoanalysis. Psychoanalysis has been strongly represented in feminist theory since the emergence of second-wave feminism, with the work of writers like Juliet Mitchell (1974) and Nancy Chodorow (1978) proving highly influential. Indeed, Lacan's post-structuralist psychoanalytic insights (and those of Juliet Kristeva, who was closely influenced by Lacan) have frequently been drawn on in feminist theory. Yet, with the notable exception of Valerie Walkerdine's work, these positions had rarely strongly informed feminist work in education. Now, however, some educational researchers are central to the body of work that sees itself as investigating the 'psycho-social', melding sociological and psychoanalytic theory and areas of exploration in order to explore individuals' experiences of social experience. Where post-structuralists such as Walkerdine (1990) see the psychic realm as discursively constituted, those drawing on the work of Klein in the 'psycho-social' movement include conceptions of selfhood and experience as pre-discursive experience. Researchers such as Helen Lucey have drawn on Kleinian concepts such as projection, splitting, demonisation, ambivalence and so on in order to analyse the constructions of pupils in terms of their gendered and social class positions (Lucey, 2001; Lucey and Reay, 2002).

A converse trend to this turn to the psychic realm, but still in reaction to the predominance of discursive accounts of gender in the 1990s and 2000s, is a return to materiality as a point of analysis. Increasingly, feminists are arguing that the discursive and the material cannot be divorced (Cohen-Shabot, 2006), and analyses based on such understandings are beginning to emerge in educational research.[4]

Hence the theoretical positions represented in current research on gender and education remain as diverse as was the case 30 years ago. Many of the perspectives represented at that time remain, though some have fallen out of favour. Marxist feminist is not so strongly represented now, though the return to structural accounts on the part of many educational researchers may herald a return to favour for such positions in the future. Social learning theories have been widely critiqued, but remain represented both in government policy materials and in some liberal feminist accounts which, for example, recommend 'role modelling' and so on to address equality of opportunities. Radical Feminism, with its focus on gendered power relations, remains strongly represented, though now manifest in a variety of forms, and the notion of 'patriarchy' has fallen out of fashion as a result of analysis of power as multiple and operated within social groups as well as between them. As we have seen, the influence of post-structuralism in this and other areas has been profound, both in terms of impact on many researchers and the reactions of others against it. Such reactions have resulted in new theoretical trajectories and developments – as usual, feminist work in education includes an eclectic range of theories, with researchers drawing on those which appear to offer a most convincing or powerful account of gender constructions and inequalities in education.

3   Social class in schooling

There has been substantial criticism of the absence of consideration of social class differences within the policy debates on underachievement and gender (especially boys') that have taken place in the past (Epstein *et al.*, 1998; Plummer, 2000; Francis and Skelton, 2005). The significance of social class for educational opportunities and successes was (re)emerging for government attention and action at the time of writing (see DCSF, 2008, *A Gender Agenda*). In contrast, a reading of educational feminists' texts from Eileen Byrne (1978) and Rosemary Deem (1978) onwards shows that differences and inequalities created through social class positioning have always occupied a central platform in British educational feminist research and writing. Key feminist thinkers were concerned about the ways in which schools reproduced the sexual division of labour (Macdonald, 1980) and the different experiences of middle- and working-class girls (Anyon, 1983). Feminists have also linked schools with wider issues about social and economic positionings: topics covered have included parent-school relationships (David, 1980; Reay, 1998; Walkerdine *et al.*, 2001); parental expectations (Reay and Lucey, 2003); and institutional selection and education policy (Lucey and Reay, 2002). This chapter begins by looking at how social class has been, and is, treated in educational policy. The relationship between social class and teaching will be used as an illustration of feminists' engagement with gender/class variables. Although there is a chapter in this book that specifically addresses gender and teaching, we chose to focus on the experiences and writing of working-class feminist teachers as an element in work on social class and education. The chapter then goes on to consider the two core themes that we return to throughout this book and which have remained central to feminist concerns – 'achievement' and 'gendered experiences of school' – in relation to what feminists have said about social class.

Education policy and social class

The emergence of second-wave feminism in the 1970s occurred at a point when social class inequalities in British education had been seen as *the* main determinant of educational success or failure for over twenty years. As was said in the Introduction to this book, the aim of the Butler Education Act (1944) was to restructure the educational system so that working-class children were able to access schools that would cater for their particular educational abilities, i.e. 'bright' working-class children were offered grammar school places if they passed the eleven-plus examination, whilst those designated as having less academic aptitude went to either technical or secondary schools.[1] Then, when the social meritocracy anticipated by this restructuring failed to materialise, and given other perceived failures of the tripartite system (Halsey, Heath and Ridge, 1980), alternative models were sought. It was at this point that the system of comprehensive schooling, which had been introduced by some Labour-dominated county councils from 1945 onwards, began to gain widespread support.

The principles underpinning comprehensive schooling were both economic but also (and particularly) intended to reduce social class inequalities. The comprehensive system ensured that all children received a full secondary education: thus the school leaving age was raised[2] (a majority of pupils in grammar schools already stayed on post-15 and achieved the qualifications necessary to access higher education, whilst secondary school children left at the earliest opportunity and prior to taking examinations [Musgrave, 1968]). Writing of the shift towards comprehensive schooling in Scotland, McPherson and Douglas Willms (1997) set out seven (albeit conflicting and contested) purposes of the system, all of which can be seen to have had significance for social class distinctions. These include key principles of: no selection of pupils by ability or otherwise at the point of transfer from primary to secondary; the 'all-through' comprehensive to be the exclusive form of schooling available; compulsory schooling should not end until children had taken public examinations (hence the raising of the school leaving age to 16); increasing access to certification; and to reduce the differences between schools in terms of the social background of their pupils; all of which aimed to eliminate the correlation between attainment and social class. The support for comprehensive schooling came largely from working-class parents and although some middle-class parents did endorse the move, it was representatives from this group that 'took the lead in organising local resistance to the disappearance of grammar schools, or in insisting on the preservation of "successful" selective schools within an ostensibly comprehensive local system' (Power *et al.*, 2003: 17).

The major debates over comprehensive schooling took place in the 1960s, but it was the 1970s when the number of comprehensive schools became such that comprehensive education became the predominant form of secondary education in Britain (Wright, 1977). Thus, educational feminists began their work at a time when social class was already firmly on the agenda. It was also a preoccupation of sociology, with many researchers focusing on working-class boys' experiences of education (Douglas, 1964; Willis, 1977; Halsey, 1980). Yet girls were conspicuously absent from these studies, apparently seen as largely irrelevant. As Walkerdine (1990; Walkerdine and Ringrose, 2006) has observed, this sociological focus on the working-class boy reflected dominant perceptions of the male manual worker as the bearer of working-class identity. Feminist research was to address this gap. In keeping with the existing social/policy concerns about the difference between middle-class and working-class opportunities, feminists drew attention to how both working-class and middle-class girls were disadvantaged in comparison to their male counterparts. For example, in the 1970s and 1980s middle-class girls were far less likely to go to university than middle-class boys (Acker, 1983; Arnot *et al.*, 1998) and the jobs open to unqualified working-class girls were less well paid and with fewer benefits (e.g. hairdressing, child-care, shop assistant) than those available to working-class boys (e.g. apprenticeships in traditional male areas such as car manufacturing, shipping, coal mining, [Wickham, 1986]).

As we shall elaborate in Chapter 6 (Curriculum, knowledge and schooling), local authorities and schools did, as a consequence of the Sex Discrimination Act 1975, develop equal opportunities policies. These policies centred on gender differences with separate 'multicultural' policies devised to address 'race' and ethnic inequalities (Arnot, 1985; Gillborn, 1995). It was only in the policy documents produced by the then Inner London Education Authority (ILEA) where social class was given the same attention as gender and ethnic minority differences. Frances Morrell (2000), writing of the development of ILEA's Race, Sex and Class policy initiatives at the beginning of the 1980s, notes how the members of the authority argued that it was important to recognise and investigate the relationship between pupils' achievement and social class, gender and ethnic origin. Morrell's (2000) account resonates clearly with the situation twenty years on when she speaks of how a key feature of the Race, Sex and Class initiatives of the early 1980s challenged the assumption that simply spending more money and reducing class sizes would, of themselves, necessarily improve pupil performance. In comparing present day government policy with that of ILEA's, Morrell finds many similarities, but observes:

> But there are differences. The most striking omission is that of social class – and that is where New Labour differs. If it is referred to at all it is in the guise of poverty or social exclusion. Whether the literal reclassification of certain groups within society will enable effective measures to be taken to eliminate underperformance by those groups is the vital question that remains for education policy after the new consensus has been established.
>
> (2000: 89)

In the 1980s, British Prime Minister Margaret Thatcher had famously declared, 'There is no such thing as society. There are individual men and women and families' (cited in Morrell, 1989: 17). Such an ideological position swept away the apparent relevance of social class distinctions, as well as the salience of social institutions, and implied that social class no longer existed in Thatcherite Britain. New Labour, under Tony Blair, adopted a similar stance. What Frances Morrell is referring to in the above quote is the way in which 'Old Labour's' commitment to tackling structural inequalities (such as social class differences) was replaced by the shift towards an 'individualised'[3] society as detailed within Third Way theories. That is, where there is a move from an industrial to a global society during which a new, direct, mutual relationship emerges between the state and the individual. This new relationship is based on the notion of 'something for something': what Fairclough (2000) calls a combined moral contractual discourse. In this way government speeches on inequalities have ceased to talk about social class differences and refer instead to inequity caused through poverty or social exclusion: problems which, according to Third Way theories, can be rectified by individuals taking up the opportunities provided by the state. An example is offered by Fairclough (2000) in his reporting of a speech by Prime Minister Tony Blair:

> Our welfare system must provide help for those who need it but the deal that we are trying to create in Britain today is something for something. If we provide jobs we expect people to take them.
>
> (Blair, 1999, quoted in Fairclough, 2000: 39)

The political ideology that combines free-market capitalism with such 'individualised' thinking has been termed 'neoliberalism'. Of course, the idea that social classes (or the inequalities created through social class differences) no longer exist, simply because they are not talked about in government policy, does not stand up to scrutiny. For example, there continues to be significant disparities between pupils' achievement in schools as a consequence of social class differences (as we will be discussing in a later section).

Social class does indeed continue to feature strongly in educational policy, even if not coined in these terms. The 2005 Government White Paper 'Higher Standards, Better Schools for All', provides a glaring example of these continued themes, and the projection of deficit onto working-class parents. The White Paper is overtly premised on notions of 'free choice' and a marketised education system responding to the demands of consumers (parents), stating the government's intention to 'put parents in the driving seat for change' (p. 2), in a system 'driven by parents and by choice' (p. 5). It is asserted that,

> If local parents demand better performance from their local schools, improvement there should be. If local choice is inadequate and parents want more options, then a wider range of good quality education must be made available. If parents want a school to expand to meet demand, it should be allowed to do so quickly and easily. If parents want a new provider to give their school clearer direction and ethos, that should be simple too. And if parents want to open a school, then it should be the job of the local authority to make this happen. (p. 20)

Yet, which parents this is targeted at, though not specified, becomes clear later in the paper, when it is recognised that not all parents will have the skills and abilities, or even 'right attitudes', needed for being 'actively involved in shaping the way forward'. It is explained that the local authority may appoint a 'suitably experienced person' to act as a 'Parent's Champion', to 'help parents understand the nature of the problems at their school and the options open to address them and then to represent their interests and help them contribute to planning the future of their children's education'. Clearly, such a person is not seen as a resource for well-educated and demanding middle-class parents, but to guide and address deficient (working-class) parents. Indeed, the demonisation of certain 'types' of parent is made overt with the observation, 'Some parents do not take their responsibilities seriously enough, and even question the teacher's right to discipline their child' (p. 11). Measures to address this include:

* extending parenting contracts and orders, so that schools can use them to force parents to take responsibility for their children's bad behaviour in school;
* requiring parents to take responsibility for excluded pupils in their first five days of a suspension ... with fines for parents if excluded pupils are found unsupervised during school hours. (p. 11)

Here we see a strong example of the 'something for something' discourse, where the 'deserving' and 'undeserving' poor are delineated by their willingness/ability or otherwise to take up opportunities offered (Bauman, 2005; Francis 2006). As Bauman has discussed, in these policies, those who do not conform are positioned as undeserving, and demonised and punished by increasingly pernicious penalties. Also, as Jane Thompson (2000) observes, though the policy mantra is about 'difference', social class remains a hidden presence throughout, as 'difference' really equates to inequalities.

Having identified the way in which social class has featured in education policy and how feminists have engaged with these, we turn now to consider debates and discussions between the various feminisms. Whilst all feminists had a concern with social class and its impact on girls' and women's experiences of education, there were some differences within feminism depending on the theoretical perspective adopted.

Social class, education and feminist perspectives

The concept of 'class' has a long history and has been widely debated (Bourdieu, 1987; Skeggs, 1997; Reay, 1998). At its crudest, the Registrar General Social Class (RGSC) scale is used which links social class and occupational skill. Over the sixty years the RGSC has been in existence, individual occupations have been reallocated to different classes, but the overall framework remains the same.

  I Professional, etc. occupations
  II Managerial and Technical occupations
 III Skilled occupations

       (N) non-manual
       (M) manual

 IV Partly-skilled occupations
  V Unskilled occupations

(Source: http://sru.soc.surrey.ac.uk/SRU9.html)

A similarly crude measure of ascertaining social class is used in schools by ascertaining children who take Free School Meals (FSM) (those who take FSM are grouped as 'working-class' or, at least, considered to be at or below the poverty line). An example from the education literature of the kinds of debates over the use of FSM as a measurement of social class helps to illustrate the problems of attempting to define social class simply through occupational skill or wealth. In a report by Cassen and Kingdon (2007) on low achievement, which was based on an analysis of the National Pupil Database), the authors observed:

> Eligibility for free school meals is an imperfect measure of disadvantage, but it is the main one in our data. Children who do take them will come from disadvantaged families, but many who do not take them, for one reason or another, may also be disadvantaged. For all that, it works much as might be expected as an indicator.

Such 'indicators' are problematic in their positioning of individuals and the hierarchical assumptions underlying these positionings, but, as Walkerdine and Ringrose (2006) observe, there are limited modes of social class categorisation available, and yet employment of some sort of class categorisation is necessary to analyse and reveal the extent of continued class segregation in Britain, and the role of education within this. However, social class is not assumed to be simply a measure of familial income or a matter of occupational skill. For a majority of social scientists in education, social class is a combination of material conditions, lived experiences and psychic investment (Reay, 1998, 2007; Walkerdine *et al.*, 2001; Maguire, 2005).[4]

For second-wave feminists, how social class was defined and understood was of particular importance to Marxist-socialist Feminists. As was noted earlier, the influence of social class in shaping educational opportunities was receiving substantial attention at the point when second-wave feminism began to emerge. Marxist-socialist Feminists were particularly critical of supposedly 'left leaning' researchers/academics who failed to take gender into account in their work on class relations. What Marxist-socialist Feminists did was define the relationship between education and the sexual division of labour (that is, the different forms of labour undertaken by women and men in the home and in the labour market). Marxist-socialist Feminists provided a radical critique of schooling by confronting the political neutrality of education. They perceived links between the ideologies and structures of schooling with the needs of capital and dominant class interests (see for example, Wallace, 1987 on female school leavers; and Wolpe, 1988, on the secondary school experience of girls in an area of London). Also, as was discussed in the Introduction to this book, feminist historians have detailed how, since the start of mass state schooling in 1870, schooling had been class and gender based.

Whilst social class was of central significance in research into females' educational opportunities, there was some criticism within feminism as to how there was a tendency for the dominant 'feminist voice' to be considered a middle-class one. As the contributors to Mahony and Zmroczek's (1997) edited collection on *Class Matters: 'Working-class' Women's Perspectives on Social Class* discuss, those women who found themselves (through their education and employment) in middle-class milieus often felt they were occupying uncomfortable positions: feelings of 'not belonging' because of the dislocation between their social class upbringings and the places they now lived/worked; there was disquiet experienced by working-class feminists utilising Radical Feminism who were being criticised for subscribing to a perspective that 'is middle-class and not interested in exploring difference between women' (Mahony and Zmroczek, 1997: 1). As was the case with many of the consequences of feminist debate, working-class feminists networked, discussed, researched and produced accounts of how gender operated alongside other aspects of identity. Given the historical precedents of teaching as a career, this area provided rich insights into how gender and social class interrelated.

Social class and women teachers

In the chapter on 'Gender and teaching' we look at how primary teaching has long been considered a 'woman's job' because of its links with 'caring' and the socialisation of young children. As such, primary teaching would apparently be as suitable for a middle-class as for a working-class woman. However, historically, teaching was regarded as the province of working-class women; as a means of 'pulling-up' from one social class to another. Indeed, Frances Widdowson's (1983) book on women who trained to be elementary school teachers between 1840–1914 and which explored the relationship between education and social mobility was called *Going Up Into the Next Class*. During this time, the majority of teachers went into teaching through the pupil-teacher route. This meant working in a classroom as a latter day 'classroom assistant' for a minimum of five years' apprenticeship. The attraction for women was that this apprenticeship offered the possibility of some form of higher education through the Queen's Scholarships. At the end of the five years, pupil-teachers received a certificate entitling her or him to sit the public examination held annually for the award. Prior to 1846, teacher trainees were expected to pay fees, but after this time those students who passed the Queen's Scholarship entrance examination had four-fifths of their college place subsidised by the government. Those who qualified were given annual maintenance grants of £25 for men and £20 for women. Those pupil-teachers who were not successful in securing a scholarship could still carry on working as assistant teachers and after three years were able to obtain their certificates by taking the 'acting teachers examination'.

A career in teaching offered women a means of independence and a chance to be economically self-sufficient. At the same time, this was really only ever an opportunity that could be taken by working-class and, to an extent, lower middle-class women. Middle-class women were not expected to work; those that did were more likely to take up positions as governesses than teachers. The majority of elementary teachers came through the pupil-teacher route and it would have been inconceivable for middle-class parents to allow their daughters to serve the five-year apprenticeship required. Training colleges were relatively cheap and provided a form of higher education but, again, middle-class parents were reluctant to allow their offspring to undertake the uncomfortable and arduous training offered by these establishments (Widdowson, 1983; Purvis, 1991).

Teaching itself occupied (and to an extent continues to occupy) a low status in the hierarchy of middle-class occupations (see Chapter 8). Its 'inferiority' as a career comes through its association with 'women's work', its (initially) cheap training (in comparison to those of other career occupations), its working-class connections and its subsequent low pay. As a consequence, whilst teaching has been seen as a 'good job for a girl' (Buchan, 1980) it has also thrown up challenges and tensions for those working-class women who did opt for this career. Many of the teachers involved with second-wave feminism contributed to the growing literature on social class, gender and education by writing of their experiences of being working-class in middle-class educational environments. Such women wrote of what it was like to be a working-class girl growing up in the 1950s on inner city, urban or suburban council estates, or living in rural communities, where education was something to aspire to but which few could realise or afford (Steedman, 1987). Those that did achieve it and secured a place in the prestigious grammar schools wrote of problems faced which were not connected to the learning of curricula knowledge; for example, embarrassing situations such as having to produce the regulation two pairs of school shoes for inspection at the start of the school year which might not have come from 'good' shoe shops (and the guilt of knowing how much parents had sacrificed in finding the money to pay for these); or working-class girls having to display their more precarious right to be occupying a place at the grammar school by completing the form asking for 'father's occupation' with 'miner', 'factory worker' or 'postman', in contrast to their middle-class school fellows who could respond 'doctor', 'lawyer' or 'architect' (Walkerdine, 1984; Evans, 1991). Women from working-class backgrounds who went on to become teachers and academics have written of situations and events which, in the words of Meg Maguire (1997: 89), were 'shaped and framed by a specific ethos which has now been displaced or at least partly eroded' or as Valerie Hey (1997a: 141) wrote, was about 'finding myself in the wrong class (code) at the wrong time' (see also Hills, 1995). Hey (1997a: 143) talks about 'translating' (her working-class accent and vernacular) in order to 'fit into academia'; something she finds necessary but also acts as an important reminder that she is '*not* an endemic member of the class that is invisible to itself' (p. 142). The point women academics such as Meg Maguire and Valerie Hey are making is that their particular experiences are borne of times when social class difference was firmly inscribed on their psyche and was perhaps more evident and recognised than is now the case; but also how social class distinction continues to be a salient factor in their contemporary places of work, and in society at large. As we said earlier, social class has not ceased to exist, but rather the central and public attention given to it in government discourses has been replaced (see also Francis and Skelton, 2005; Francis, 2006). Indeed, there is significant evidence to indicate that social class is of greater import today than is recognised in public consciousness.

At this point we want to take up the themes at the core of this book: gender and achievement and gendered experiences of schooling.

Gender, social class and achievement

The debates on gender and achievement have changed from a second-wave feminist focus on girls, to a contemporary policy focus on boys. As we stated at the beginning of this chapter, one of the major criticisms made by feminists and pro-feminists (see Chapter 7) of the debates and discussions around boys' underachievement has been the absence of any consideration of the significance of social class when exploring patterns of achievement (Gilbert and Gilbert, 1998; Raphael-Reed, 1998; Lingard and Douglas, 1999).

An example of how social class interrelates with gender and ethnicity to impact on achievement can be seen by looking at the performance of pupils in English – a subject which is presumed to be 'feminine' and to appeal to females. As such, it is assumed that girls, as a group, are better at English than boys, as a group. Certainly, the statistics provided by the government statistics gateway show that when children sit their examinations in English at ages 7, 11, 14 and then GCSEs, girls consistently outperform boys.

Table 3.1 Gender gap in English – percentage of those attaining prescribed levels

	Boys (%)	*Girls (%)*	*Gap (%)*
KS1 Writing	75	86	11
KS2 English	76	85	9
KS3 English	68	81	13
GCSE English	53	68	15

DCSF Gateway Statistics for 2007.

If we undertake a further breakdown of the Key Stage 2 results, some larger gaps than the nine per cent shown on Table 3.1 between boys, as a group, and girls, as a group, emerge. (KS2 is taken as an example, and it should be noted that the pattern is the same across all Key Stages). As Table 3.2 shows, looking at the English results of boys and girls according to whether they do or do not take Free School Meals (FSM), there is an apparent gender gap of 32 per cent between girls who do not take FSM (88 per cent) and boys who do take FSM (56 per cent). However, this articulation would not be an accurate reflection of the gender gap, as girls who take FSM are not doing as well as boys who do not take FSM, even within this so-called 'feminine' curriculum subject (English). Thus social class redefines how the 'gender gap in achievement' should be discussed.

Table 3.2 Percentage of pupils achieving level 4 at Key Stage 2 English: gender and social class

Girls – non-FSM	88%	Boys – non-FSM	80%
Girls – FSM	69%	Boys – FSM	56%

DCSF Gateway Statistics for 2007.

When ethnicity is considered alongside social class and gender, yet a different picture is revealed. One that indicates that although gender gaps are evident between groups of girls and groups of boys from different minority ethnic groups, social class does not have the same effects across all ethnic groups. That is, whilst being working-class (using FSM as an indicator of social class) impacts strongly on the gender gap at Key Stage 2 English for White British children, with the gap widening for those taking Free School Meals, it appears to make less difference to some other ethnic groups (see Table 3.3).

Table 3.3 Percentage of pupils achieving level 4 at Key Stage 2 English: the differential impact of social class on majority/minority ethinic groups

Non-FSM	*Boys*	*Girls*	*Gender gap*
White British	80	88	8
Pakistani	70	79	9
Black African	74	84	10

FSM	*Boys*	*Girls*	*Gender gap*
White British	55	68	13
Pakistani	60	72	12
Black African	58	67	9

DCSF Gateway Statistics for 2007.

However, Table 3.4 illustrates the impact of social class (as indicated by FSM) on achievement within and across different pupil groups. We can see how the impact is particularly strong for the majority group of White British pupils, with gaps of 25 per cent for boys, and 20 per cent for girls, respectively. The table also illuminates a point we shall develop in Chapter 4: that social class has been found to impact somewhat less strongly on the achievement of some minority ethnic groups (Archer and Francis, 2007). For example, we can see from Table 3.3 that although the achievement of children of Pakistani origin is somewhat affected by social class, with a gap of 10 per cent between those boys taking Free School Meals and those not, and a smaller gap of 7 per cent between Pakistani girls according to FSM, these gaps are far smaller than the gaps for White British pupils according to FSM. As we will elucidate further in the next chapter, it is thought important to note the complexity at stake beyond social class, as is illustrated by the overall higher performance of White British children at Key Stage 2 English compared to their Pakistani and Black African counterparts.

Table 3.4 Percentage of pupils achieving level 4 at Key Stage 2 English: gender, ethnicity and social class

	Non-FSM	*FSM*	*Gap*
White British boys	80	55	25
White British girls	88	68	20
Pakistani boys	70	60	10
Pakistani girls	79	72	7
Black African boys	74	58	16
Black African girls	84	67	17

DCSF Gateway Statistics for 2007.

There is always a danger of creating a 'hierarchy' of inequalities when considering the impact of gender, social class and minority ethnic status on educational opportunities and achievement when considering these alongside each other. Feminists in education would strongly contest such a move, urging instead for a recognition that it is the interrelationship of these that illuminates how it is productions of learner identities that lie at the heart of achievement (Connolly, 2004; Francis and Skelton, 2005; Archer and Francis, 2007).

In terms of explanations for these social class achievement gaps, feminists have been at the forefront of those attacking 'deficit' approaches which locate blame for underachievement with working-class parents and pupils. We do not intend to draw out the literature here, but especially in the 1950s and 1960s there was a strong movement in the social sciences to explain social class difference as due to poor parenting (specifically, mothering [Bowlby 1953]): assumptions of middle-class superiority, and of working-class practices as deficient, underpinned this work, in addition to expectations about gender. It was assumed that working-class practices must be *compensated for* in order to improve their children's achievement. As we have seen from the extracts from the White Paper (2005) discussed above, these discourses remain strongly evident in current policy-making, with assumptions that while middle-class parents should be active in directing their children's educational pathways (and the education system as a whole), working-class parents should listen to the direction of teachers and other agency workers for the good of their children (in other words, they should 'know their place').

Instead, feminist researchers concentrating on social class issues have conducted devastating studies of the ways in which working-class children and their parents are systematically rubbished and excluded by the educational system. Valerie Walkerdine and Helen Lucey (1989) undertook a discourse analytic study of the construction of mothering as socially classed, looking at how mothers are expected to inculcate liberal values of democracy and individualism in their children, and how working-class mothers are pathologised for their different values and priorities. Reay and Ball (2001) also show how it is these very negative experiences of education that influence working-class parents' tendency not to 'pressure' their children in terms of their educational achievement. Much has been made of working-class parents' lack of 'pushing' and low expectations of their children's educational achievement in relation to their middle-class counterparts. Yet Reay and Ball have shown how it is these parents' painful memories of their own experiences of being devalued and made to feel stupid and worthless by the education system that influences their approaches with their children. They wish to avoid setting their children up for the same disappointments, and therefore encourage them simply to 'try their best', playing down pressure. Diane Reay also traces these patterns in the interface between parents and school in her book *Class Work* (1998), where she shows how teachers related very differently with parents according to social class. Some working-class parents who attempted to engage with their children's teachers felt intimidated and patronised, and were viewed differently by teachers to middle-class parents (who were usually respected, if sometimes feared!) Drawing on Bourdieu, Reay argues that the working-class parents lacked the cultural capital needed to command effective engagement from the school. Similar themes are taken up by Gillies (2006), who uses the notion of emotional capital to argue that whereas middle-class mothers experienced their relationships with the school as positive and intimate, working-class liaisons required a different sort of emotional investment, given that they were often centred around challenging injustice, against a backdrop of feelings of stress and low self-worth. These studies all illuminate how teachers' and other educationalists' low expectations and stereotypical views of working-class pupils and parents impact on their achievement via self-fulfilling prophesies that serve to alienate pupils, often provoking disengagement (see e.g. Reay, 2002; O'Brien 2003; Reay and Lucey, 2003; Walkerdine *et al.*, 2001). In these studies, then, 'deficit' is firmly consigned to the education system and social policy, rather than to working-class individuals.

Having illustrated the ways in which social class impacts on educational achievement, we now turn to a closer consideration of gendered and classed experiences and perceptions of education.

Gender, social class and educational experience and trajectories

Researchers of social class and gender in education have traditionally been attuned to the place and experiences of working-class pupils within education (e.g. Anyon, 1983; Walkerdine, 1984; Weiss, 1989) Given the sociological focus on working-class boys in the 1970s it is not surprising that early feminist work tended to be on girls, but later, a focus on the relationality of gender, and recognition of the interplay of different facets of social identity in educational experiences, meant that researchers increasingly focused on diverse samples. As Reay (2006) maintains, a distinction between feminist and other work on class is the feminist 'focus on gendered and racialized class processes rather than class positioning' (p. 340). This growing attention to diversity also coincided with a trend towards masculinities research in the 1990s, which meant that the focus on class and *boys* in school was maintained. While much of this work is feminist or pro-feminist, the recent policy concerns about underachieving boys have sometimes been especially targeted on certain groups of boys, specifically Black boys and White working-class boys (Francis, 2006). Consequently, there is an increasing amount of 'grey-literature' on working-class boys and how to ensure their educational engagement. Given that we devote a later chapter to boys and schooling (Chapter 7), we attempt to cover some of this research there. As such, we shall target *this* discussion on research on *girls*.

Girls' perceptions of their futures have been shown to have changed significantly since the early second-wave feminist research on this topic. Researching in the 1980s, Spender (1982), Gaskell (1992) and others found that girls planned to work until they were married, and then either to assume the role of secondary breadwinner, or cease work altogether. However, over the last three decades, schoolgirls' occupational aspirations have both broadened and become more ambitious (Sharpe, 1994; Miller and Budd, 1999; Francis, 1996, 2002). Girls tend now to see their chosen career as reflecting their identity, and as a vehicle for future fulfilment, rather than as simply a stopgap before marriage (Riddell, 1992; Wilkinson and Mulgan, 1995). Whereas Spender (1982) and her contemporaries found that secondary schoolgirls listed an extremely narrow and highly gender-stereotypical range of (non-professional) occupations, contemporary research has shown secondary schoolgirls to aspire to a much broader range of occupations, including some stereotypically masculine jobs (Sharpe, 1994; Wikeley and Stables, 1999). Gendered preferences remain evident in the attributes of the jobs selected by girls, which tend to be categorisable as caring or creative (Francis, 2002; Francis *et al.*, 2003), but girls certainly tend to higher aspirations than used to be the case.[5]

Such 'choices' are not equally open to all girls, however. 'Choices' are facilitated or constrained by institutional barriers; and by young people's particular environments, and the sorts of routes and aspirations which they consequently see as achievable or suitable for 'people like me' (Archer and Yamashita, 2003). Social class clearly has a strong impact here, as does 'race'. For example, one of us conducted a study with pupils of diverse ethnic origins in London schools, and found the mainly working-class girls in the sample to be highly ambitious, often citing professional jobs as their preferred future occupation (Francis, 1996, 2002). A different light has been shed on these findings by research that has sampled more widely beyond urban environments: this research illustrates how ethnicity and locality were influential in the former study, as the largely White working-class girls in the wider studies held less ambitious and more gender-stereotypical preferences for future occupations (Warrington and Younger, 2000; Francis *et al.*, 2005). Of course, the practices of schools and careers staff in perpetuating these patterns has been noted, via their channelling girls down stereotypical classed, 'raced' and gendered routes (e.g. Rolfe, 1999; Francis *et al.*, 2005). Jayne Osgood (2005) highlights the implication of policymakers in such practices, in her interrogation of recruitment drives for childcare workers by the DCSF's SureStart unit: while ostensibly 'open to all', the language of the advertising masks the perpetuation of a gendered and classed childcare workforce due to the conditions, gendered perceptions and (low) status of childcare work.

These points about constrained and directed routes are supported by work on 'race' and occupational aspiration, which illustrates how minority ethnic girls often hold higher aspirations than their White counterparts, and how these aspirations are less affected by social class than in the case of White girls. For example, British South Asian and Chinese girls are particularly likely to opt for professional careers (Lightbody, 1997; Francis and Archer, 2005), and Mirza (1992) has shown how African-Caribbean girls were both more ambitious, and more ready to opt for non-gender-traditional jobs, than were White girls. These findings again reflect institutional effects on gender constructions – for example, Pang (1999) discusses how the encouragement of young British Chinese to enter into the professions illustrate families' seeking of secure and comfortable, as well as respected, positions for their offspring, in contrast to the hard life which many first-generation Chinese migrants endured in the catering trade. Likewise, Mirza's sample of African-Caribbean young women were less constrained by gender stereotyping due to their recognition for the need for self-reliance given the institutional barriers to Black male employment. Yet the very institutional inequalities that facilitated the ambition of these young people also constrained their progress on preferred occupational paths: Mirza found such barriers impact on the young women too, so that they eventually tended to pursue known 'safe routes' in occupations where substantial numbers of Black women are employed (such as occupations in the health service and social care). Likewise, Pang (1999) showed how many young British Chinese professionals ended up returning to the catering trade due to the racial 'glass ceiling' that many of them encountered within their professional career.

Hence what this work on 'choice' of school-to-work trajectories illustrates is how limited these apparently free choices are – limited by social constraints, in spite of neoliberal claims that such choices are available and facilitated for all. Yet, as we have seen, neoliberalism positions inequalities of outcome as the result of individual inadequacies, rather than recognising the role of social institutions that this body of work on social class and gender highlights.

Much of the research on gender, social class and education has, in the past, tended to focus on working-class experiences and perceptions in order to redress the situation in which these were viewed and adjudged through the 'middle-class gaze'. More recently, explorations into social class and education have started to problematise middle-class normativity. For example, middle-class girls and their (highly pressured) educational trajectories form part of Walkerdine, Lucey and Melody's study (2001). Diane Reay, Gill Crozier and David James have undertaken research into white, middle-class parents who have made a decision to send their children to the local comprehensive school rather than, as might be expected, sending their children to selective or exclusive schools. Rather, the parents in their study have a commitment towards schools characterised by its diverse – in terms of social class, gender and ethnicity – pupil population (Reay *et al.*, 2008). Reay and her colleagues consider how some of these parents' intentions of 'thinking and acting otherwise' may offer hope for a 'reinvigorated democratic citizenry', in which left-leaning middle-class parents see themselves as responsible for increasing social equality. On the other hand, their careful research conversely documents the practices of privilege and distinction that such parents may fall prey to within the localised practices of the state's school environment. Hence concluding that,

> Within a contemporary era of neoliberalism that valorises competition, individualism and the market, even these white middle classes who express a strong commitment to community and social mixing struggle to convert inclinations into actions.
>
> (Reay *et al.*, 2008: 238)

Others have sought to ascertain whether, in today's 'individualised' society, it is possible to identify 'cultural lifestyle choices consistent with dominant middle-class parenting practices' (Maier *et al.*, 2008). However, the work of Reay and others would seem to suggest that clear trends are maintained according to class, as we shall see subsequently.

Working-class girls

We have seen how, while working-class girls may be outperforming working-class boys at school, middle-class girls *and* boys continue to exceed their achievement. The tendency to present middle-class girls' achievement as representative of all girls insidiously hides the underachievement of many working-class girls, thus masking continued social inequality (Lucey, 2001). The heightened focus on achievement indicators within British education is intermeshed with notions of 'standards and effectiveness' which have been in the policy ascendancy since the late 1980s (Arnot *et al.*, 1999). A repetitive trope in such policy has been the notion of 'excellence'; with the production of 'excellence' (i.e. high achievement) positioned as a central concern. Yet as Helen Lucey (2001; Lucey *et al.*, 2003) has observed, the very concept of 'excellence' depends on the continued presence of its opposite: failure.

Helen Lucey and Diane Reay have collaborated to produce a body of work showing how middle-class children tend to benefit from institutional practices of selection and from schemes to promote 'excellence' within state schooling (Lucey, 1999; Lucey and Reay, 2000; Reay and Lucey, 2003). They analyse how particular resources and selective programmes, ostensibly conceived as enabling meritocracy via provision of development to gifted working-class children, work in practice to construct working-class failure. They argue that it is actually middle-class children who are more likely to be chosen for such schemes, and that of course in any case the schemes are available only to a small minority of pupils. However, the schemes serve an important symbolic function, as the existence of these schemes can be used to suggest that opportunities have been provided – hence the mass 'failure' of working-class pupils must be of their own making rather than due to inequalities in the system. Hence Lucey's findings with Reay (Lucey and Reay, 2000) show how the marketisation of schooling and notions of 'free choice' and 'opportunity' characteristic of neoliberal education policy function to set up the 'failure' of working-class girls early on in their lives.

In contrast to middle-class families, where parents tend to decide which secondary school their children will attend (Reay and Ball, 1998; Walkerdine *et al.*, 2001; O'Brien, 2003), in working-class families such decisions are often taken by girls themselves. Different values and lack of 'educational capital' means that working-class girls tend to rely on social networks rather than parents to direct their decisions around school choice (O'Brien, 2003). Lucey and Reay (2000) demonstrate that middle-class girls are more likely to be offered a place at their school of choice than are their working-class contemporaries (Black boys are shown to fare especially badly in this process). These patterns of inequality continue throughout educational trajectories. Walkerdine *et al.* (2001) found that the few working-class White girls in their study who had succeeded in gaining undergraduate degrees had done so via extremely fragmented and diverse routes to their higher education; in strong contrast to the smooth and predictable routes pursued by their middle-class counterparts in the study (see also Reay *et al.*, 2005). Such evidence illuminates how apparent 'free choices' are actually far from equal, and are strongly mediated by social class and 'race'.

Feminist research has emphasised the devastating psychic costs of difficult educational experiences, and positionings as 'failing', for working-class girls. For example, Maeve O'Brien (2003) discusses how these painful experiences for the working-class Irish girls in her study led to their educational disengagement: 'working-class girls internalise that the effort required to achieve high academic performance is too gruelling, too lonely, unsociable and stressful' (p. 251). O'Brien labels this process ' "moving out" rather than "moving on" ' (p. 251), and this may be a key facet of working-class girls' relative underachievement. Indeed, such negative experiences and consequent disassociation frequently account for girls' full disengagement and absence from education (Osler and Vincent, 2003). Osler (2006) maintains that these girls are victims of various sorts of violence at the hands of schooling (interpersonal, institutional and structural). Clearly such processes are internalised, impacting on the self-image of these girls, particularly as they are positioned by contemporary individualist discourses as responsible for their own underachievement. This point is illuminated by Lucey and Reay (2000), who found that working-class girls relegated to schools not of their choice believed that, as they had ended up at 'rubbish schools', they too must be 'rubbish' (hence setting up painful relationships with education and potential consequent disengagement). Likewise, Archer *et al.* (2003) interviewed young people who had not engaged in education beyond 16, and found that these respondents expressed embarrassment, guilt and shame at this 'lack', irrespective of the reasons for their non-participation.

Hence, the neoliberal demand for individuals to consider themselves responsible for their life trajectories and the acquisition of opportunities available to them, has become a strong theme in research on gender and class in education. It is in a similar vein that Carolyn Jackson (2006) notes that recent moral panics around 'laddettes' and 'binge drinking' are coupled with concerns about respectability and social class (indeed, considering the panics around gin drinking in the eighteenth century, Evans *et al.* [2008] link these to current panics around obesity, single-motherhood and so on, arguing that such moral panics are inevitably targeted at, and demonise, working-class women). Jackson (2006) maintains that although 'laddette' attitudes may be demonstrated by middle-class girls and young women, the fact that the term is drawn from the notion of the 'lad', associated with working-class boys and young men, gives it working-class connotations. She argues further that the 'excessive' behaviours that delineate the 'laddette' are associated with 'undesirable' and 'unrespectable' working-class lifestyles (see Skeggs, 1997; 2004). Hence while some middle-class girls may be able to adopt the attitudes of the laddette as 'cultural omnivores' (Skeggs, 2004), Jackson argues that working-class laddettes are constructed as overstepping boundaries and representing all that is bad about their working-class backgrounds. She and Archer *et al.* (2007) also note how such behaviours in girls, though ostensibly performing aspects of traditional masculinity, are actually constructed in a context of (hetero)sexualised hyper-femininity, and hence do little to seriously challenge or disrupt the gender order. Such themes of respectability and responsibility emerge strongly in the findings of Archer *et al.*: they show how boys identified by the school as 'at risk of dropping out' were happy to present themselves as 'hard' or 'bad'; but in contrast their female contemporaries – although frequently engaged in conflict with teachers – maintained that they were not 'really' bad, but 'good underneath', and valued education (though often did not enjoy school). Their practices of 'speaking their mind' – framed by the girls as agentic and authentic – is shown by Archer and her colleagues to be in tension with normative (middle-class) productions of femininity, and hence drew them into conflict with the school. Their consequent 'bad girl' reputations were often regretted later, when the girls sought to remake themselves in their final years of schooling to 'come good'. Hence the moral entrapment of these young working-class women in discourses of self-responsibility and respectability, in which they are positioned as failures, is clearly illustrated.

Of course, in addition to these psychic burdens precipitated by educational underachievement, there are the significant economic implications. Economic consequences of educational underachievement may be particularly acute in the light of the 'qualification inflation' (Ainley, 1998) resulting from the expansion of Higher Education in the UK: education credentials are increasingly important in securing 'good' jobs.

Middle-class girls

It has been argued that the key explanation for changes in the configuration of gender and achievement patterns between the early 1980s and the 1990s was the rapid educational attainment of middle-class girls – middle-class girls are now doing as well as (and in some cases exceeding) middle-class boys (Reay, 2001). As we have seen, with the introduction of the National Curriculum in 1988, girls quickly caught up with boys at maths and science within compulsory schooling, whereas the reverse did not apply to boys' achievement at literacy and language subjects. As Walkerdine *et al.* (2001) observe, expectations of 'excellent' achievement for daughters as well as sons have been the norm within middle- and upper-class families for some time, and their analysis of the data from the middle-class girls in their study shows the pressure that such expectations can place on students. In some of the middle-class families, success was so expected that anything other than 'excellent' grades was perceived as failure. Hence feelings of, or worries about, 'not being good enough' characterised the talk of middle-class girls from an early age (Walkerdine *et al.*, 2001). Even extremely high-achieving girls expressed anxiety and a lack of confidence about their educational performance. Walkerdine *et al.*, (2001) observe that it was as though these girls could '*never* be good enough' to meet the expectations of their parents (see also Lucey and Reay, 2000). It is via such findings that Lucey (2001) argues that portrayals of (middle-class) young women as 'having it all' and 'in control' are somewhat illusory.

Such research has also highlighted the tension between heterosexual femininity and high achievement (Walkerdine, 1990). Girls receive strong messages that in order to be seen as successful women in contemporary society they must be considered physically attractive, as well as high educational achievers (Hey, 1997b; Walkerdine *et al.*, 2001). Yet this is a particularly challenging combination to achieve, given the powerful associations between cleverness and unfemininity/asexuality (Walkerdine, 1989; Reay, 2001). It has therefore been argued by a number of researchers that there are fundamental psychic contradictions in being an educationally achieving girl, pincered as girls are between discourses of compulsory heterosexuality that foreground gender difference, and discourses of academic application which suppress difference (Walkerdine, 1990; Hey, 1997b; Reay, 2001). Being a popular or 'successful' girl depends on particular interweavings of aspects of identity and performance, including ethnicity, social class, academic achievement, 'beauty', knowledge of and access to popular culture and so on (Reay, 2002; Ali, 2003). The achievement of such balances may be particularly challenging for those girls that do not fit the 'norm' of White, middle-class girlhood, including those girls who have fulfilled neoliberal expectations in 'remaking' themselves as middle-class (Walkerdine and Ringrose, 2006); but even for White, middle-class high-achieving girls, there are psychic tensions bound up with maintaining (or failing to attain) such balances. Lucey (2001) and Walkerdine *et al.* (2001) discuss the extent to which the behaviour of these girls is constrained, arguing that the cost of the suppression of femininity and sexuality involved in being an academic achiever can lead to anxiety and stress. It is suggested that these psychic costs are evidenced in the increase in self-harm and eating disorders which particularly (though not exclusively) affect middle-class girls (Reay, 2001, 2006; Evans *et al.*, 2004; Walkerdine, 2003).

So, even for high-achieving girls, the occupation of the masculine position of academic achiever is fraught with difficulties and costs. As we have reported in various parts of this book, 'natural brilliance' continues to be constructed as a male attribute, meaning that the success of these girls is rarely recognised or affirmed. Given this, as we have argued elsewhere (Francis and Skelton, 2005), it is little wonder that they internalise feelings of 'never being good enough', for they are not, and can never be, boys.

This being said, middle-class White girls' educational success clearly represents class privilege and reproduces class capital in the relatively well-paid and high-status[6] occupations which many of these girls go on to pursue which, as we have seen, is far from being the case for many girls. Some research has drawn out the ways in which girls themselves, as well as their teachers, are implicated in constructing and policing classed boundaries, by drawing on discourses of achievement and morality (e.g. Reay, 2002, 2006). An especially disturbing feature of these constructions on the part of middle-class pupils is their conflation of working-class identity with (low) ability (Mac an Ghaill, 1994; Reay, 2006) – a conflation which, as we have seen, is expressed via many vehicles, including government policy. The casual arrogance of some middle-class girls in Reay's (2006) study, and their evident feeling of 'natural' authenticity in their contemptuous Othering of working-class children, reminds us of the ways in which class binaries, like those of gender and 'race', locate power and authenticity in one side of the binary, while positioning the Other as lack. As Hey (2006) observes, 'the privileged absorb a dominant and corrosive awareness of their power' (p. 306).

Forward thinking

Hence, while current work on gender and social class builds on themes attended to by second-wave feminist researchers (and in some key cases is conducted by the same women), this work has gained in quantity and strength – perhaps in order to address the heightened inequalities that have widened rather than narrowed in the last thirty years with the application of free-market and neoliberal government policies (including within education). New questions that such researchers are exploring include the notion and costs of 'upward mobility' (Walkerdine, 2003; Walkerdine and Ringrose, 2006); building on the analysis of meanings and experiences of 'moving', or even 'escaping', from one class to another (Mahony and Zmorczek, 1997; Walkerdine, 2003; Hey 2006). Other innovative points of exploration include how to negotiate the theoretical problematics of avoiding deficit constructions of working-class families while critiquing the reproduction of educational inequalities (Hey, 1997a,b; Walkerdine 2003); and psycho-social explanations for why some girls from similar family circumstances negotiate education differently to their siblings (Edwards *et al.*, 2006); 'remaking' of classed and gendered identity, and the neoliberal imperative of self-responsibility for doing so, has also become a major point of critique, with a number of researchers pointing to the implications this has for working-class girls' internalisation of their 'failure'

(Lucey and Reay, 2002; Archer *et al.*, 2007), and others engaging the reflective practices of neoliberal subjecthood.

Theoretically, this work has engaged many of the dilemmas faced by those working on 'race' (see Chapter 4): for example, while autobiography and 'standpoint' has been used effectively to recount and authenticate classed experiences, to reflect on the political and psychic costs of 'success' or 'moving on', and to highlight inequality (see, for example, Steedman, 1982; Mahony and Zmroczek, 1997), such positions have also been critiqued for their reification of the 'personal voice' (see Hey, 2006, for discussion). Valerie Hey (2006) draws on psychoanalytic theory in order to provide an account of the anxieties and tensions at stake, arguing that these autobiographical narratives have a validity beyond the personal, as they 'can tell us how class is now un/done as a relational concept and what is at stake in its contemporary configuration' (p. 206). As we saw in Chapter 2 and in the work recounted in this chapter, the psycho-social has been increasingly seen as a fruitful theoretical avenue for work on gender and social class, offering both accounts of the psychic internalisation of class and gender and the consequences; and accounts of individual differences within social groups. Additionally such theory can provide powerful metaphors in the analysis of data. A second, strong strand of contemporary theorising of social class and gender in education has drawn on Bourdieu and his concepts of various social capitals – economic, social, cultural and symbolic – to which individuals have different levels of access depending on their social class, and which work to reproduce existing class inequalities. In Chapter 2 we noted how feminists particularly concerned with social class issues have increasingly turned to Bourdieu, arguably reflecting a response to the apparent limitations of postmodern theoretical positions for explaining and/or analysing persistent structural inequalities.

Centrally, this corpus of work retains an emphasis on identifying and highlighting inequalities; the role of education policy and institutions within this; and the psychic and economic costs of such inequality.

4 Ethnicity, gender and education

For feminist educationalists writing of women teachers and girls in schools in the twenty-first century the importance of considering how gender interacts with social class, ethnicity, sexuality, religion and so forth in shaping identities is accepted. This has not always been the case. We have seen in Chapter 2 how Black Feminists' critiques regarding the 'Eurocentric' concerns and the often discriminatory practices of White Feminists shaped theoretical developments in feminist theory. Also, a tracing of the literature across the years from the early days of second-wave feminism demonstrates how the analysis of various 'isms' (sexism, racism, heterosexism) have evolved from the first feminist texts when they were discussed as impacting separately and discretely on schooling experiences. At the same time, educational feminism has always shown an awareness of, if not always a sensitivity to, 'race' and minority ethnic positioning. This chapter will chart the development of research on gender and ethnicity in education, focusing again on our dual themes of educational achievement and educational experiences. However, before looking in more detail at the discussions within feminism on ethnicity and gender in relation to education it is appropriate to give a brief outline of the backcloth against which these debates took place. The tensions that emerged between multicultural/anti-racist education and equal opportunities/anti-sexist education resulted in schools having distinct and often contradictory equality policies.

Multicultural/anti-racist versus equal opportunities/anti-sexist school educational policies

In the UK the Sex Discrimination Act 1975 and the Race Relations Act 1976 were both products of the civil rights movements that were started in the USA in the 1960s. As Madeleine Arnot wrote in 1985 'it would be easy to assume that race and gender are somehow a "natural pair" of policy problems' (p.1) and it was a relatively easy task to point to how 'Black people' and 'women' (White women) both experienced discrimination and prejudicial treatment. However, as Arnot (1985) went on to say, attempting to identify similarities between the two cases concealed how the combination of gender and ethnicity shaped the experiences and opportunities of Black women. As was argued by several feminists,[1] it was too simplistic to assume that Black and White people constructed gender identities in the same ways, given their differential access to societal power, which was a consequence of their differing histories and being shaped by different social institutions (Carby, 1982; Phoenix, 1987; Williams, 1987).

It was some years before these exhortations began to be heard, which meant that for a considerable period of time schools and local authorities were operating with policies that set up a number of contradictions. Jenny Williams (1987) noted that although anti-racist and anti-sexist policies at the 'strong' end of the policy spectrum, with their focus on power inequalities (see Chapter 6), appeared to be on the same wavelength, there were different emphases. Anti-racist policies gave prominence to the need for White teachers to amend their behaviour and attitudes towards Black pupils in a way that anti-sexist policies did not focus on the need for male teachers and boys to reflect on their behaviours towards women teachers/girls. Anti-sexist policies advocated single-sex classes for girls, women only support groups and assertiveness training which, if applied to Black pupils would have precipitated concerns over segregation and incitement. Furthermore, race equality policies were seen to be more politically controversial and featured in both local and national politics whilst gender was not taken up by any of the political parties in the same way. Whatever the differences, it is fair to say that, at least in the early days, there appeared to be far greater awareness in second-wave feminist writings of the interplay of gender and ethnicity in informing girls' educational experiences and opportunities (Fuller, 1980; Arnot, 1985; Weiner, 1985) than in the work of those focusing on multicultural/anti-racist education (see, for example, Troyna, 1984; Cashmore, 1987). At the same time, as we observed at the beginning of this chapter, Black Feminists disputed apparently unproblematic constructions of 'womanhood' used by various feminist perspectives.

Such challenges first emerged among Black women's campaign groups in the United States (see e.g. hooks, 1982; Lorde, 1984; Hill-Collins, 1991; or Wheeler, 2007, for elaboration). Black Feminist and 'Womanist' critics took issue with the traditional (White) feminist assumption that all women share a common and primary oppressor (hooks, 1982; 1995), and charged White Feminists with racist practices (Wallace, 1995). In Britain during the late 1970s and early 1980s, campaign groups such as the Organisation of Women of Asian and African Descent (which included some feminists), Southall Black Sisters, Wages for Housework and others were challenging the White Feminist status quo and demanding attention to the specific issues facing Black women.[2] As Wheeler (2007) succinctly explains, such critiques fed and drew on the development of feminist 'standpoint theory' (see Hartsock, 1986, 1999; Hill-Collins, 1991), which saw identity (gender, 'race', class, etc.) as giving access to particular knowledges on the basis of experience, and hence insights into particular world perspectives which provided epistemic validity; but further, the accounts of Black Feminists demanded feminist attention to the specific issues facing Black and minority ethnic women. They also called for greater recognition of how Black and minority ethnic women are positioned in society and the difficulty they encountered in privileging one form of oppression over another, because of how those oppressions interconnected and affected their lives (Carby 1982; Amos and Parmar, 1984; Collins, 1990). The significance of the Black Feminist standpoint is that it offers Black Feminists a 'third space' (Mirza 1997) between the margins of gender, class and 'race' through which they can articulate their own experiences and challenge dominant (White) ways of thinking – and by so doing create new knowledge.

The influence of identity politics impacted strongly on the field of gender and education in Britain, in terms of both theoretical and empirical contributions. Black Feminists began to apply the theoretical debates around identity politics and standpoint theory to the case of education (see, for example, Carby, 1987; Phoenix, 1987), and in conjunction a proliferation of studies emerged in the early 1980s that focused specifically on the experiences of Black and Minority Ethnic girls in educational settings. What is interesting, and sets these earlier studies apart from current ones is two key points: first, early studies tended not to focus (at least primarily) on educational achievement patterns and gaps; and second, they were focused on the experiences of *girls*.

Early studies and what they showed

So, for example, feminist educational studies in the late 1970s and early 1980s drew attention to a number of 'commonsense' (pathologising) presumptions about the experiences and potential of different cultural groups, especially in relation to Black girls (Fuller, 1980; Wright, 1987). These studies showed the devastating effect of teacher assumptions of 'disruptive attitudes', 'broken English' and so forth on pupils' educational achievement, with Black and minority ethnic pupils often consequently perceived by teachers as 'unsuitable' for top exam classes (or indeed labelled as having Special Educational Needs). Cecile Wright (1987) identified the lack of recognition among teachers at how Black children's 'negative' behaviours were often related to disillusion and response to the racism (overt and covert) that they endured daily in the school system. Wright observed how Black girls in her study often sought to avoid subjects taught by racist teachers, and as such their curriculum choices were circumscribed (see also hooks' autobiographical account, 1982). Such accounts provide the backdrop to findings by Fuller (1980), Lees (1993) and Mirza (1992) that African-Caribbean girls tended to be, as Lees put it, 'learning oriented but alienated from school' (1993). These findings were of particular significance because, not only did they demonstrate similarities between teacher attitudes and expectations of Black girls and boys but also highlighted how gendered, and consequently, different, these were.

The interest in the 1970s and 1980s on research on sub-cultures in schools offered evidence of how teachers' expectations of working-class White and Black boys' academic potential and (mis)behaviours were in tangent with these groups' disaffection for schooling and actual behaviours, i.e. one helped to create the other (Lacey, 1970; Driver, 1980). In contrast, high teacher expectations were linked to higher academic achievement and classroom conformity, and as we know, there was an assumption that the findings of research into boys would be applicable to girls too (Skelton, 2001). Feminists challenged these taken-for-granted conclusions: researchers such as Lambart (1976) and Fuller (1980) showed how Black girls adopted different attitudes to school, which did not necessarily engage either conformity or resistance as commonly conceived. For example, Fuller (1980) found that the educational 'subculture' the Black girls in her study engaged in involved employment of strategies designed to enable them to take control of their school and future lives (rather than having both controlled by others), by proving themselves academically. These girls also had confidence in their own abilities in terms of being both Black and female. The 'subculture' Fuller identified was underpinned by the girls' rejection of negative stereotypes associated with being Black and female and the limited type of opportunities available to Black women. Qualifications were seen by these girls as essential to challenging 'race' and sex discrimination in employment. Riley (1985), however, suggests that Black girls were committed to education through their own sense of responsibility (i.e. to their families, but this was reflective of Black parental expectations that both males and females should work; thus education becomes important to gaining employment), rather than to prove their self-worth as Fuller suggested. Like Fuller, Amos and Parmar (1981) identified a resistance to education institutional practices amongst Black girls. They showed how they challenged racism and sexism in renegotiating their educational experiences. This resistance/achievement binary involves Black girls challenging stereotypical assumptions on the one hand and achieving on the other (Mirza, 1992). Their resulting behaviours can be read as education oriented but their achievement is not due to teachers having higher expectations of them or positively encouraging them to achieve, rather, due to their own determination (Mirza, 1992).

These studies drew attention to the racist and discriminatory perceptions of minority ethnic girls among educationalists at the time, and how these manifested in lower expectations of these girls (with consequent potential for a self-fulfilling prophesy to emerge), and in pathologisation of their classroom behaviour.

Such work began to highlight the varying ways in which different minority ethnic groups of girls were positioned, with a resulting manifestation in differing experiences and issues of concern. For example, the writing of Wilson (1978) pointed out that the experiences of British Asian girls in schools was not the same as those of British Black girls, with Osler (1989) and others also identifying how, while Black girls were constructed by teachers as too loud and 'unladylike', South Asian girls were conversely positioned as too quiet and obedient. As Brah and Minhas (1985) and others have pointed out, this construction of South Asian girls as 'too quiet' is premised on notions of parental oppression, 'pressure' and tyranny that White teachers often hold in relation to South Asian families (and sometimes East Asian families too; see Archer and Francis, 2007). The impact of such constructions of South Asian girls as being 'quiet' can be that they become 'invisible' in the classroom, and 'systematically forgotten or ignored when it comes to demands on teachers' time' (Brah and Minhas, 1985) – this in turn may have implications for their educational performance and outcomes. In contrast Black girls were visible, much to the frequent disapproval of White teachers. Where teachers hold stereotypical expectations of behaviour of particular ethnic groups 'this may lead to different ... classroom treatment' (Mirza, 1992: 53). Brah and Minhas (1985) noted further that when South Asian girls did not conform to the stereotype of quiet and passive, teachers treated their behaviour more severely than when similar behaviours were exhibited by girls from other ethnic groups (see also Connolly, 1998). Hence feminist work began to illuminate the differences in treatment and experience of girls according to their ethnicity, in contrast to the more simplistic approaches adopted previously.

This empirical work was complemented by critiques of previous assumptions about Black children and families evident in the research and educational policy literature. For example, the notion of the matriarchal Black family (originally mobilised by the influential Moynihan Report in the United States, which premised its arguments that Black underachievement was caused by matriarchal family structures on misogynist assumptions and blindness to racism) was subjected to devastating critique by Phoenix (1987) and Mirza (1992). These Black Feminists drew attention to the negligible difference between numbers of absent fathers in White and Black families, and argued that it is racism rather than family structure that impacts on gender relations within Black families, causing different manifestations of gender in comparison to White families. For example, that racist social structures impacting on Black male employment mean that the gendered breadwinner/dependent dichotomy traditional in White families is less evident in Black families – with a consequent impact on Black girls' perceptions about the importance of education and career. Such analyses again drew attention to the ethnicised and racialised specificity of gender relations, emphasising how White women's experiences could not necessarily be generalised to Black (Mirza, 1992, 1997). Such concerns were extended further to social class: attention was drawn to the interplay of social class with 'race' and gender. For example, Reynolds (1997) has explored the differences in Black women's experiences within and between different social classes.

What we have argued in this section is that many feminists writing about education were, from the start of second-wave feminism, aware of the significance of 'race' in discussions about girls and women teachers' at school. However, in the 1970s and 1980s theoretical (and political) persuasions were such that it was more likely for researchers to focus on 'girls' *or* 'race' and pupils' experiences. The impact of Black Feminist research and writings on the wider field can be witnessed by the ways in which increasingly, towards the end of the 1980s, gender research in education recognised diversity of experience, examining the different experiences and gender constructions of girls within these studies according to ethnicity (and sometimes social class). For example, Sue Lees' (1993) study drew a sort of typology of girls' behaviours and engagement in education, and related 'race' to this, arguing that many of the African-Caribbean girls in her study appeared to fall within the category 'Academic but Anti-school'. Other studies showed increasing attunedness to the impact of ethnicity, with researchers recording the ethnicity (and social class) of all respondents as well as their gender, and analysing the distinct performances of different groups of pupils according to 'race', social class and gender.[3]

Theoretical issues regarding a proliferation of identities

The kind of 'typologies' approach represented in Lees' study regarding educational engagement has, of course, been applied to gender identity (e.g. Mac an Ghaill, 1994; Sewell, 1997). Such approaches illustrate some of the theoretical tensions linked to attempts to analyse more than one discrete factor of identity. On the one hand, as the early researchers of gender and ethnicity argued, to focus on a single aspect of identity (e.g. gender) can render findings relatively meaningless and support discrimination by marginalising the different needs and experiences of minority ethnic respondents. Yet on the other hand, attempts to simultaneously analyse more than one social category invoke a raft of theoretical difficulties. Such issues were already being debated in feminist theory outside education: the additive notion of 'Triple Oppression' (by gender, 'race' and class) (see Carby, 1982) that ostensibly addressed the multiple forms of discrimination/disadvantage experienced by some women, was critiqued as being an inaccurate and oversimplified descriptor of women's experiences, and as evoking an infinite quantity of 'additions' (for example, sexuality, dis/ability, age, religion, and so on). Hence social categories ('race', gender, social class and so forth) were not to be seen as fixed aspects to be added on top of one another, but rather as interacting or 'intersecting' aspects of identity (e.g. Mirza, 1997).

This latter notion and the terminology associated with it has, however, proved problematic in itself. Description of social identities and inequalities as 'intersecting' or 'cross-cutting' have been subject to critique for a range of reasons: these include the argument that such terms evoke a sort of Venn diagram of identity, with fixed, boundaried aspects of identity overlaying one another, hence ignoring the fluidity, interwoven complexity, and holistic manifestation of aspects of identity (Cealey Harrison and Hood-Williams, 1998; Francis, 2001). As Archer *et al.* (2001) have observed, the notion of multiple, intersecting categories can also imply that separate fixed identity components can simply 'slot' (or interlock) together, or be 'added on' to one another. Such perspectives do not adequately acknowledge the complexity of social experience (Brewer, 1993). Cealey Harrison and Hood-Williams (1998) argue that systematic analysis of intersecting, multiple social categories is unworkable in practice, pointing out that potentially a very large number of categories could be of equal importance (they list factors such as religion, sexuality, age and so on in addition to gender, ethnicity and social class, noting the possibility of more). They observe that beyond the analytical challenge in applying all theses categories in any meaningful sense, the 'weight' of each factor as meaningful/impacting on each individual is not easily identifiable.

Moreover, the basis for these categories was extensively critiqued: clearly the status of sex/gender has historically been a central point of debate in feminist theory; but in other fields of identity studies attention turned to interrogation of 'commonsense' conceptions of 'race' and ethnicity, social class and sexuality.

In the field of ethnicity, an important contribution was made by Stuart Hall's non-essentialised theoretical approach. In particular, his conceptualisation of 'new ethnicities' (1992) understood ethnic identities as always 'in process', constructed through social, cultural and discursive processes, and integral to the production of broader social identity. This theoretical position contested popular perceptions of ethnic groups as homogenous, fixed entities; maintaining rather that ethnic boundaries are actually fluid, contextual and contested. Hence ethnic delineations, 'cultures' and so on are, like ethnic identities, forever 'becoming' (Hall, 1992; Anthias and Yuval-Davis, 1992) and of course, as Anthias and Yuval-Davis observe, these ethnic identities are inflected by other aspects of social identity such as social class and gender (Anthias and Yuval-Davis 1992).

The issues around categorisation of ethnic groups can be traced through gender and education research, as in the late 1970s and early 1980s researchers often chose to analyse only according to two or three different 'ethnic' groups (typically White and Black, or sometimes White, Black and Asian).[4] It might be argued that in the early 1980s these categories were more representative of ethnic diversity than is the case in contemporary times, but even then these categories in no means addressed the existing diversity and nuance of ethnicity as represented in the UK. Again, such limitations were being addressed in broader debates around categorisation and terminology. In the 1970s and 1980s the term 'Black' was advocated as a political identity which could unite all 'people of colour' (all those not White) as experiencing racism in White societies, and in challenging such racism. However, this political identification did not suit everyone. First, the evocation of dark skin by the word 'Black' was alienating to some, with various (particularly South East and East Asian) minority ethnic commentators maintaining that they did not experience themselves as 'Black' (Modood, 1994). Indeed, the identification with 'Blackness' made it difficult to incorporate challenges to racism against White minority groups such as Irish and (increasingly) Eastern European migrants. Second, because the narrow identification appeared to marginalise the needs and identities of some groups (e.g. South Asians; see e.g. Modood, 1994; also those with hybrid/hyphenated identities; see, e.g. Werbner and Modood, 1997; Anthias, 2001). The term 'Black' never addressed religious ethnicisation and racism (such as in the Jewish case), which of course has become heightened with the recent rise of Islamophobia in the West. As Archer and Francis (2007) observe, the complexity of the contemporary British scene in terms of ethnic identities and identifications – albeit often 'racialised' – works to challenge and disrupt unitary notions of collectivity organised around colour-based or geographic-heritage categorisations. 'New' migrants, especially refugees and asylum seekers, are subject to exclusionary, racialised and racist practices, as are Muslims; yet such practices often do not fit comfortably in previously applied categories of cultural and biological racism.

Of further political concern is the way that Whiteness tends to have been ignored in studies of gender and education (Charles, 1992; Phoenix, 1997; Nayak, 2001;

Reay *et al.*, 2007). In this the field can be seen as no worse than other areas of social research, and yet clearly the underpinning assumption that, if minority ethnic subjects are not present, ethnicity is not an issue (see Gaine, 1995, or Kannen and Acker, 2008, for critique), is deeply problematic, hence demanding redress. As Maylor and Read (2007) show, this lack of attention to Whiteness and corresponding assumption that ethnic identity equates with *minority* ethnic identity carries through to teaching practice within schools. The consequence is an exoticisation and Othering of 'ethnic' identity and culture (a common criticism of the application of multicultural approaches in schools; see Brah 1994) and an anxiety or resentment among many White pupils that they do not have an ethnic identity (Maylor and Read, 2007). Moreover, research by Reay *et al.* (2007) highlights the importance of empirical data in this field. Examining the practices of urban middle-class White parents who had bucked a social class trend by choosing to send their children to their local school, Reay *et al.* (2007) found disturbing patterns in which middle-class 'aquisitiveness' and appropriation emerged, in their extraction of 'value' from the minority ethnic Other. Some minority ethnic pupils and parents were valued by these White middle-class parents (though in rather stereotypical and patronising terms), while other groups – particularly Black families and White working-class families – were seen as excessive and pathologised.

Hence calls have been made to researchers across the social sciences for further interrogation of Whiteness and exploration of ethnic majorities. Without critical attention to them, dominant ethnicities and Whiteness remain 'hidden' (by normalisation) and their manifestation in racialised identities and inequalities unexamined (Charles, 1992; Anthias 1992; Bonnett, 2000).

Such 'hidden' identities also apply to some extent to mixed heritage identities, albeit for rather different reasons. Children of mixed heritage comprise the fastest growing pupil population, yet evidence suggests they are often ignored in the classroom/curriculum (Cline *et al.*, 2002; Tikly *et al.*, 2004). Their experiences are beginning to be addressed, including in terms of gender, and feminists have been at the forefront of those dispelling myths of 'confused identities' resulting from 'culture clashes' that have traditionally been projected on to mixed heritage pupils (see e.g. Tizard and Phoenix 2002; Ali, 2003a, b; Dewan, 2008).

We turn now to consider how these theoretical insights have played out in more recent research into gender and school identities. As we have stated, two of the central concerns of early second-wave feminists which are as pertinent today are 'achievement' and 'gendered experiences in schools' and we shall pursue these themes here, attending first to research on the interaction between gender and ethnicity in educational achievement.

Gender, 'race' and achievement

One of the most influential British contributions to the field of gender, 'race' and education has been Heidi Mirza's book *Young, Female and Black* (1992). This publication differed from many of its predecessors in its focus on gender, ethnicity and *patterns of educational achievement*. As we have seen, previous studies had tended to examine the educational experiences of minority ethnic girls, and the perceptions of their teachers: Mirza's study engaged these areas too, but included a strong focus on attainment. In particular, Mirza launched a devastating attack on previous work on Black pupils' achievement, wherein, she argued, generalisations were made about Black educational attainment exclusively based on the (under)achievement of Black boys. Mirza conducted analysis of the quantitative data on educational achievement as well as her own qualitative data to show how the notion of 'Black underachievement' was a myth as applied to Black girls: Black girls were doing as well as their White counterparts, and rather better in some areas (such as regards take-up of post-compulsory education and subsequent achievement therein). It was the (dramatic) underachievement of Black boys that was skewing the results for 'Black children': the lack of attention to gender and subsequent lack of differentiation was causing misleading and pejorative statements in relation to Black girls.

As we have noted elsewhere (Francis and Skelton, 2005; Archer and Francis, 2007), the situation is now since changed, with almost a reverse situation emerging in the ignorance of Black girls' underachievement due to the furore concerning the underachievement of Black boys. Arguably this contemporary attention to the educational performance of Black boys has been precipitated by the rise in policy preoccupation with educational achievement, and we shall turn to this issue next before elaborating our point in relation to the absence of attention to Black girls.

We have expanded elsewhere upon how a particular 'socio-economic moment' in government policy-making mobilised a series of discursive practices that precipitated concern with boys' 'underachievement' (see Francis and Skelton, 2005; also Chapter 7). The rise and hegemony of human capital theory and neoliberalism in formulating policy-makers' perceptions (with the premise that to ensure a nation's affluence and influence it must supply increasingly skilled and flexible workers to compete in the global marketplace) had an especial bearing on education policy. As we have shown, this manifested in a preoccupation with educational 'standards and effectiveness' (initiated by the Conservative governments in the 1980s and early 1990s and maintained by the New Labour administrations since 1997; [Francis and Skelton, 2005]). Standards and effectiveness have largely been measured in terms of achievement at different official tests (which also proliferated during this period); especially GCSE results (tests taken at the end of compulsory schooling). A tool seen by policy-makers as making school performance transparent (and aiding parent 'consumers' in their choices in the new education quasi-market) was the publication of 'League Tables', which depicted the relative achievements of a school's pupils at GCSE exams. Crucially, these League Tables were broken down by gender: their analysis revealed vividly for the first time that boys were not outperforming girls in the way that had (apparently) been assumed.

The ensuing 'moral panic' (as many feminists have branded it) around 'boys' underachievement' involved a great deal of anxious articulation among both journalists and politicians; but the new attention to achievement in relation to different facets of identity (e.g gender) also highlighted further discrepancies in overall achievement on the basis of other aspects of social identity, including ethnicity. The concern among policy-makers at the time can be evidenced in their commissioning of key pieces of work analysing the impact of aspects of social identity on educational achievement. Prime examples include the reports by Gillborn and Gipps (1996) and Gillborn and Mirza (2000), which were based on quantitative analysis of patterns of educational achievement according to ethnicity, social class and gender, funded by OfSTED. Increasingly too the Department of Education (in its various manifestations: first Department for Education and Science, then Department for Education and Employment [DfEE], then Department for Education and Skills [DfES], and currently Department for Children, Schools and Families [DCSF]) developed and maintained its own, openly accessible, quantitative data on achievement according to aspects of social identity.

What the Gillborn and Gipps and Gillborn and Mirza studies showed was that gaps *between* groups according to social class and ethnicity were larger than gaps *within* ethnicity and social class groups according to gender. Hence they argued from their analysis that ethnicity and social class were more significant as predictors of educational success than gender, having a greater impact on achievement. This was clearly an important finding in relation to the continuing policy and media preoccupation with gender and achievement. Such findings did not appear to dampen this fervour around gender at the time they were published. (Perhaps this is explained by the extent to which the 'moral panic' was so entrenched, with various political explanations for this discursive hegemony [Epstein *et al.*, 1998]; or perhaps because a counter-reading of the data showed that in terms of language and literacy subjects at least, girls consistently exceeded boys within their ethnicity and social class groups [Francis and Skelton, 2005; Skelton *et al.*, 2007]). Yet, as we saw in the previous chapter, recently social class has begun gradually to re-emerge (albeit faintly) in policy writings on educational achievement (see, for example, DfES 2007). Certainly concerns with ethnicity and achievement have been in the ascendancy for a significant period.[5] It may be argued that such concerns emerged, like the concerns about boys' achievement more widely, at a specific social moment, which combined tensions around particular manifestations of masculinity (with the notion of a 'crisis of masculinity' as a back-drop) with concerns about educational achievement as patterned by social identity. Hence, coinciding with the publication of quantitative analysis around ethnicity and achievement came studies of masculinity as performed by Black boys in school (e.g. Sewell, 1997; Connolly, 1998). Such studies drew attention to the stereotypical perceptions of Black boys held by teachers, including lower expectations of achievement and behaviour, and the potential impact of such stereotypical expectations on both exclusion rates and (under)achievement among Black boys.

The concerns raised by such work, and by quantitative analysis showing that Black boys (especially those of African-Caribbean heritage) are one of the most significantly underachieving social groups[6] in educational terms, has led to a plethora of government funded studies aimed at raising the educational achievement of Black boys (e.g. Blair and Bourne, 1998; DfES, 2006; Demie, 2005). As with the broader discourse on the 'underachievement' of boys more generally, hypotheses have been drawn that explanations for this underachievement may be found in factors such as the lack of 'identity matching' or available minority ethnic 'role models' within the teacher population; and studies have been undertaken to investigate such assumptions (e.g. Carrington 2002; Maylor *et al.*, 2006). As in the case of 'gender matching' in the teacher workforce, studies of the notion of Black male teachers as automatic positive role models for Black boys – consequently engaging them with education and hence aiding their achievement – have shown this premise to be deeply flawed and problematic (Carrington 2002; Maylor *et al.*, 2006; Maylor (forthcoming). However, what is evident here is the amount of both research energy and government resourcing on investigations of Black boys' underachievement – the focus being very much on the *boys*. Although Black girls are underachieving in relation to their White counterparts,[7] they are entirely ignored in the policy debate which focuses on Black boys' underachievement – encouraging the assumption that because Black girls are outperforming Black boys, their achievement is not an issue, but as we have spelled out elsewhere, this is far from the case (Archer and Francis, 2007).

For example, when we look at the results for KS2 in 2006, we can see that Black Caribbean girls are underperforming in relation to White British boys and girls at both maths and science (though they outperform White British boys at English); and the largest gap therein – that between Black Caribbean girls and White British boys at science, is 14 per cent (63 per cent of Black Caribbean girls attained level 4 and above at KS2 maths in 2006, compared to 77 per cent of White British boys; see Skelton *et al.*, 2007). Of those pupils gaining the marker of five A*–C grades at GCSE in England in 2006, Black girls significantly underperform overall in comparison with their White counterparts, as Table 4.1 illustrates.

We can see from Table 4.1 that there us a 10 per cent gap between those Black Caribbean girls and White girls not taking free school meals in terms of proportions gaining 5 A*–C grades (65.6 per cent of White British girls; 55.9 per cent of Black Caribbean girls). Although, again, it is interesting to note that among the far smaller groups of those children taking free school meals, there is a 10 per cent gap in achievement between Black Caribbean girls and White British girls gaining 5 A*–C grades, in this case favouring Black girls. Overall however, when the numbers are combined, 62 per cent of White British girls gain 5 A*–C grades, compared with only 53 per cent of Black Caribbean girls. Yet this point is ignored by media and policy commentary, which continues to focus exclusively on the (under)achievement of Black boys (with research funding also targeting this specific issue), and, as Ward and Robinson-Wood (2006) have shown, minority ethnic girls continue to be under-represented in more general debates on children's educational experiences.

Table 4.1 Achievements at Key Stage 4 GCSE and equivalent in 2006 by ethnicity, free school meals and gender (females)

| | Non FSM | | | | FSM | | | |
| | % achieving | | | | % achieving | | | |
Ethnicity	Eligible pupils	5 A* to C	5 A* to C including E and M	Any passes	Eligible pupils	5 A* to C	5 A* to C including E and M	Any passes
Girls White	217,990	65.7	52.0	98.3	26,901	31.6	18.4	93.8
White British	212,013	65.6	51.9	98.3	25,655	31.3	18.1	93.8
Irish	939	70.8	59.7	98.1	192	32.8	22.4	93.2
Traveller of Irish Heritage	36	41.7	27.8	88.9	33	3.0	0.0	69.7
Gypsy/Roma	70	15.7	7.1	72.9	69	5.8	4.3	82.6
Any other White background	4932	68.9	55.8	98.1	952	43.5	26.6	96.6
Mixed	5346	66.4	52.7	97.9	1474	40.4	25.1	95.3
White and Black Caribbean	1978	58.9	42.7	97.8	647	38.2	20.6	94.4
White and Black African	475	67.2	53.5	97.5	165	44.2	29.1	95.2
White and Asian	1036	77.4	67.9	98.1	196	42.9	34.2	95.4
Any other mixed background	1857	68.1	54.7	98.1	466	41.2	26.2	96.4
Asian	12,881	70.6	56.5	99.0	5111	56.7	36.5	98.3
Indian	5732	78.3	66.6	99.5	749	62.6	45.5	98.0
Pakistani	4249	60.5	43.0	98.4	2359	52.4	31.2	98.0
Bangladeshi	1322	64.4	46.5	99.4	1628	59.7	38.5	99.3
Any other Asian background	1578	75.0	64.5	98.7	375	59.5	43.5	96.8
Black	7601	59.3	44.5	98.5	3344	43.9	28.2	97.3
Black Caribbean	3333	55.9	39.4	98.9	1054	41.6	23.9	97.3
Black African	3348	62.9	50.4	98.4	1956	44.5	30.4	97.4
Any other Black background	920	58.8	41.5	97.4	334	47.3	28.7	96.4
Chinese	954	84.9	73.6	98.7	130	80.0	60.0	99.2
Any other other ethnic group	1521	66.3	52.9	97.4	796	53.1	33.4	96.4
All Pupils[3]	252,625	65.7	52.0	98.3	38,625	37.0	22.3	94.9

Source: standards.dfes.gov.uk/genderandachievement/understanding/analysis/

Contemporary trajectories

Recent research has continued to draw and build on the early work established by Black Feminists and other theorists of gender, ethnicity and education. Some work has developed the explorations of the experiences of girls from particular minority ethnic groups and their positionings according to, as well as their performances of, gender and ethnic identity. Examples include the work of researchers such as Shain (2003) and Ahmad (2001) examining the educational experiences of South Asian girls; Ali (2003a) and Tizard and Phoenix (2002) on dual heritage girls; and Archer and Francis' analysis of the educational positioning of British Chinese girls (Archer and Francis, 2007). This body of work has also broadened to include research on boys as well as girls, including for example, Muslim boys (Archer, 2003). However, research studies specifically focusing on the gender identities and performances of particular minority ethnic groups in relation to education, and the inter-relation of ethnicity and gender in their performances of selfhood, remain relatively few and far between. This under-representation of ethnicity research with a strong focus on gender was noted in our collection of key contributions to *Gender and Education* journal (Skelton and Francis, 2005) and may be considered a cause for concern.

What has grown more common is research extending subtle analysis of multiple aspects of identity to the gender performances among multi-ethnic groups of pupils. Notable examples here include Connolly's examination of constructions of gender, ethnicity and social class in primary school (1998); Ali's study of dual-heritage girls (2003a); work by Reay examining parental interaction with schools (1998) and the peer-relations and gender constructions among different groups of primary school girls (2001); Archer's work exploring constructions of gender, ethnicity and educational aspiration/engagement among urban youths (Archer and Yamashita, 2003; Archer *et al.*, 2007); and Renold's work on high achieving girls (2007). These studies, and others like them, share a common approach in their understanding of gender and ethnicity as socially constructed or performed, and their analysis of diversity in such performances among a variety of groups. Similarly, some researchers have extended such conceptual analyses to educational policy and its impact in the classroom, applying post-structuralist discourse analysis to examine the ways in which discourses of gender and ethnicity shape such policy and produce individual subjects in particular ways (Youdell, 2003; Archer and Francis, 2007; Kenway *et al.*, 2006) These lists of studies could go on: we have used a few studies with particularly strong attention to ethnicity as exemplars here, but it is probably not over-complacent to say that a majority of studies in the field of gender and education that include minority ethnic respondents now include consideration of ethnicity in their analysis. Analysis of Whiteness arguably remains under-represented, but is increasingly brought under scrutiny (e.g. Frankenburg, 1993, 1997; Ware, 1992; Kehily and Nayak, 2007).

This attention to diversity and plurality of ethnic and other forms of identity reflects the theoretical trajectory from identity politics and 'standpoint theory' (assuming the authenticity of different 'voices' representing particular identity groups), to developments in poststructural and postcolonial theory, that are drawn on by researchers in education. These theoretical positions have often been drawn together under the banner 'critical theory', and share a concern with power as well as diversity and critique. Some postcolonial theory has been criticised by post-structuralist commentators for slippage into identity politics or modernist epistemology: for example, Chun (1996) accuses Said's influential book 'Orientalism' (1978) of evoking a 'real' Orient which is misrepresented or distorted by the West. Chun and others go on to deconstruct the very notion of ethnic identity itself. Such approaches are prey to common criticisms of poststructuralism: that is, that they fail to adequately acknowledge the material actuality of power differentials (in this case, racism) which operates to interpolate individuals to construct their identities accordingly. As Soper (1990) argued so cogently with Derrida's claim that women should abandon reference to gender to further the cause of equality, one may cease allusion to gender, yet it does not prevent one falling prey to sexism or male violence – the same may be said of ethnic identity and racism (Ang, 1998).

Yet these debates aside, post-colonial and post-structural theorists continue to influence work in gender and education. For example, Archer (e.g. 2003; Archer and Yamashita, 2003; Archer *et al.*, 2007) has drawn heavily on the work of Stuart Hall in her studies of urban youths, exploring his conceptions of hybridity and 'new ethnicities' in relation to particular groups of pupils, as well as attending to their gender and social class identities. Ringrose and Renold apply metaphors developed by Deleuze and Guattari (1987) such as the nomad, the rhizome, and 'lines of flight', to their analysis of the diverse and complex identities of high-achieving girls (Renold, 2006) and girl bullying (Ringrose and Renold, 2007). Other researchers have drawn on structuralist semiotic and post-structuralist ideas in order to deconstruct the discourses shaping the production of gender and ethnicity in education. For example, Archer and Francis (2007) unpick the relational discourses of 'race', gender and educational achievement evident in teacher's talk to show how different dichotomies manifest in relation to the ideal and 'Other learners'. This work critiques the normalised but unspoken discursive construction of the 'ideal' pupil as White, middle class and male, and how this model remains stable in spite of variations in educational achievement (see also Rollock, 2007).

A focus on the practices and constructions operated by educational institutions and their staff has been retained in recent research. In their study of excluded secondary school pupils from different ethnic groups (White, Asian and African-Caribbean), Wright, Weekes and McGlaughlin (2000) sought to explain how changing educational policies affected the school processes which led to exclusion. Schools were found to vary in their exclusion policies: the conflict between schools and pupils was related to the sanctions schools deployed towards pupil resistance. In turn, pupil resistance and their responses to sanctions were mediated through the gendered and racialised positions of the pupils. Significantly, the researchers discovered that teachers saw differences *between* the behaviours and explanations for the behaviours of White pupils, whilst Black pupils – boys and girls – were regarded and treated as if they were a homogenous group (and believed to be far more likely to be disruptive than other ethnic groups). Similar findings are recorded by researchers such as Sewell, 1997; Osler and Hill, 1999; Frosh *et al.*, 2002; and Youdell, 2003. The influence of 'race' and gender on teacher perceptions and behaviour management needs to be continually scrutinised, especially as such perceptions impact on pupil exclusions: African-Caribbean males are three times more likely to be excluded than White pupils (Parsons *et al.*, 2005; Bull, 2006; DfES, 2006), and like their male counterparts, African-Caribbean girls are disproportionately excluded (Osler *et al.*, 2002). A strong illustration of the ways in which gendered and racialised stereotypes/teacher expectations of behaviour are likely to negatively influence pupils' educational outcomes.

Conclusion

This chapter has attempted to chart the progress of research on gender, 'race' and ethnicity in education, from early accounts of the experiences of particular groups of minority ethnic pupils in the classroom, through 'standpoint' and identity political positions, to the frequently post-colonial and/or post-structuralist analyses of contemporary research in the field. We have also observed a change in focus (represented both in work on gender, ethnicity and education, and in research on ethnicity and education more broadly) from classroom experiences to educational achievement and outcomes. We have argued this to reflect the contemporary policy concern with achievement; yet this is in no way to devalue the importance of such work, or to downplay the significance of achievement gaps in patterns of educational achievement according to ethnicity. Clearly these gaps may be seen as the product of the various stereotyping and direct/indirect discrimination recorded in educational research from the 1970s to the present day.

The existence and durability of these educational achievement gaps according to ethnicity constitutes a schooling scandal in its own right. In terms of gender however, we would argue that the new scandal is the lack of attention to minority ethnic girls – and specifically, Black and minority ethnic *girls'* underachievement. As we have shown, this may be argued to be particularly the case for African-Caribbean girls. We seem to have come full circle, as the studies of minority ethnic girls' experiences of schooling, emerging from second-wave feminism in the late 1970s, were prompted by the absence of attention to these girls and/or critique of their positioning in raced and gendered discourses. It seems timely to launch a new critique of old practices.

5 Sexualities and sexual harassment in schools

Looking back over the last three decades at the literature on gender and education, it is understandings of 'sexualities' that have often been especially critical in informing and transforming feminist knowledge and thinking. In the early years of second wave feminism consideration of sexualities emerged in discussions on female teachers and pupils' sexual orientation (Trenchard and Warren, 1984; Squirrel, 1989) and the sexual harassment of females at school (Whitbread, 1980; Lees, 1986; Herbert, 1989; Holly, 1985). As more sophisticated theories around notions of 'difference' began to influence feminism, there was a shift away from 'global' concepts of women (see Chapter 2) towards one which allowed explorations of the discourses that constitute 'women'. This more complex approach includes that work influenced by Foucault's geneaological examination of the historical production of sexuality: such theorising has led to analyses of 'sexual subjectivities' where sexuality is seen as culturally, socially and historically situated (Weedon, 1987). Some feminists have long argued that gender and sexuality are inseparable (e.g. Rich, 1980) and later in the chapter we elaborate how this inseparability is being increasingly commented on in recent feminist work.

The aim of this chapter is to explore the key themes raised by second-wave feminists examining issues of sexuality in education, and how these themes have been developed and added to in contemporary work. As educational achievement has rarely been formally considered in relation to sexuality (given that records on sexuality are not kept), our focus in this chapter is on aspects of *educational experience* in relation to sexualities. The research and literature on sexuality, gender and education covers a number of areas, which intersect in more recent theorising. For readers new to feminism and education it is probably most useful if we trace how sexuality(ies) have figured in, and impacted on, debates and discussions on education and schooling.

One of the central tenets of early second-wave feminism was 'the personal is political'. This was to recognise that inequalities experienced by women were not solely located in public places such as politics, the labour market and the economy, but extended to the potential for exploitation and oppression in women's domestic and emotional lives (Eisenstein, 1984; Whelehan, 1995). Here, the power of heterosexual expectations was shown to frame the lives of girls and young women in terms of 'getting a boyfriend', followed by marriage and motherhood.

Adrienne Rich (1980) referred to 'compulsory heterosexuality' whereby girls had little choice over their sexuality but were constrained to demonstrate their 'attractiveness' (to men) through their ability to 'catch a husband' (on whom they would then be reliant for economic and emotional security). Sue Lees (2000: 260) quotes one of the girls in her study as saying 'I will get married when I've had my life': thus, she argues, 'in other words, the choice of getting married becomes a negative one – of avoiding being left on the shelf'.

Also, for Marxist-socialist Feminists, the sexual division of labour within the family echoed that of the division of labour in the economy with the 'masters' being the husbands who controlled the 'labourers', i.e. their wives who carried out the tasks of domestic servants (Pateman, 1988). However, unlike the division of labour in the workplace, where such unequal relationships between 'employer/master' and 'employee/worker' were obvious and open to challenge, the inequalities between husbands and wives were masked within 'natural' and 'taken-for-granted' familial relationships. For example, women's emotional labour, the care of a couple's children and domestic work in the home, went unrecognised and unremunerated. The consequences of this have become widely known, with the increase in the breakdown of marriages resulting in more women living in poverty. Family responsibilities have meant more women than men are single parents and more women than men take on part-time, low-skilled jobs, thus not accumulating the level of pensions that will enable a comfortable old age (Albeda and Tilly, 1997; Ginn, 2003). Furthermore, feminists have recorded how gendered inequality in heterosexual relationships often underpins/results in domestic violence, and observed how marital breakdown has also exacerbated the extent and levels of domestic violence against women (Wilson and Daly, 1998; Humphreys and Stanley, 2006).

During second-wave feminism, lesbian feminist work launched an important challenge, both to feminist theorising, and more broadly to the heterosexist social assumptions supporting patterns of family life in contemporary society. On the one hand, lesbian feminists were at the forefront of those critiquing the patriarchal, oppressive nature of heterosexual relationships, within which gender equality was inbuilt and perpetuated (e.g. Rich, 1980; Dworkin and MacKinnon, 1985; Dworkin, 1987; Jeffreys, 1986). Some of these women examined the nature of heterosexual sex, arguing that heterosexual sexual practices were in themselves oppressive and even violent to women, in their reflection and actualising of gender power inequalities (Dworkin, 1987; Jeffreys, 1986, 1987, 2005). Such arguments supported practices of 'political lesbianism' (Leeds Revolutionary Feminist Group, 1981; Jeffreys, 1986) and separatism, demands for which challenged feminist theory and practice in the 1970s and early 1980s.[1] Demands for such practices presented challenges to hetereosexual feminists, who sometimes complained of feeling excluded, and/or that they had to justify their sexual choices to practising lesbian feminists, who might present as 'more feminist' than them on these bases. Such complaints were, of course, experienced as ironic by many lesbian feminists, given the homophobia to which they were daily subjected due to the overwhelming heterosexism of society at large. However, more generally the campaigning work of lesbian feminists drew attention to the heterosexist tendencies of the broader feminist movement, and forced feminist introspection in this regard.

How do these concerns around sexuality relate to feminists' work on education and schooling? Feminists and pro-feminists writing on this area have observed that whilst issues around sexuality have been central to feminist understanding and theorising, it has taken longer for them to be recognised in debates and discussions on equity in education than either 'race' or 'social class'. In 1989 Gillian Squirrel commented on how 'within mainstream academic research it would appear that sexuality and education are not thought a suitable coupling' (p. 87). As Debbie Epstein and Richard Johnson (1998: 1) later explained:

> Putting the terms 'schooling' and 'sexuality' together is the stuff of which scandal can be, and often is, made. ... This may be partly because schooling stands rather on the 'public' side of public/private divisions while sexuality is definitely on the private side.

When Epstein and Johnson talk about 'the stuff of which scandal is made' they are referring to issues around sexual orientation and, in particular, anxieties around paedophilia. Whilst these are of import to feminists/profeminists in education, this interpretation of 'sexualities' and schooling is, as Epstein and Johnson indicate, just one aspect of a broader concept. In order for us to trace and explore various aspects of sexualities and schooling, including sexual orientation, sexual harassment, sexual cultures, sex education and 'romance relations', we will begin with the 'stuff of scandal' and focus here on teachers' sexual orientation and working with children.

Teachers' sexual orientation and working with children

We do not wish to spend time focusing on media reportage of incidents where teachers have had sexual relationships with secondary age pupils (though we do revisit the issue of such relationships under 'romance relations' below). Instead we will explore pro/feminist literature on how (actual or presumed) sexual orientation has informed notions of who is 'suitable' to teach children.

Heterosexuality has been of critical, yet largely unspoken, significance in discourses of 'suitability' for teaching. Feminist historians of the teaching profession and teacher unions have drawn attention to how constructions of sexuality have shaped women teachers' career opportunities and experiences. We have spoken of 'compulsory heterosexuality' and certainly, for most of the twentieth century (and before), marriage was seen to be the goal of all women. At one stage, a 'marriage bar' was introduced into teaching whereby a single female teacher would have her contract ended when she married (this ran from the 1920s to the early 1930s). The reasoning for the marriage bar was that a woman would not be able to fulfil her professional responsibilities as a teacher alongside those of her personal, family commitments. In reality, the marriage bar was a means of preventing unemployment amongst newly qualified teachers.[2]

The distinction between married women and single women teachers was used by one of the teacher unions, the National Association of Schoolmasters (NAS) in their battles to secure better pay deals for men teachers (Littlewood, 1995; Oram, 1999). In her discussion of the treatment of women teachers in the documents produced by the NAS, Margaret Littlewood (1995) observed how the term 'married women' was used alongside comments on 'true womanhood'. In contrast, single women teachers were characterised as 'unnatural' in that they were desexed, celibate, advocates of women's rights. Thus, women teachers were in a no-win situation: they were either single teachers employed on full contracts but were positioned as frigid or 'abnormal' (i.e. lesbians) or, if married, regarded as more sexually and personally fulfilled but without the benefits of a teaching contract.

In the early part of the twentieth century, discussions on single-sex versus co-educational schooling included concerns regarding the sexuality of women teachers and the impact of these on pupils. (Blount [2000] discusses how these debates were also extended to men teachers, who were also scrutinised in terms of sexuality.) At the same time as these debates were taking place (around the 1920s), there was an increased interest more generally in sexuality, and experts such as the sexologist Havelock Ellis, and later, the pioneer of birth control, Marie Stopes, spoke widely on the subject. Indeed Marie Stopes was one of the most outspoken opponents of single women teachers working in single-sex schools. In 1926 she argued against the imposition of the marriage bar on the grounds that any school with a high proportion of unmarried women teachers would damage the growing child's mental health and sexual development. Single women teachers were portrayed by Stopes as not only dangerous to children but because they had failed to get married, they were vitriolic and jealous towards married women colleagues. Also, Stopes seemed to believe that, if they chose or were unable to marry, single women teachers leaned towards lesbianism (and that this latter was problematic). This is what Oram (1999: 103) refers to when she notes how 'sexology and psychology had also categorised lesbian sexuality for the first time, and created an ambiguous overlap with spinsterhood'. As Faraday (1989: 38) says of Stopes:

> According to her observations, lesbian teachers came in varying degrees of unwholesomeness, from the 'slightly erotic and almost hysterically affectionate' through to those 'indulging in intense and repeated physical experiences with a member of their own sex'.

The problems of being pathologised as 'other' (than heterosexual) has placed pressure on both women and men teachers up to the present day (Epstein and Johnson, 1998; Berrill and Martino, 2002; Blount, 2004), with many gay and lesbian teachers finding it easier not to 'come out' to colleagues (Spraggs, 1994; Khayatt, 1997). Also, as Ferfolja (2007) points out in her account of lesbian teachers who choose to stay 'closeted' and pass as heterosexuals in school, where heterosexual teachers can draw on their personal experiences and histories in their teaching and relationships with pupils, such opportunities are denied to

LGBT[3] teachers, thus inhibiting their pedagogical approaches. These practices were analysed and challenged by various feminist/gay activist groups in the 1980s, with various pamphlets and interventions drawing attention to the implication of heterosexist practices for gay teachers and pupils, and encouraging heterosexual teachers to be attuned to inclusion in their own practices. Notable examples are from left-leaning London organisations including the Greater London Council and ILEA. Yet this was to change with the instigation of the Conservative 'Clause 28' legislation, as we shall see below. However, as Coffey and Delamont (2000) report, some LGBT teachers have 'outed' themselves in order to challenge the heterosexist nature of schooling and curriculum and, importantly, to provide lesbian and gay pupils with positive images of their sexuality.

Today it is the sexual orientation and sexuality of men teachers of young children that appears to receive the most attention. In research studies, men teachers frequently talk of awareness (and wariness) of the physical and emotional contact required in working with young children (Skelton, 1991, 2003; Thornton, 1998; Johnson *et al.,* 1999; Smedley, 1999; Sumsion, 2000; Carrington, 2002) and this seems to be of even greater concern for gay men than for heterosexual men teachers (Allan, 1993; King, 2000), which is perhaps not surprising given Sargent's (2001: 47) observation that 'suspicions of homosexuality and the conflation of gayness with paedophilia are powerful sanctions that carry legal implications'. Ferfolja (2007) discusses the closely associated ways in which gay women teachers negotiate their sexualities at work, often feeling compelled to 'pass' as heterosexual: this illuminates how powerful heterosexual normativity remains within educational institutions in spite of the introduction of some more liberal legislation with regard to gay rights.

We have started by dealing with issues around sexual orientation because, as we said at the beginning, it is one aspect that receives significant attention. However, feminist discussions on sexualities and schooling comprise more than this one facet. Two key themes which come under the umbrella of sexuality and which have featured in discussions from the start of second-wave feminism are sex education, and the impact of sexual harassment on education and schooling.

Sex education

The main concern for second-wave feminists was how sex education was taught in schools, and the central points of concern – including, for example, the sex education curriculum, and the point at which sex education is addressed in schools – remain feminist preoccupations to the present day (Measor and Sikes, 1992). For the most part, the sex education taught in schools was simply about biological reproduction, contraception and sexually transmitted diseases, what Lenskyj (1990: 217) called 'a plumbing and prevention approach'. Not only have feminists noted the problematic (and often inaccurate) presentation of heterosexual sex acts as something 'done to a woman by a man', with women presented as bereft of sexual pleasure and action, but they have also railed at the heterosexist silencing of 'other' manifestations of sexuality. An ongoing feminist criticism has been the lack of attention paid to the emotional elements of relationships within the sex education curriculum. Before considering these issues in more detail it is worth setting out the UK educational policy requirements on sex education at various times, as this policy has informed the boundaries of sex education in schools.

As Alldred and David (2007) observe, since the nineteenth century Western societies have traditionally tended to construct children as 'innocent' and non-sexual, and sex and sexuality as to some extent 'taboo' and ideally removed from the realm of children. Such constructions cause the education of children about sex, and the age at which such education is undertaken, to be controversial. Education policy typically reflects prevalent social assumptions that children are not sexual or sexually aware, and hence their education about sex to be potentially 'dangerous' or contaminating. Alldred and David's book *Get Real About Sex* draws on qualitative data and policy analyses to provide an interrogation of the impact of socio-political trends on views around sex education, and the ways in which these discourses play out in education policy. British education policy clearly reflects the level to which sex education is politically contested and sensitive: this is illustrated for example by concerns to empower parents and to adequately reflect the concerns of institutions articulating different moral views of sex education. Such concerns are illustrated by The Education (No. 2) Act 1986, which took powers over sex education away from local education authorities (LEAs) and gave them over to school governors. These powers included the right to decide whether sex education should be taught at all. The school governors were obliged to inform and consult with parents and were also given the power to allow individual parents to withdraw their children from sex education. Importantly for feminists concerned about the emphasis on heterosexuality at the expenses of other forms of relationships, this Act prioritised 'the family' (as narrowly conceived):

> Where sex education is given … it is given in such a manner as to encourage those pupils to have due regard to moral considerations and the value of family life.

> (Education Act 1986)

These trends expressing social homophobia and conservative desires to 'protect innocent children' were arguably at their most manifest in the Conservative government's introduction of the infamous 'Section 28'. Section 28 of the Local Government Act 1988 amended the Local Government Act 1986: the amendment stated that a Local Education Authority *'shall not intentionally promote homosexuality or publish material with the intention of promoting homosexuality'* or *'promote the teaching in any maintained school of the acceptability of homosexuality as a pretended family relationship'*. This openly homophobic stance (the phrase 'pretended family relationship' is glaring in its spite) provoked numerous large-scale demonstrations across the UK, but the amended bill was nevertheless instated, with devastating effects in schools. Teachers and other educationalists were worried that the provision of children's access to any materials that portrayed gay relationships in an unproblematic light might be considered to be 'promoting homosexuality' and hence many refrained from providing access to such materials. For gay teachers the issue was particularly acute, as even being openly 'out' within school might potentially be considered to be promoting homosexuality (in addition to the point of having to survive within a created climate in which homosexuality was specifically and overtly pathologised). Teachers were even afraid to discuss gay issues with students who were questionning their own sexuality, or who were experiencing homophobic bullying.

The Education Act 1986 was superseded by the Education Act 1993 which required all maintained primary and secondary schools to have a written statement of whatever policy they adopted on sex education and to make it available to parents on request. Sex education remained the responsibility of school governors. The Act granted the *general* right of withdrawal and made adjustments to sex education in the National Curriculum to allow this. The governing bodies of all secondary schools were required to make sex education provision (outside the National Curriculum) for all pupils (through Personal and Social Education [PSE]). Primary school governing bodies had the right to decide not to offer sex education outside the national curriculum. Parents had the right to withdraw children from all or any aspect of sex education, apart from aspects contained in the national curriculum, in both primary and secondary schools.

Still under a Conservative administration, a circular from the Department for Education and Employment (DfEE) was distributed in 1994 (5/94) which provided schools with guidance to their responsibilities regarding sex education. In primary schools the advice was that sex education should,

> ... prepare pupils to cope with the physical and emotional challenges of growing up, and to give them an elementary understanding of human reproduction.
>
> (DfEE 5/94)

Whilst in secondary schools, sex education should:

> ... encompass, in addition to facts about human reproductive processes and behaviour, consideration of the broader emotional and ethical dimensions of sexual attitudes.
>
> (DfEE 5/94)

New Labour came to power in May 1997, but it was not until July 2000 that new advice was drawn up by the DfEE – *Sex and Relationship Education Guidance.* As we have noted, criticism of earlier sex education had been its narrow focus on biological reproduction at the expense of excluding discussion on human emotional relationships. For example, in 1988, when the National Curriculum was introduced, sex education was located in the science curriculum (that is, a focus on sexual reproduction and sexually transmitted diseases). However, not many science teachers were happy with this or felt equipped to deal with it. As a consequence they would often avoid teaching it.

It can be assumed that, by focusing on the mechanics of reproductive biology and the dangers of pregnancy and sexually transmitted diseases, the intention in sex education during the 1980s and 1990s was to reduce the incidence of these. Clearly these aims were not very successful as the number of teenage pregnancies in 1998 were over 100,000 conceptions to teenagers of which over 8000 were to girls under 16 (*Sex and Relationship Education Guidance* 2000). New Labour's approach to Sex Education was intended to pursue the 'good practice' identified in other countries. For example, a research study by Ingham (1997), involving interviews with young people in The Netherlands and the UK found a marked difference in attitudes. The young people interviewed in the UK complained of the context-free nature of their sex education, which contrasted significantly with the perceptions of young people in The Netherlands, who had encountered a more liberal sex education which, for many, begun in the primary school and had included many of the issues that British young people had identified as missing. Such findings are also echoed in studies by Forrest (2006) and Alldred and David (2007): Forrest finds that a gulf has emerged between young people's knowledge of sex from outside school (where sex and sexuality is presented as more fluid and pleasure-oriented); and that provided in-school, which remains largely about policing sexual activity. Alldred and David similarly found British children and parents to perceive the sex education offered in school as completely divorced from 'real life'.[4] Whilst the aim has been to give greater credence to emotional relationships in the document *Sex and Relationship Education* (2000) it has been heterosexual relationships, to the exclusion of all others, that have been centralised. In the following quote the emphasis on the (heterosexual, nuclear) family is as strong as in earlier conservative policies on marriage:

> As part of sex and relationship education, pupils should be taught about the nature and importance of marriage for family life and bringing up children … pupils should learn the significance of marriage and stable relationships as key building blocks of community and society.
>
> Sex and Relationship Education Guidance (2000: 4)

It is then rather contradictory for the Guidance, on the one hand, to positively advocate heterosexual relationships as they have here, but then go on to argue that the various forms of sexual orientation should not be 'promoted':

> [Sex and relationship education] is about the understanding of the importance of marriage for family life, stable and loving relationships, respect, love and care. It is also about the teaching of sex, sexuality and sexual health. It is not about the promotion of sexual orientation or sexual activity – this would be inappropriate teaching.
>
> Sex and Relationship Education Guidance (2000: 5)

Of course recently in Britain gay 'marriage' has been institutionalised in the form of 'civil ceremonies' legally recognising gay committed relationships (though retaining the significant semantic distinction from *marriage*, which remains an exclusively heterosexual preserve). The Equality Act, which came into force in April 2007, requires schools to meet the needs of *all* its pupils and parents, and as is observed on the No Outsiders Project website (Atkinson, 2008), the DCSF guidance on Sex and Relationship Education does require schools to recognise non-heterosexual as well as heterosexual relationships, and to recognise that there are loving and stable relationships outside marriage. Yet there is little evidence that 'alternative' family configurations are being presented within sex education in the majority of schools. Indeed, this is something that the 'No Outsiders Project'[5] is attempting to address, for example via work with teachers and within literature provided for children in primary schools.

In addressing some of these obvious policy prejudices and contradictions, feminists have been drawing attention to 'the discourse of desire' noting that it is more or less missing from sex education in schools except in the context of male desire as danger (Kehily, 2002; Allen, 2004). What is being suggested is a move away from 'Sex Education' to 'Sexuality Education' (Mellor and Epstein, 2006), which celebrates diversity and pleasure and is more inclusive of young people's perspectives. Lees (1993) and Fine (2003) have argued that a feminist sex education framework would interrogate sex-gender inequalities inherent in current social expectations and constructions of sexuality, and Chilisa (2006) points to the need to ensure that students are enabled to interrogate the ways that 'race' and ethnicity are positioned in such constructions. As we have seen, other researchers agree that a combination of such moves would make sex education more relevant to the lives of young people (Alldred and David, 2007).

A second theme that has absorbed feminists' interests in writing on education across the years is that of sexual harassment.

Sexual harassment

It was Radical Feminism that drew attention to gender-power dynamics in the classroom and illuminated the ways in which sexual harassment functioned in schools (Jones, 1985; Mahony, 1985). The term itself is a fairly new one although the associated behaviours date back as long as men have had social control over women (Thomas and Kitzinger, 1997). Wise and Stanley note that it was a group called Working Women United, based in New York state, that came up with the term in the mid-1970s, but:

> There seems to have been no mention of any such animal as 'sexual harassment' in the English press, certainly none that we could find, before the reporting of American sexual harassment cases and the review of feminist and feminist-influenced books on the subject at the end of 1979.
>
> (1987: 30)

As such, it was not until the 1980s that the term 'sexual harassment' began to be applied to those practices in schools and other educational institutions, whereby, for example, female teachers and girls would be subjected to male obscenities or remarks about their physical appearance and being, literally 'manhandled' (Whitbread, 1980; Jones, 1985; Lees, 1986; Wood, 1987; Ramazanoglu, 1987). At the same time, as Carrie Herbert (1989) has pointed out, sexual harassment has been notoriously difficult to define and there is much confusion around the issue. What was clear is that sexual harassment had little or nothing to do with sexual emotions but was all about power exerted through sexual means of one group or individual over other groups or individuals. June Larkin (1994) refers to it as 'sexual terrorism' in her descriptions of how young women were made late for school through being stalked by predatory males on their way there, and having to take refuge in shops, trains, or side alleys in order to escape their attentions.

The definition of sexual harassment articulated by the National Union of Teachers (NUT) in 1986 stated that it was 'Any uninvited, unreciprocated and unwelcome physical contact, comment, suggestion, joke or attention which is offensive to the person involved and causes that person to feel threatened, humiliated, patronised or embarrassed'. This was a development of the definition put out by the Trade Union Congress in 1983 which had added the clause that the actions needed to be persistent as well as unwanted. What the NUT recognised by not reproducing in its definition the rider that it had to be 'persistent', was that an action only needed to take place once for it to be harassing – for example, a girl having her breasts grabbed as she walked along the corridor to her next lesson did not need to have this occur on a regular basis before she was regarded as having a right to get upset! What made sexual harassment particularly difficult to tackle is that for something to be determined as such depends on the subjective perception of the recipient. For example, a teacher may witness a group of boys commenting within a girl's hearing about how 'fit' she is. The teacher might well intervene as such behaviour could be seen as sexually harassing and certainly transgresses what is appropriate within the school environment. However, the girl might consider the comments to be 'teasing' or even welcomed as a compliment. It is this kind of dilemma that has prompted discussions over what is *sexist* harassment and how this differs or overlaps with sexual harassment[6] (Epstein, 1997; Robinson, 2005). As such, in addition to current policies on sexual harassment (The Employment Equality [Sex Discrimination] Regulations, 2005), the then Department for Education and Skills issued guidelines on what it termed 'sexual bullying' (see DCSF 2008):

Sexual bullying impacts on both genders. Boys are also victims of girls and other boys. A case of proven sexual assault is likely to lead to the exclusion of the perpetrator. In general, sexual bullying is characterised by:

- Abusive name calling
- Looks and comments about appearance, attractiveness, emerging puberty
- Inappropriate and uninvited touching
- Sexual innuendoes and propositions
- Pornographic material, graffiti with sexual content
- In its most extreme form, sexual assault or rape

It is interesting to note that it was felt important to mention that boys as well as girls are subject to bullying and harassment. Although equal opportunity policy statements have not necessarily stipulated that sexual harassment was something only experienced by girls/women, its association with dominant power structures meant that, in the past, there have been questions over whether men can be victims of sexual harassment (Lee, 2000). Explorations into the construction of masculinities as well as research into the school experiences of LGBT pupils and teachers has shown how some boys and men can be subjected to sexual bullying (Epstein *et al.,* 2003).

Writing on how gender can be conceptualised, Connell (1987) has used the notion of hegemonic masculinity[7] to detail how a dominant form of masculinity is constructed in relation to women and other (subordinated) masculinities. A key aspect of hegemonic masculinity is that it is heterosexual. Studies of boys and girls at school have shown how being perceived as being anything 'other' than dominant, heterosexual and male leads to physical and verbal intimidation and violence. There are numerous accounts of how boys utilise homophobic language to denigrate other boys. Askew and Ross' (1988) study of an all boys school recalls how unaggressive, quieter boys 'took the place of girls ... by providing a "butt" for proving masculinity' (p. 39). Barrie Thorne (1993: 116) observed how young boys who did not do well at sports or played with girls would be called 'sissy', 'faggot', 'fag' or 'girl'. Boys who attempt to challenge, or even just try to avoid engaging with heterosexist bullying of others, tend to invoke similar kinds of reactions. Pat Mahony (1985: 47) wrote of an incident whereby a boy who attempted to challenge the sexist behaviour of his male teacher was similarly positioned as 'not a proper male':

> One case emerged of a third year boy in a single sex school ... The teacher had suddenly announced to the class: 'Quick lads there's a naked woman running across the playground.' All the boys with the exception of S ... leapt up and rushed to the window. Then he said: 'Alright you can sit down now, I was just checking you were normal.' S ... said: 'I think that's sexist sir'. ... He [the teacher] commented: 'Thank you S ... now we know who isn't normal'. After school S ... was threatened, comments such as 'poof', 'S ... is a woman' and worse were shouted.

As we have seen, during the 1980s there was strong activist attention to homophobia in schooling, and various materials and interventions produced to challenge such practices in schools and elsewhere (though somewhat submerged in the 1990s by Clause 28). However, the increasing influence of post-structuralist theories on feminist thinking facilitated new conceptions of the ways in which sexual/sexist harassment, sexual bullying and the impact of heterosexism on gender identities could be understood. Hence, literature on sexualities, gender and schooling has, more recently, focused attention on sexual cultures and sexual subjectivities. For example, as we have observed, one of the problems in tackling sexual harassment has been the difficulty of trying to arrive at definitions and shared understandings of what it actually involves. Deborah Chambers and her colleagues (2004) have argued that the difficulty of identifying sexual harassment has been because it is seen as simply 'incidents' which occur. They make the case that sexual harassment should not be separated from understandings of cultural contexts of youth but rather these are 'a set of practices embedded in the everyday collective culture of teenagers and a central part of the peer regulation of teenage sexual identities' (Chambers *et al.*, 2004: 398). The evidence for this, they argue, can be found in the wealth of literature that points to how sexual bullying is an everyday feature of school life and, rather than claiming it is 'widespread', it should be acknowledged as 'the norm' (p. 411). Kerry Robinson (2005) makes a similar point, and one which has been raised by profeminists researching masculinities and schooling, about how sexual violence is used by boys, individually and collectively, as a means of negotiating relationships within their friendship groups (see also Walker, 1988; Mills, 2001; Martino and Pallotta-Chiarolla, 2003; Epstein *et al.*, 2003; Phoenix *et al.*, 2003).

An important strand of work on sexuality and sexual harassment which we must not ignore here is the involvement of Western-based feminists in research on these topics in education in 'The Global South' (traditionally referred to in World Bank terms as 'the developing world'). A major consideration for these feminists (often working with colleagues in Asia, Africa and elsewhere) has been the Millennium Development Goals (MDGs) and their drive towards 'Education For All' by 2015 (Unterhalter, 2007). Gender inequalities weigh more heavily on females than males in a number of ways. First, two-thirds of those who have no access to education are women or girls. Indeed one of the aims of the MDGs is to attain gender parity (where equal numbers of boys and girls enrol at school). However, girls and women remain disproportionately excluded from education in many countries due to a range of deeply embedded factors including customs, laws, practices and institutional processes (Gordon, 1996; Stromquist, 2000). Contributors to a collection by Aikman and Unterhalter (2005) offer what are often harrowing accounts of the obstacles encountered by girls and women in their attempts to secure an education. The chief impediments to girls' and women's education include (apart from the privileging of an education for boys), the early marriage of girls, their domestic responsibilities, the fact there are too few government schools (many of which are severely overcrowded and unsanitary), schools setting themselves up as hostile environments in which low expectations of girls were held; and the issue of girls' safety when they are at school (for example, male teachers sexually harassing girls and using them to run errands, fetch water and cook).

Furthermore two-thirds of HIV sufferers in the Central African Republic are made up of girls and young women. Contributing to this rise is the number of men teachers having sex with their pupils (Dunne *et al.*, 2006). For example, Dunne *et al.*, report,

> ... the study in Kenya by Omale (1999) reported sexual harassment and incidents of rape of girls on the way home from school with [male]

teachers found guilty of having sex with primary students and in some cases impregnating them.

(Dunne *et al.*, 2006: 87)

As Lynn Davies wrote in 2004, this is:

not about male lusts but part of the cultural system of schools which helps reinforce and revise relationships of power and authority between males and females ... and between material and ideological differences between local and larger world systems. (p. 66)

These kinds of issues have raised more questions for feminists, not least how these might be approached. Feminists have pointed to the different trajectories of western feminist thought compared to the theories and perspectives of feminists in non-western countries (Aikman and Unterhalter, 2005; Fennell and Arnot, 2008). Clearly, a substantial portion of contemporary western work is highly theoretical, drawing on complex ideas from Butler, Foucault, and on Queer Theorists (often influenced by the former thinkers). Much of this work in education is empirically based, albeit theoretically articulated, and the No Outsiders project led by Elizabeth Atkinson and Renee DePalma (2008) demonstrates the possibility of applying such nuanced ideas pragmatically to educational interventions.[8] Nevertheless, it has been suggested that while these highly 'academic' accounts may be applicable to identify and examine often-nuanced issues in basically liberal Western settings, they are too subtle for application to the stark, often more obviously visceral issues of sexual inequality in educational settings in the Global South. This theoretical dissonance has become a point of some anxiety and debate among Western feminists that work with colleagues from, and/or analyse gender and education in, the Global South. At the time of writing, no consensus has been arrived at regarding the ways in which western and non-western perspectives and theorising might be harmonised. Indeed Shailaja Fennell and Madeleine Arnot (2008) have raised the question of whether it is feasible to attempt to merge the very different strands of western-based gender studies and with that of non-western development studies, or to keep them apart.

Having provided an outline of some of the key issues and findings on work on sexual harassment, we turn now to focus more specifically on the more recent attention that has been given to the closely related field of sexual cultures.

Sexual cultures

One of the reasons why there is a sense of 'discomfort' in linking sexuality and schooling is because of longstanding notions around 'childhood innocence'.[9] Yet the (adult) idea that children do not have any knowledge or feelings about sexuality are challenged just by watching the games of 'kiss-chase' or listening in on conversations about 'boyfriends', 'girlfriends' and 'who loves who' that take place in primary school playgrounds (Redman, 1996; Epstein, 1998; Skelton, 2001).[10]

Indeed, as a significant body of work has elaborated, schools are highly sexualised spaces. What this means in terms of sexual cultures is that young children do not just 'learn' about sexuality in a way that suggests they simply imbibe information about it, but employ and negotiate knowledge about sexuality 'articulating it in diverse ways within their friendship cultures while forming their own social realities' (Mellor and Epstein, 2006: 382; see also Chambers *et al.,* 2004; Renold, 2005; Youdell, 2006).

Second-wave feminist studies of sexual harassment were radical, not just in their attack on male power, and their identification of the subjugation and abuse of females in educational institutions, but also in identifying schools as sites of sexuality. Recent ethnographic and theoretical work has elaborated these themes to reveal how binary norms of gender and sexuality are inherently linked and perpetuated through practices in schools (Duncan, 1999; Hey *et al.,* 2001; Martino and Pallotta-Chiarolli, 2003; Epstein *et al.,* 2003; Renold, 2005; Nayak and Kehily, 2006). Emma Renold (2000: 309) has commented that the majority of feminist studies in primary schools had previously focused on gender relations and failed to notice 'how sexuality, and specifically heterosexuality, is part of the everyday experience in the worlds of primary school children'. It is these linked practices of gender and sexuality and the (unequal) power relations they bear that underpin the sexual harassment of girls, and of boys ascribed insufficiently masculine, or 'gay', in educational institutions. As Duncan (1999) and Renold (2000) have documented, it is possible for sexual harassment to be practiced by girls – indeed many feminist researchers have noted how girls are inculcated into the policing of sexual behaviour via name-calling and abuse of other girls. Yet as Mills (2001) asserts, these behaviours (especially the more visceral behaviours) are more usually practiced by boys, as would be expected given their investment in the gender regimes practiced within schools.

Recently this body of work has been informed by Butler's notion of 'the heterosexual matrix' (Butler, 1990), as an effective metaphor via which to analyse sexuality in educational sites. This is the metaphor Butler applies to the discursive configuration resulting from the meshing together of two binaries – that of gender, and that of sexuality (both of which, of course, Butler sees as illusory constructions). The heterosexual matrix explains the privileging of both masculinity and heterosexuality, but also importantly conceives them as integrally linked. Butler's theoretical work in this area (e.g. 1990, 2004) is important and appealing to researchers of sexuality in its powerful articulation of the impact of this matrix on those 'othered' by the norms imposed by it. Her notion of certain 'othered' lives (in terms of those who do not conform to binary heterosexist models of sexuality, but also those who do not fit binary models of gender) as rendered 'unintelligible' via the matrix, has lent powerful theoretical tools to the ethnographic accounts of many feminist education researchers. Butler's accounts facilitate articulation of the extent and effects of homophobic and misogynist abuse in British schools, which are rampant and often considered unremarkable or inevitable by teachers. The introduction of new equalities duties in British schools demands that pupils are not discriminated against on the basis of their gender and sexuality, and it remains to be seen whether this new legislation will have an impact on the 'low-level' abuse which seems currently to be a consistent feature of secondary school life (and to some extent, primary school life). Indeed, Butler's terminology includes the notion of the 'unliveable' life – those lives which are constructed as untenable in their unintelligibility (lack of recognisable fit with norms of binary gender difference and heterosexuality), and that may therefore be forcibly altered, or ended via homophobic 'policing' and punishment (Butler [2004] discusses homophobic murders, and the normative medical practices pathologising and disciplining intersex and trans bodies, to illustrate her point).

Hence one of the key arguments made by earlier feminists working on issues of sexuality, that gender and sexuality are inseparable (e.g. Rich, 1980), is being increasingly commented on and developed in recent feminist work. This recent work argues that schools themselves facilitate the production and reproduction of children's sexual and gender relations (Renold, 2000, 2005). Hence feminist researchers exploring issues of sexuality in education have been increasingly attuned both to the structural role of the school in perpetuating gender/sexuality binaries, and in the manners in which children take up and demonstrate their gender/sexuality. This of course includes the immense pressure that children encounter in schools to conform to other children's views of what is 'normally desirable' (views which of course reflect the broader values of society). Ground-breaking studies like that of Bronwyn Davies (1989), which documented the myriad, continual and complex ways in which young children delineate their gender identities have been extended to the field of sexuality: those working in this area have begun to document the minutiae of signs and practices which pupils use to construct their gendered sexualities.

For example, Deborah Youdell's (2005: 253) ethnographic research with 15–16-year-old girls showed, through an analysis of their day-to-day practices (e.g. hairstyles, clothes, linguistic styles, physical games, bodily deportment) how sex-gender-sexuality are joined together in 'complex constellations'. These practices are carefully documented in Emma Renold's work with primary school children (e.g. 2000, 2005, 2008). Renold draws attention to the signs used by pupils in their signification of gender and sexuality, be these practices of 'naming' (including name-calling) or the clothes they wear. She and others document the pressures of 'compulsory heterosexuality' in children's constructions of their gender/sexual identities (Renold, 2006a, 2007), and draw on Butler to reveal the ways in which discourses reflecting the heterosexual matrix converge to position some children as 'impossible subjects' (who then risk ostracism or bullying). Mindy Blaise (2005; Blaise and Andrew, 2005) has applied these approaches to her work with children in the early years, demonstrating the ways in which productions of sexuality via the heterosexual matrix are evident among even very young children. Clear themes of embodiment and 'adornment' (Youdell, 2005) emerge from these close analyses – themes which Atkinson and DePalma (2008; DePalma and Atkinson, 2007) both at once acknowledge and disrupt with their study of constructions of sexuality on an on-line website (where, of course, participants are 'disembodied'). They found however that participants to the on-line forum tended to 're-embody themselves, consciously or unconsciously, in ways that invoke social meanings and effectively import socially constructed power asymmetries into the virtual space' (2008: 192). Hence Atkinson and DePalma maintain that the virtual space is as much prey to 'power plays' as are physically embodied spaces.

An important element of this work on sexualities has been the attention to 'race' and social class in addition to gender. Mac an Ghaill's study (1994) and following work made an important contribution in analysing the intersection of different facets of identity in production of sexuality, and this approach has been taken up and developed by other researchers, who have variously documented the ways in which ethnicity may facilitate or close down particular constructions of gender/sexuality (e.g. Sewell, 1997; Connolly, 1998; Martino and Pallotta-Chiarolli, 2003). This work has developed the ways in which complex discursive configurations between racial (racist) discourses and those around social class, sexuality and gender produce 'raced' and 'classed' bodies in particular ways. For example, Black boys and girls, and White working-class boys and girls, are seen within school institutions as more sexual than other groups of pupils. Black boys, particularly, are constructed (and sometimes construct themselves) within racist colonial discourses of virile Black male sexuality (Connolly, 1998). Conversely, other groups of pupils tend to be constructed by teachers and pupils as less sexual, or in the case of boys, more effete (see Connolly's discussion of some pupils' construction of South Asian boys). Archer and Francis (2007) discuss how these constructions are applied to British-Chinese pupils, with British-Chinese girls especially being positioned by teachers as asexual (almost as automatons) and 'unhealthily repressed'. The discourses applied to Black and White working class students reflect historic European eugenicist themes based on Cartesian notions of a split between body and mind, whereby 'mind' is associated with human development, and body (incorporating sexuality and reproduction) with under development/bestiality. Hence the working classes and 'colonial hordes' were seen as fecund, fertile/virile, in a dichotomy with the White bourgeois/upper class who saw themselves as more developed intellectually but (in the case of women) more delicate and less fertile.

A good example of this work on the intersections of 'race', sexuality-gender, and social class, is that on teenage pregnancy. Feminists have challenged the ubiquitous policy notion of the 'problem' teenage mother (often Black and/or working class), looking instead at these young women's motivations and ways of managing, and celebrating their resilience. They have also launched a devastating attack on the construction and treatment of these young women by educational policy and institutions (e.g. Phoenix, 1991; Phoenix *et al.*, 1991; Luttrell, 2003). This work reveals the interplay of 'race', social class and gender in the perceptions and practices that socially pathologise and stigmatise these young women.

One of the issues to have emerged as post-structuralism became influential in feminist educational work in the late 1980s and 1990s is the notion of desire, and its infusion in educational relationships and settings. Valerie Walkerdine (1990) observes how educational relationships are steeped in desire: desire to achieve, desire to please, for some working-class students desire to 'escape' poverty via educational success, and so on. The sexual 'edge' to these educational relationships and desires is foregrounded by researchers such as Alison Jones (1999, 2001), Bronwyn Davies (Davies and Saltmarsh, 2006) and Mindy Blaise (2005). Jones and Davies have both attended to the desires for and by girls' to be compliant and pleasing, and the discipline with which this is inculcated by institutions and by girls themselves. They focus particularly on girls' writing practices as an illustration of the bodily practices and constraints girls engage to produce 'beautiful writing', and their desires to please the teacher and achieve in this regard. Clearly such practices reflect and contribute to broader, sexualised constructions of desirable femininity. Blaise (2005) inspects relationships between early years practitioners and children in their care, noting how physical contact and relationships between early years educators may be highly gendered and sexualised, yet how such relations are often ignored or misrecognised within early years practice, which sees children as innocent or non-sexual (see also Walkerdine, 1988). Such work emphasises the ways in which all aspects of the education system are both steeped and implicated in the construction and reproduction of sexualities, within which inequalities are embedded.

Conclusions

We have attempted to show the scale and power of feminist work in the field of sexuality in education. Second-wave feminist researchers lifted the veil over schooling to reveal the extent of sexual harassment and sexual denigration against girls practiced therein, and the ways in which education institutions themselves were complicit with these practices. They highlighted the ways in which such harassment functioned as an integral aspect of the maintenance of the gender order, teaching girls (and women teachers) to 'know their place'. Other aspects of schooling sexuality, such as the curriculum subject of sex education, were also critiqued as espousing both masculinised and conservative perceptions. Work on sexual harassment and bullying has more recently developed out to the important identification and analysis of homophobia in educational institutions, and in turn to the general application of heterosexist practices in policy, curriculum and classroom relations. Subsequent work has been attuned to the interaction of different aspects of identity (such as social class and 'race') with gender-sexuality, and has developed ethnographic approaches and often applied post-structuralist and queer theory to the study of sexuality as reflected in all aspects of education. This recent work involves close explorations of discursive and embodied productions of gender-sexuality, but central to it is the retention of a powerful critique of inequalities and the pernicious effect of the normalising discourses that render certain, non-traditional constructions of gender-sexuality as 'unintelligable' and even 'unliveable'.

6 Curriculum, knowledge and schooling

The introduction to Dale Spender's (1982) *Invisible Women* begins with the statement 'Schools cannot teach what society does not know'. Her point was that the knowledge children were taught in schools was 'male knowledge' in that it was written largely by men, about men and from a male perspective. Hence, in terms of the *content* of what pupils were being taught, women's knowledge, writing and viewpoints were either unknown or unrecognised. This identification paved the way for research and initiatives on the school curriculum that, first, revealed how what was being taught in schools was 'male centred' and, second, offered ways in which women's knowledge could be included. Since these initial forays into examining links between gender and curriculum, feminists and pro-feminists have provided insights into how girls and boys locate themselves in relation to specific subjects as a means of constructing their identities, e.g. being good at and enjoying English is discursively constructed as doing femininity (Rowan *et al.*, 2002; Martino and Pallotti-Chiarolli, 2003). The same has been shown to pertain to teachers' engagement with pupils whereby their expectations of pupils' abilities, motivations and interests for a subject are related to their own knowledge and understanding of, and training in, that subject (Ivinson and Murphy, 2007).

We have chosen to structure this chapter around the two 'types' of curricula identified early on in second-wave feminism that were practiced in schools. First, there is the official curriculum, that is, subjects that are taught, and the content of these. As well as the topics included (and excluded), feminists have analysed the resources used to deliver the subject areas, considered whether they are 'masculine' or 'feminine' subjects, and looked at this in relation to pupils' subject choice. Yet beyond this 'official' curriculum, as Spender went on to show in *Invisible Women*, the structure and organisation of school processes and practices are also of significance in terms of their perpetuation of the gender order. These 'hidden' aspects of schooling which contributed towards a positioning of pupils along gendered lines were referred to as the 'hidden curriculum': within this, feminist researchers have analysed patterns of interaction, the way children are treated, and classroom management strategies (Delamont, 1980; Stanworth, 1983; Whyte, 1983; Kenway and Willis, 1990; Sadker and Sadker, 1994; Gaine and George, 1999; Skelton and Francis, 2003).

Feminists in the UK, Australia and North America have reported on investigations into not only the content and assessment of curriculum subjects but how schools have been organised and classrooms managed along gender segregated lines (Kelly, 1981; Best, 1983; Thorne and Luria, 1986; Yates, 1987). What these explorations showed was that girls were hampered by having to look at subject knowledge through a masculine lens and in being continually reminded through classroom routines and practices that they, as pupils, were different to boys as pupils. In addition, gendered assumptions about 'girl pupils' and 'boy pupils' have, and continue to, inform the attitudes and behaviours of teachers and students, which, despite the current assumptions that schools are biased against boys, have been found time and again to discriminate against girls (AAUW, 1992; Gilbert and Gilbert, 1995; Reay, 2001; Renold, 2006b).

This chapter takes the various sectors of mainstream education in turn to identify how inequalities in both the overt and hidden curriculum have been articulated and addressed from the early days of second-wave feminism to the present day. We will begin by looking at feminists' explorations of the school curricula, concentrating first on the 'official' curriculum and related materials, and then on the aspects deemed to constitute the 'hidden curriculum'.

The official curriculum

The official curriculum varies from country to country, and many countries have a 'National Curriculum'. As Carrie Paechter (2007) observes, it is rare for National Curricula to explicitly address gender equality, though a few countries do (she cites Sweden and South Africa as examples). Paechter notes the relative commonality of curricula internationally. However, as she argues elsewhere (Paechter, 2000), the official curriculum is deeply imbued with gender, as are the teaching and learning practices that attend it.

Gendered subjects

Gender bias in curriculum materials is explored in a later section, but here we want to skim a couple of the key curriculum areas where there have been substantial bodies of feminist research. Clearly, feminist works since the 1970s have extended to a diverse range of subject areas, and to cover them all in any detail would comprise a book in itself. It is not our intention to attempt that here; rather, we have chosen to focus on the three subjects areas promoted as 'key subjects' in contemporary English education policy: mathematics, literacy/English and science. This approach risks excluding subject areas which have been the focus of extensive feminist work: these include, for example, sex education, ICT, and physical education. Curriculum areas that have benefited from substantial feminist input also exist beyond the school curriculum (notable examples include Women's Studies, Black Studies, and – in previous decades at least – Teacher Education). For overviews of feminist work in such fields (and including the topics covered here), see, for example,

Paechter (2000, 2004); or Bank's edited collection *Gender and Education: an Encyclopedia* (2007).

While female literacy rates in 'the Global South' tend to remain low in relation to males (Robinson-Pant, 2004), girls in 'the Global North' traditionally outperformed boys at literacy and their national language. In Britain, girls' success at literacy and English tended to go unexplored by second-wave feminist researchers – given their agenda, attention tended to be focused on subjects at which girls underachieved, rather than succeeded. Lee's (1980) evocation of boys' underachievement at literacy as a product of their masculinity constituted a rare exception. The closest related work tended to apply content analysis to fairy stories and other texts, exploring the 'gender roles' illuminated therein. Bronwyn Davies' (1989) work exploring the gendered and age-related discourses of morality underpinning such texts revolutionised this field, and drew attention to children's own literate practices – and to the ways in which these were shaped by gender discourse. Since the mid-1990s, however, there has been closer research attention – including feminist – to literacy, as a result of the furore on 'boys' underachievement' (as we have argued elsewhere, it is boys' dramatic, international, underperformance at language and literacy that skews their achievement so significantly that the impression is given they are underachieving more broadly).

Non-feminist commentators have often argued that the English curriculum is 'feminised', and that more 'boy-friendly' learning materials need to be introduced to engage boys. Feminists have argued instead that as it is boys' constructions and performances of gender that impede their ability/desire to engage with English; the focus should be on changing boys, rather than necessarily changing the curriculum (Rowan, *et al.*, 2002; Martino, 1995). Some feminists, such as Millard (1997, 2003), Guzzetti *et al.* (2002), and Marsh (2000, 2003) have analysed boys and girls' literary practices in close detail and suggest changes to the curriculum that would be beneficial to both boys and girls (including, for example, greater use of ICT and of popular cultural texts). Davies and Saltmarsh (2006) have urged caution, noting the 'importance of interrogating the role of such (popular) texts in producing neoliberal subjectivities and social relations which serve the economy in both implicit and explicit ways' (p. 242). Davies (2003; Davies and Saltmarsh, 2006) has rather been interested in the ways in which literate practices both gender students and are drawn on by students to perform their gendered subjectivities. For example, how girls' writing practices represent their embodied gender as well as their learner identities in their neat, constrained, diligent productions of writing; in contrast to boys' less constrained, untidy and space-dominating practices. Productions of gender distinction are also evident in the content of their writing. As Kanaris (1999) observes of children's written stories, they reveal 'a strongly gendered view of reality, where society's stereotypical notions of boys as doers in a world of action and girls as recipients, even in their own stories, are produced and reproduced' (p. 264). Both Kanaris, and Davies and Saltmarsh emphasise the ways in which the replication of such discursive positions via literate practices are preparing boys and girls for differently invested gender identities – and hence inequalities – beyond schooling.

Reviewing the debates on gender and ability in mathematics, Boaler and Sengupta-Irving (2006) observe that girls are outperforming boys at maths in several developed countries (including, for example, Japan and Sweden) and equalling them in some others; but that girls' lower rates of participation in mathematical sciences – which heightens at each level – remains an international phenomenon. They claim therefore that 'girls and women are systematically discouraged from entering mathematical and scientific fields', and that that this disassociation begins at school (Boaler and Sengupta-Irving, 2006: 205). Earlier research on gender and maths explored these issues, and found girls to be less confident, and less convinced of the usefulness of maths than boys (e.g. Leder, 1982; Hart, 1989). This notion of a lesser valuing of the subject among girls was confirmed by Ethington (1992), who found that girls perceived maths to be a subject where males dominate (see also Fennema *et al.*, 1981). Patterns of interaction whereby boys communicated with the teacher more and gained more positive feedback than girls were demonstrated to occur in maths classrooms (Becker, 1981). In addition, the pedagogic practises that tend to characterise maths lessons (individual, competitive working, question and answer sessions and so on) have been shown by a body of feminist work to be alienating to girls who, due to their social constructions of femininity, tend to prefer 'connected knowing' (see e.g. Becker, 1995), and collaborative learning environments (Boaler, 1997, 2002; Lucey *et al.*, 2003).

It has been claimed, however, that earlier intervention work such as the GAMMA (Gender and Mathematics Association) project that sought to 'compensate' for girls' lack of confidence and engagement with maths were to some extent missing the point. Research by Walkerdine (1988, 1989) and Boaler (2002) challenges work that sees girls' lesser engagement with maths in deficit terms, critiquing instead the prevailing discourses around maths and learning (and resulting teaching practices) which position maths as 'quintessentially male' and pathologise and disadvantage girls. Some feminist scholars have consequently conceived an alternative mathematics that operates within a feminist epistemology (e.g. Burton, 1995). Simultaneously researchers have drawn on insights from post-structuralism (e.g. Mendick, 2005, 2006) and psychoanalytic theory (e.g. Lucey *et al.*, 2003) to examine the dis/investments that pupils have with maths, in relation to their gendered subjectivities and their performances of gender in educational environments.

The debates and research findings on gender and science often overlap with those pertaining to mathematics. As with maths, feminist research began by identifying girls' under-representation in science within and without school and analysing some of the reasons for this (see e.g. Thomas, 1990; Hanson, 1996). As Blickenstaff (2005) has recently argued, the different factors contributing to female under-representation in the study of science and in science careers are diverse, multifaceted, and interwoven. He identifies many of the issues we have considered above in relation to maths, including low teacher expectations of girls' abilities and interest in science; teaching practices that tend to alienate girls; girls' perception of science as irrelevant to their lives; a 'chilly climate' for girls in science classes which encourages their perception that science is a male domain; and what Blickenstaff calls 'an inherent masculine worldview in scientific epistemology' (2005: 372). Responses to these analyses begin with those that sought to compensate girls and then in more radical work that critiqued the gendered epistemology of science and science teaching practice (see Kenway and Gough, 1998, for elaboration). Research has also become gradually more attuned to the impact of other aspects of social identity and context on girls' engagement with science (Brickhouse *et al.*, 2000). As in the case of maths, some feminists have interrogated the masculinist epistemology of existing discourses around science and of science education practices; inspiring Calabrese Barton (1998) to set out her vision for a feminist science education (see also Rosser, 1997). Calabrese Barton and Brickhouse (2006) warn against a blanket view that women do not engage with science, pointing to the greater proportions of women than men entering medical school in the US and UK, and women's agricultural activism in India, as prominent examples of this engagement. However, they note the discipline-specificity of engagement, and the lack of women in positions of influence.

School reading materials

A good deal of attention was given to the reading schemes and books that children came into contact with when arriving at school (Stones, 1983). Glenys Lobban's (1975) study of the six most popular reading schemes used by schools in the UK showed how these schemes identified certain jobs, activities and temperamental dispositions as gender specific. She found that, in contrast to the thirty-three occupations shown for adult males, only eight were given for adult females and these were mum, granny, queen, princess, witch, teacher, shopkeeper and handywoman about the house. When one compares this to images of males who were largely represented in various forms of paid employment, Lobban demonstrated how young girls were offered little to aspire to outside of being responsible for others or an outcast! Similar findings were made by Aileen Pace Nilsen (1975) in her analysis of fifty-eight award-winning picture books published in the USA. She coined the phrase 'the cult of the apron' in finding that of the few (twenty-five books) that did contain an illustration of a female, all but four of these depicted the female as wearing an apron – and this was irrespective of whether it was a human female or a rabbit, chicken, horse or sheep! In the 1990s publishers did make attempts to redress such sexist images in their schemes, however these did not always produce the intended gender equality.

Research undertaken by one of us (Skelton, 1997) compared gender narratives in two of the older reading schemes in the UK (*Janet and John* and *Ladybird*) with more recent schemes (*Reading 360* [more often referred to as Ginn], *Flying Boot* and *The Longman Book Project*). When carrying out a content analysis of the images of masculinity and femininity in the books the situation had certainly improved. Content analysis was one of the strategies used by second-wave feminists to interrogate children's reading matter. It has more recently been seen as a somewhat problematic strategy in that it has often been applied in conceptualisations of gender as something which is 'fixed' and immutable. At the time, though, it provided a means of evaluating the kinds of messages that children were receiving about gender in the books provided for them by schools. Feminists such as Lobban and Nilsen were concerned with the greater prevalence of male images in early reading books and that they were portrayed undertaking a different and wider range of activities to those of females. Furthermore, the language used was gender biased with 'fireman' rather than 'firefighter' or girls described as 'giggling' whilst boys 'laughed'. Few of these books contained representations of minority ethnic groups and those that did were rarely positive portrayals (Dixon, 1977). The schemes produced in the 1990s were more sensitive in the use of language and did provide illustrations such as mum working on a word processor, dad baking and shopping, and the (White) central characters with friends from minority ethnic groups. However, post-structuralist (see Chapter 2) analysis of these schemes indicated that the books had changed little in their narratives, if not actively reinforced inequalities between the characters.

A post-structurualist analysis of these reading scheme books differed to that of content analysis by going beyond the superficial aspects of the language and looking at the text as a vehicle by which meaning is produced (Walkerdine, 1990). This means considering not only the content but also the metaphors, forms of relationship and patterns of power and desire that were created in the text. When this approach was used with the older schemes, *Janet and John* and the *Ladybird* series (referred to colloquially as 'Peter and Jane' books), it was not surprising to find that the boys made more demands, gave more instructions ('Look at me Janet!' 'See me Jane!'), were given more of the adults' attention and engaged more in conversations with their parents than their sisters. Also, the girls (Janet and Jane) would often ask their brothers' opinions ('What shall I have John?') or request permission to join in with them ('Jane says, "Please can I play with you?" ') whereas the boys never acted in these ways with their sisters. The storyline in one of the early *Janet and John* books (*Out and About*) concerns mum and dad shopping for a new cap for John. Janet appears in many of the illustrations but whilst the voices of John, mum and dad are heard, she does not does not speak for the first 18 pages. When she eventually does speak it is to admire the cap which their parents have bought for John.

Analysis of the newer reading schemes revealed similar narratives about males being of greater significance than females. The 1990s version of Level 1 of *Reading 360* (Ginn) showed that the text had not changed since the earlier 1970s version. What had changed were the illustrations, which in themselves told a story; and, as teachers know when teaching reading, the illustrations in early readers provide a story and clues to the limited vocabulary that accompanies them. As Jackson and Gee (2005: 116) have pointed out in referring to Chatton (2001) 'in the context of messages children receive about gender then, illustrations play a significant role in conveying ideas about the meaning of being male or female to young children'.

The only word to appear in the first book of *Reading 360* was 'Look' but the illustrations in the revamped scheme introduced the reader to the traditional family which appears in reading schemes of mother, father, two children (one boy, one girl) and a dog. In the six books that make up Level 1, the boy is the centre of attention, closely followed by the dog which he has been given as a birthday present (in Book 1). By the end of the six books, the reader has learned the names of the boy (Ben) and the dog (Digger). In naming the boy and the dog greater opportunities are provided for involvement in the story lines as one of the functions of early reading books is to use repetitive vocabulary. Hence, Ben is the one who occupies all the pages of the final book in the first level which is about the family moving house. Here Ben speaks to the removal men, asking if he and his sister can help them and then goes off searching for his dog who has got lost, all the time engaging his parents in conversation. In all of the six books, the sister only gets to speak once. 'Janet' might have been silenced in the first 18 pages of *Out and About* but at least the reader was told her name. The sister in *Reading 360* is not given a name until Level 2 books. Moreover, looking through the later levels shows no change to the situation for girls, as again the sister is found to be asking permission of her brother to join in his activities which, as she is clearly older than Ben, suggests something of a worsening in gender power inequalities between siblings in the more recent versions of these reading schemes.

Feminist research demonstrated that such patterns existed in other school materials beyond reading schemes. Jean Northam's (1982) investigation of maths textbooks found that the number of images of women and girls steadily decreased then disappeared as the maths scheme progressed. Angel Bailey (1988) discovered that where girls were represented they were frequently shown helping boys (e.g. recording results for a boy who was weighing himself, holding a stake whilst the boy hammered it into the ground). Again, this illustrates boys as active subjects; girls as their passive helpmates. In a study of primary history textbooks, Cairns and Inglis (1989) found that only 14.8 per cent of the content dealt with women. They identified a skewed preoccupation with military and political history, whilst cultural and religious dimensions – which were more likely to carry references to women's involvement – were omitted. Apart from the books, resources such as Lego, Meccano and other building and science kits would be packaged in boxes with illustrations of boys on the front thereby marking these out as suitable only for boys (Browne and France, 1986).

Examples thus far have referred to primary teaching materials, but similar results were found in analysis of secondary school curriculum resources. For example, investigating maths text books, noted of just one of six maths text books in a series:

> 31 images depicting men only, four showing females only (of which one is advertising Spain and another singing), and four scenes including both males and females, but in a ratio favouring males. In the quiz show on page 11, the token female is also the token black and of course she is not winning.

Other examples are found in Burkhardt's book (1981) in which photographs depict extremely negative images of women and girls who are wallpapering across the door of a room (p. 43), as prizes to be won by competing males (p. 67), as onlookers whilst the boys cheer *Match of the Day* (p. 146), as items to be scaled down from fat to thin (p. 154) etc.

In Janie Whyld's (1983) edited collection of essays on gender and secondary school subjects it was apparent that the absence of females in school books was not relevant only to the 'masculine' subjects of physics, mathematics and technology but was the same for the 'feminine' curriculum areas of English and humanities. It was found that women had been rendered insignificant or invisible in secondary school English and social studies books (Scott, 1980). In contrast, history, geography and science books were full of references to male pioneers and scientists (Walford, 1980; Turnbull *et al.*, 1983; Kelly, 1987) whilst mathematics and modern language textbooks assumed the reader was always male (Hingley, 1983; Abraham, 1989).

The concern with curriculum materials has been maintained in gender and education research to the present day, although the theoretical lens applied to such studies has developed. Often more recent research in this area has applied post-structuralist ideas to explore the discursive productions underpinning school reading and curriculum texts. However, as Sue Jackson and Susan Gee's post-structuralist examination of illustrations in 100 early school readers used in New Zealand schools over a period of 50 years revealed, images of masculinity and femininity in terms of the characterisation of men, women and children had changed little (Jackson and Gee, 2005). Here they noted the consistency of presentation of the normative, gender-divided, heterosexualised nuclear family, with mother and father occupying traditional roles: he as wage earner, she as nurturer and domestic worker. Boys were depicted within similarly traditional masculine positionings, involved in adventures and sports pursuits – hence as physically able, and as active, agentic subjects. Where there was some change was in the portrayal of girls, some of whom, in the more recent readers, were shown dressed and engaged with activities more traditionally associated with males. At the same time, Jackson and Gee (2005: 126) observe that 'in doing so, however, markers of traditional femininity, such as long hair, posture or dresses, preserved connotations of femininity, thereby avoiding undermining it'.

In a subsequent paper, Sue Jackson (2007) reports a study in which she asked young children for their interpretations of illustrations in early readers. Jackson observes how these illustrations functioned as a cultural resource producing meanings around gender, but also analyses how children bring their own understandings drawn from other contexts to make sense of these representations. In this study she found some less stereotypical productions of gender in both the illustrations (which Jackson conceives within notions of new 'empowered' femininities produced in neoliberal contexts), and in children's readings of them. However, dominant constructions of masculinity *as* dominant remained ingrained in the texts and difficult for the children to read otherwise.

Research drawing on these kind of analyses of curriculum materials and children's books and stories, as well as on Davies' (1993, 1997) work using deconstruction of such texts to encourage children to reflect on gender constructions, now comprises a substantial body of intervention work. For example, Wing (1997), Yeoman (1999) and Balfour (2003) recount their work using stories with children in different parts of the world (e.g. Yeoman in Canada, Balfour in South Africa) to facilitate children's critiquing of gendered texts. Both Wing (1997) and Yeoman (1999) found that exposure of pupils to 'disruptive' non-gender traditional texts and critical reading activities (crucial to support the disruption – see Davies, 1989) can help to challenge dominant gender discourses and to open up alternatives. Balfour (2003) agrees that such approaches are not only effective in encouraging social critique, but also shows how these practices extend pupils' language use.

Curriculum subject preference and subject choice

At the time when second-wave feminists began to explore gender inequities in schooling, primary and secondary schools were very different to each other. Primary education was dominated by notions of child-centredness, whereas secondary schooling was all about preparing pupils for skills that would secure their futures in the labour market (and for some, this meant further and higher education). As such, curricula had two main pathways: academic subject knowledge for those who were deemed capable of passing examinations and vocational training for those who were not. These two pathways had more significance for social class than for gender (see Chapter 3) with more middle-class pupils taking subjects which allowed them entry to higher education whilst more working-class children were channelled into vocational subjects (Marland, 1983). Yet, there were gender discriminatory practices too: for example, in the UK the '11-Plus' exam results that pupils were required to achieve in order to gain entry to the academically oriented grammar schools were set higher for girls than for boys,[1] and – partly as a result of such practices, and partly because of the lower expectations of teachers, academics, family members and girls themselves regarding female abilities and prospects – women were under-represented in universities.[2]

What was very strongly evident was that boys and girls tended towards different subject choices at school and in post-compulsory education. A report on *Curricular Differences for Boys and Girls* (DES, 1975) noted that girls were inclined towards both academic and vocational humanities subjects (e.g. art, English, cookery, music, childcare, hairdressing and catering). As these subjects led to lower paid and often less secure jobs, then one of the strategies adopted by schools following the Sex Discrimination Act (1975) in the UK was to avoid timetabling a science/technical subject against an arts/humanities subject; but, this in itself was soon found to be insufficient as boys and girls continued to pursue gender-stereotyped choices (Burchell and Millman, 1989; Gaskell, 1992).

It was girls' disinclination towards the maths and science subjects that generated particular concern in the USA, UK and Australia. Leone Burton's (1986) *Girls Into Maths Can Go* noted that prior to the Sex Discrimination Act, 1975 (in the UK), much of the work on female participation in mathematics had been carried out by feminists in the USA. For example, Maccoby and Jacklin (1974) explored sex differences in achievement; Brophy and Good (1974) looked at how teacher attitudes and expectations impacted on girls' achievements in maths; Fennema and Sherman (1977, 1978) investigated the reasons girls decided to pursue or reject mathematical study. One possibility that was given immediate consideration was the extent to which boys and girls' achievements and interests in the areas of maths and science were due to biological factors. Any such hypotheses were refuted as no grounds for biological or genetic differences could be found in any of the research studies on participation and success rates in maths/sciences (Harding, 1980; Licht and Dweck, 1983). There was some anxiety about the actual success in examinations of girls but generally those girls who did participate alongside boys were found to do about as well. Jan Harding (1980) discovered that there was no difference between boys and girls' 'O'-level success in science in terms of percentage passes. Licht and Dweck (1983) found that girls' mathematical achievements were equivalent to those of boys during their elementary schooling (but gaps did begin to appear at the time pupils entered junior high school). Feminists working in the maths and science fields had more wide ranging concerns regarding the presentation and engagement with these subjects by teachers and pupils. It was argued that maths and sciences were constructed in ways that made it clear these were 'male' subjects and unsuitable for girls; also that stereotypical attitudes about the interests and potential of girls meant they were often steered towards lower-level qualifications in these subjects, e.g. in the UK more girls took the less prestigious CSE examinations than 'O'-levels which would have allowed the opportunity to pursue the subject at a higher level.

Thirty years on, curriculum subject preference and uptake is one of the areas reflecting persistent gender inequalities. This is in spite of the somewhat altered patterns in gender and educational attainment, and in Britain, the introduction of the National Curriculum. Gendered curriculum preferences and uptake are now more likely to be conceived as reflecting gender discourses of selfhood and appropriate behaviour rather than as agentic 'choices' (see e.g. Paechter, 2004; Francis, 2006). However conceived, these trends carry women and men down particular school-to-work routes, reproducing gendered inequalities (including pay gap, etc.) in their future lives.

Contemporary findings on gendered curriculum subject choice

Since the introduction of the National Curriculum in Britain, girls and boys have been forced to take the same core subjects up to age 16. This had a significant impact in reducing the previously endemic gender difference in curriculum subjects pursued by secondary school pupils (see e.g. Arnot *et al.*, 1999, for analysis). However, discrepancies remain: for example in the numbers of pupils entered for

GCSE exams in traditionally gendered subjects (Francis and Skelton, 2005). There have been more positive research findings too: for example, schoolgirls in both co-educational and single-sex schools in England now have slightly more diverse subject preferences than was the case two decades ago. Girls' preferences have even been found to include some traditionally masculine subjects: for example, maths appears relatively popular (Miller and Budd, 1999; Wikeley and Stables, 1999; Francis, 2000; Francis *et al.*, 2003). However, stereotypical patterns persist, particularly regarding pupils' *least* favourite subjects (Francis, 2000; Francis *et al.*, 2003) and this has been shown to be the case even in single-sex schools: a study found single-sex schoolgirls' dislike for 'hard' science subjects to be pronounced (Francis *et al.*, 2003). This finding undermines a key feminist argument for single-sex education; namely the notion that single-sex schooling allows girls to flourish at non-gender traditional subjects in the security of an all-female environment. The findings demonstrate that constraints on girls' preferences are not just a consequence of boys' classroom behaviour in mixed-sex schools, or of their gender constructions resulting from classroom interaction with boys: even in single-sex schools, gendered trends persist in terms of subject preference. Educating girls in a single-sex environment cannot eliminate the impact of gender discourses prevalent in the wider society which girls take up as integral features of their construction of femininity.

Such gender difference remains strikingly apparent in the non-mandatory subject areas at Key Stage 4, particularly in 'training routes' such as GNVQs and vocational GCSEs, where uptake remains highly patterned by gender and class. As soon as choice is reintroduced for 'academic' subjects at post-16, gender re-emerges as a key factor in uptake, with subject choice at 'A'-level and undergraduate degree level vividly gendered (see Francis, 2006 for elaboration). Indeed, at this level, the persistence of the trends in curriculum subject choice identified in the feminist literature of the 1970s and 1980s is striking. The propensity for young women to take up arts, humanities and social science subjects, and young men to opt for subjects such as maths and the 'hard' sciences, recorded by the likes of Sharpe (1976), Spender (1982), Stanworth (1983) and Kelly (1987), remains the case today. For example, the Department for Children, Schools and Families data shows vastly more men than women taking 'A'-levels in maths and physics (though interestingly, no longer in chemistry) and girls more often taking language and social science subjects (with the exception of economics, see DFES Statistics Gateway at http://www.dfes.gov.uk/rsgateway/DB/SFR/s000630/SFR01-2006v1.pdf for details). Notable distinctions to the picture painted by second-wave feminists are that women are now tending to perform better than their male counterparts, and are taking 'A'-levels in greater numbers (see Francis and Skelton, 2005, for detailed analysis). This is also the case at degree level, where women are receiving higher proportions of 'good' degree awards, and entering Higher Education in greater numbers than men; but where the subjects pursued by men and women remain strongly delineated by gender. For example, nearly three times as many women as men are studying languages, four times as many study education, and women also predominate in the humanities, creative arts, and social sciences. They maintain their traditional numerical dominance of biology at undergraduate level and constitute the vast majority of those pursuing subjects allied to medicine.[3] Men overwhelmingly outnumber women in engineering and computer science and, to a lesser extent, in the physical sciences and maths. Hence the subjects that undergraduates pursue still tend to reflect the gendered construction of subject areas as masculine or feminine, and hence as more appropriate for one gender or the other (see Paechter, 2000). It is imperative to recognise that these gendered choices have strong consequences for the types of career that students are able to pursue, and hence on future occupational opportunities, status and remuneration (Thomas, 1990; Francis, 2002; DTI, 2004; Madden, 2004).

Recent work has illuminated how these 'choices' are inflected by 'race' and social class. For example, there remains a tendency for working-class young men and women to follow vocational rather than academic routes: this tradition has been analysed in terms of the low expectations of career advisors and teachers (Rolfe, 1999; Francis *et al.*, 2005), but also of the working-class alienation from education institutions (Reay and Lucey, 2003; Archer *et al.*, 2007) and of the narrower, local sources of information to which working-class pupils have access (Archer and Yamashita, 2003). The work of Walkerdine, Reay, Lucey, and Archer among others (e.g. Walkerdine, 1990, 1997; Reay, 2002; Reay and Lucey, 2003; Archer, 2006; Archer *et al.*, 2007) has made a powerful contribution to understanding working-class pupils' psychic and emotional investments and resistances to educational practices that systematically pathologise them. In terms of ethnicity, it has been shown that girls from certain minority ethnic groups tend to less gender-stereotypical subject preferences and choices than their White working-class counterparts (e.g. Mirza, 1992; Biggart, 2002; Francis and Archer, 2005). This may be due to a variety of factors, including the impact of 'race' stereotyping on career guidance; the impact of ethnicity and/or diasporic experiences on the construction of gendered subjectivity; teacher expectations; and pupils' recognition of the constraints of racism in the employment market (see Mirza, 1992, or Archer and Francis, 2006, for discussion).

Paechter (2004) reminds us that these subject preferences and 'choices' occur within the parameters of an educational curriculum which remains itself inherently gendered and classed (as well as 'raced'). She argues that the contemporary curriculum remains 'firmly rooted' in the elite male curriculum developed in the nineteenth century to enable upper- and middle-class boys to manage their estates, or to enter the professions. Hence the curriculum reflects enlightenment values in which rationality is elevated over empathy (Paechter, 2004): this valuing of abstraction and 'reason' is reflected in the enduring status hierarchy of subjects, in which traditionally masculine subjects such as maths and science are viewed both as more difficult and more important than traditionally feminine subjects like languages and arts (Thomas, 1990; Harding, 1991; Francis, 2000; Paechter, 2000). Hence these constructions are imbued with power and lack: it is not simply that the subjects which men and women pursue tend to differ; rather, power and status are disproportionately invested in those subjects more frequently pursued by men, and those often pursued by women tend to be positioned as 'softer', easier and more esoteric.

Gender and the hidden curriculum

The impact of pedagogic philosophies

Initially, the focus of research into gender inequalities was the secondary or high school. This was because 'girls start school doing rather better than boys, and gradually fall behind during secondary school' (Platt and Whyld, 1983: 16). During the primary/elementary school years large-scale studies of children's achievements pointed to the fact that, with the possible exception of mathematics, girls consistently outperformed boys (Gorman *et al.*, 1988; Foxman *et al.*, 1991; Gipps and Murphy, 1994). It was because girls were seen to achieve and the fact that at primary school all pupils took all subjects that contributed to the idea that gender discriminatory practices were not a feature of this sector of education (Oakley, 1981a; Whyte, 1983; Millman and Weiner, 1985). In addition, the commonly held perspective of 'child centredness' tended to foreclose discussions of equality. Alexander (1984) set out four elements identifiable in child-centred ideologies:

- *Sequential developmentalism*: the idea that all children progress through 'natural' and 'ordered' stages of development in linear ways. Fundamental to child-centred approaches was the notion that the child had to have reached the appropriate level of 'readiness' before being able to be taught certain skills;
- *Individualism*: where teachers needed to respond to children as unique individuals – a former day version of what is currently being called 'personalised learning';
- *Play as learning*: play was regarded as 'the' means of young children learning;
- *Childhood innocence*: the idea that children were ingenuous and pure; that is, whilst they were capable of misbehaviour they did not possess the means of deliberately and maliciously cause harm. As such, they needed to be 'protected from the harmful and unpleasant aspects of the outside world' (p. 22). As such, this denied the conception of children as active agents.

It was the emphasis on 'the individual' in child-centred philosophy which seemed to convince teachers that they were not exposing pupils to gender discrimination (Walkerdine, 1983; Skelton, 1989). A focus on the 'individual child' allowed teachers to invoke the use of 'natural' gender differences. Valerie Walkerdine (1983) showed that the language used in child-centred education to describe the ideal pupil as inventive, creative and enquiring were actually characteristics associated with boys. Walkerdine argued the implication for girls was that, as they were often noted to be conscientious, passive and conforming to rules, then they were seen as inadequate learners because 'instead of thinking properly, girls *simply* work hard' (1983: 84). Also, within child-centred philosophy the teacher's job was not to teach as such but to facilitate the learning environment for children. As children are aware from an early age how important it is to be seen as a 'proper girl' or 'typical boy' then they would take up gendered activities and behaviours, which would then be facilitated or even encouraged by the class teacher as a means of enabling their 'individual needs'. Studies showed that even on occasions when girls might want to take up non-traditional gendered behaviour this was not always possible. For example, a Year 4 class were observed working on the topic of 'Houses' and were told by the teacher they could select from a range of tasks. The result was that the boys were found constructing an electrical circuit for a doll's house whilst a group of girls designed patterns for curtain materials (Skelton, 1989). In interviews, several of the girls said they had wanted to experiment with the electrical circuit, one would have liked to build a bird table and another had opted for the pottery wheel to make household pots. When asked why they had not followed up their 'learning needs' they said that the boys had got to the electrical circuit and the pottery wheel first and the fact that there were a group of boys already working on the bird table had put the other girl off. What could be seen to be the major obstacle here lay in the way that child-centred philosophy both masked the ways in which gender discriminatory practices were being lived out in the classroom and also, did not allow for the teacher to actively intervene in order to disrupt such gendered behaviours (Younger *et al.*, 2005; Warrington *et al.*, 2006; Keddie and Mills, 2007).

That gender equity was not thought to be of consequence in the 'child-centred' world of primary schools meant that the practices in which boys and girls were constantly reminded of their gender and that they needed to be treated differently were accepted as part of everyday school life. It was through this 'hidden curriculum' of schooling that gender difference and discrimination was continually reinforced.

Our own work has recently shown how stereotypical assumptions of gender difference are increasingly seeping into teachers' thinking as a result of the enduring focus on boys' achievements, and the suppositions of 'natural gender differences' on which policy and media commentary in this area have tended to be based. These assumptions of difference affect teachers' curriculum planning and classroom practices in relation to particular subject areas. This quote from teacher Louise Fletcher is illustrative (see Skelton and Read, 2006: 115):

Louise Fletcher: May be if we're talking about, for example if we're talking about ehm diets, things that we eat. Obviously you don't play on the fact that if you eat too much fat you're going to be fat, because the girls have got this thing about obviously looking good and no matter what age, I mean they start at a very early age, even now they'll talk about being fat or thin. Ehm, and the boys obviously … if you're looking at them, then you're more pushing 'You need to eat the right food because you need to be healthy to do all these sports', they do more sports than the girls.

(Female, White, Old House, NE)

As can be seen, the problem here is that teachers might well fail to recognise the significance for assessment and pupil learning of encouraging particular approaches or framing the content in specifically gendered ways (see Section on Assessment, this Chapter).

Organisation and management

It was common practice for primary schools to complete attendance registers with separate lists for boys and girls (Whyte, 1983) as well as having gender segregated cloakrooms and playgrounds (Byrne, 1978; Deem, 1980; Skelton, 1988). Studies by Sara Delamont (1980) and Lesley Holly (1985) found that many primary schools adopted dress codes which forbade female teachers and girls to wear trousers. Second-wave feminist researchers analysed how these various gendered practices sent boys and girls implicit messages that; (a) they are different, and have different roles; and (b) concerning how this difference should be understood (for example, girls' skirts encouraged modest behaviour such as crossing legs and not sprawling, and impeded physical activity).

Day-to-day management procedures frequently relied on gender as a means of organising the pupils. Incidents were recorded where teachers would pit girls against boys in quizzes, or set 'races' to complete work or to tidy up at the end of a session. Children were frequently recorded being asked to line up at the door in 'boys' and 'girls' lines, and often were recorded in two separate 'boys' and girls' columns on the class register. (Hough, 1985; Windass, 1989). Occasionally gender stigma would be used to control children's behaviour: for example, a teacher might tell a boy that if they did not behave then he would be made to sit with the girls (Marland, 1983).

These practices of the 'hidden curriculum' remain very evident today, although they may be more frequently analysed as productions of gender discourse rather than deliberate inculcation of 'gender roles' on the part of educational institutions. The attention given since the mid-1990s by governments across the Western world to problems of boys' achievement has had something of a negative impact for girls in schools (see more detailed discussion in Chapter 7). Teachers are encouraged to pay attention to the gendered learning needs of boys (in particular) and girls, a consequence of which has been organising and delivering curricula in highly gendered ways, and often with preferential attention to the perceived needs of boys. In a study of the perceptions of 300 7–8-year-old pupils in the UK and their teachers on gender, we discovered that a majority – 71 per cent – of the teachers planned curriculum activities along gender stereotyped lines (Skelton and Read, 2006: 115). For example,

> *Luisa Perez*: No other than, I mean, every half term we have a gift I give out, you know, for working hard – an award system – and I would buy a present for a girl and a present for a boy. A girl would probably get something like Barbie clothes or boys something like to do with football. So I would use

gender in that certain time but not for teaching them. (Female, White. Delving School, SE).

Ewan Griffith: I bought some nice football cushions which the boys want to sit on, it means they don't move around the carpet.
Int: Yeah.
Ewan Griffith: So that's worked nicely because each of those three boys, each like football anyway and it's like, oh that's a treat, if you're not going to sit on it, I'll have to give it to someone else.
Int: Right, so it's like an incentive for them to sit?
Ewan Griffith: Yeah, but the other children that are good, I'd never think of doing that…Terrible, I probably wouldn't buy the girls those cushions. (Male, White, Bree School, SE).

Ewan's words are particularly indicative of the continuities here, as he not only introduces clearly (stereotypically) gendered incentives for the boys, but also focuses exclusively on the boys while taking the girls for granted. It could well be that the emphasis and interest by government and media on boys' underachievement has served to encourage teachers to focus particularly on gender differences and, in so doing, encourages teachers to replicate 'taken-for-granted' conventional interests in their management and reward systems (Skelton and Francis, 2003; Browne, 2004; Connolly, 2004).

A further example of gendered classroom organisational practice that has experienced something of a revitalisation in contemporary times is the use of single-sex classes. Single-sex schooling was often seen by feminists as benefitting girls, for example allowing them to experiment with traditionally masculine subjects free from the ridicule and intimidation of boys (Laviguer, 1980). Within co-educational environments, pro/feminists often advocated single-sex classes as spaces where boys or girls could work through issues specific to their gender, such as bullying and harassment (boys) and assertiveness skills (girls) (see e.g. Reay, 1990 or Salisbury and Jackson, 1996, for examples). However, although the evidence has tended to show that girls, rather than boys, are more likely to benefit from single-sex schooling in terms of their academic achievement (see Tsolidis and Dobson, 2006; Leonard, 2006), single-sex classes have recently been held up as a panacea to address 'boys' underachievement in Britain, Australia, the US and elsewhere (see e.g. the edited collection by Bleach, 1998 or Hoff Sommers, 2000). There is very little evidence for the success of such strategies: as Younger *et al.* (2005) argue, such strategies in themselves are unlikely to be effective (and may even be detrimental in the case of boys) unless they are contextualised by a holistic and concerted approach to the deconstruction of 'gender cultures' in schools (see also Warrington and Younger, 2003).

In keeping with the findings of Mollie Warrington and Mike Younger, is a study by Ivinson and Murphy (2007) into how single-sex teaching actively mitigates against students' access to subject knowledge. Gabrielle Ivinson and Patricia Murphy show in their book *Rethinking Single Sex Teaching* how a number of factors come together in complex ways to inform how learning is mediated. They argue that the following come together in the constitution of a 'teaching arena':

- Historical legacies of knowledge and gender;
- Professional teacher training in a curriculum subject;
- Contemporary education policies;
- Media representation of gender as fixed, innate and dichotomous;
- Institutional pressures: 'The Year of the Boy' and the strategy of single-sex classes.

(Ivinson and Murphy, 2007: 171)

One example they provide of how these factors converge was in design and technology when the teacher was teaching 'joins' to single-sex classes. The teacher was male and, of course, design technology is traditionally seen as a masculine subject. With the boys' class the teacher inculcated them into 'a community of practice' by providing them with a history of joins throughout the ages and how 'men' (generic) have used them to develop, create and serve in daily life. He brought the talk into the present day by referring to materials 'you' (the boys) would buy from *B & Q* (a large hardware retailer in the UK). Ivinson and Murphy summarise his approach with the boys by saying 'The history of joins was the history of man and the masculine valence of the lesson aligned with the historical legacy of resistant materials or handicrafts as a male domain' (2007: 64).

In contrast, the same subject of 'joins' was presented to the girls class by relating the topic to the domestic sphere. Whereas the boys were positioned in the teacher's approach as the 'producers' of technology, the girls were located as simply 'users' thereby placing them outside the subject. Furthermore, the teacher used technical terms with the boys but changed these into 'user friendly' language for the girls. It is teachers' perceptions of students' predilections and abilities, depending on their biological sex, that contributed to them being positioned as 'insiders' or 'outsiders' to the subject. Ivinson and Murphy (2007: 174) carefully set out the pitfalls and the possibilities of single-sex teaching when there is a clear awareness and understanding of the interrelationships of 'the influence of gender identities associated with curriculum subjects; the imperceptibility of gender emerging in classroom practices; and typical gender patterns of practice'.

Teacher attitudes

As we have just illustrated in our discussion of the research into single-sex teaching by Ivinson and Murphy (2007), the knowledge, understandings and beliefs of teachers is a key factor within what used to be called the 'hidden curriculum'. Eileen Byrne wrote in 1978:

Teacher attitudes are almost certainly the dominant influence on how children develop in school; they may well be more accountable than they realise for the persistence of different interests, activities, and levels of achievement in boys and girls. (p. 82)

Feminist research into this area showed how many teachers assumed that boys would be more badly behaved than girls and adjusted their management styles accordingly by, for example, selecting topics which were aimed at boys' interests such as 'Dinosaurs' or 'Space Travel' (Clarricoates, 1980; Skelton, 1989). In centralising boys' perceived learning needs, then, no consideration was given to girls, presumably on the basis that their conscientious approach to school work would see them through.

As one class teacher observed, boys made greater use of non-verbal language than girls and, as a result, 'boys dominated the discussion – not by strength of argument, nor even by their ability to articulate … but (–) added power to their contributions by constant movement (and) jostling for attention' (Lee, 1989: 28). Also, boys were perceived to be more likely to take 'risks', for example, putting themselves forward to respond to a teacher's question even when they did not know the answer (Spender, 1982; Whyte, 1983). Perhaps because of their more boisterous and assertive behaviour in the classroom, some teachers seemed to interpret 'more confident' as 'more able', despite the fact that girls in the primary school were outperforming boys (Clarricoates, 1980; 1987).

This research into teacher attitudes indicated that many teachers were influenced in their dealings with pupils by gender-specific preconceptions. There was a generally held view that 'typical girls' were cooperative, conscientious workers in the classroom (Browne and France, 1986; Skelton, 1989). In effect, girls were viewed as the 'conformist plodders' whose hard work was the reason for their educational achievement. In contrast, 'typical boys' were deemed dominant, demanding and difficult but far more rewarding to teach (Stanworth, 1983; Davies, 1984; Clarricoates, 1987). At the same time, boys were judged by teachers to be more 'naturally talented' (Belotti 1975; Walden and Walkerdine, 1985). Such views of boys being 'better' than girls were often found to be retained even when teachers were faced with conflicting evidence: the teachers in Clarricoates' (1980) study of four primary schools responded to her query regarding who scored the most highly in tests by referring to girls, e.g. 'Oh the girls naturally' (p. 29). Perhaps it was because boys generally were found to take up more of the teachers' time through their behaviour and demands for attention (Paley, 1984) that their more boisterous presence in the classroom led to their being perceived as more able learners. Whatever the causes, teachers' perceptions were of boys as 'more capable of learning' than the girls (p. 33). As one teacher commented 'Although girls tend to be good at most things, in the end you find it's going to be a boy who's your most brilliant pupil' (Clarricoates, 1980: 33).

These issues around teachers' lower expectations for girls and their bearing on girls' self-perception were found to impact from elementary education right up to the later years of schooling. A particular area of interest among researchers of secondary schooling concerned girls' (absence of) self-confidence. Writing on the situation in the United States, Sadker and Sadker (1994) reported on a national survey of nine to fifteen year olds which showed that boys tended to far higher levels of self-esteem than girls. Also, it was discovered that girls began with more self-esteem in elementary schools, but it then began to slide off in high school. Hispanic girls demonstrated the sharpest drop-off in confidence, from 68 per cent in elementary down to 30 per cent in high school. The explanations for this were myriad; from feeling alienated from curriculum subjects at which they had once felt they were capable, to the receiving of implicit messages that it was boys who are really the bright ones (Pipher, 1994; Sadker and Sadker, 1994).

Michelle Stanworth (1983) drew attention to the phrase 'the faceless bunch', a term used by one of the male pupils in her study of students in a college of further education, to describe the inability of many teachers and boys to recall the names of the girls. She argued that this failure to identify the girls as individuals would undermine their self-confidence. Certainly girls had a lower opinion of their capabilities than boys and also interpreted any failure at school work in different ways to boys. Whereas boys accorded their failings to lack of effort, girls attributed them to lack of ability (Jones and Jones, 1989; Stables and Stables, 1995).

As we highlighted in Chapter 4, the studies undertaken in the early days of second-wave feminism also revealed how teachers' perceptions and expectations of pupils' classroom behaviour, ability and achievement were inflected by ethnicity as well as by gender. As we saw in Chapter 4, whilst White and Asian girls were frequently perceived as compliant and hardworking, the opposite view was held of Afro-Caribbean girls. Teacher interactions with Afro-Caribbean girls were similar to those with their male counterparts, whereby Black pupils generally received a disproportionate amount of negative assessment, discipline and feedback, reflecting teachers' (lower) expectations (Fuller, 1980; Wright, 1987).

Recent research suggests that the differential perception of girls as achieving through hard work and boys as innately clever continues. This work shows how girls and boys are 'read' by teachers according to gender constructions that insist on locating talent and ability in the masculine, in spite of any contrary material evidence. For example, two highly able Year 6 (11–12-year-old) girls in Renold's (2001) study were not seen as talented by their teachers but as 'bossy', 'overconfident' and 'not as clever as she thinks she is' (p. 580). Teachers in Maynard's (2002) research of a primary school saw underachieving boys as 'having innate if untapped potential' (p. 67)!

Of course, the child-centred ethos of the primary schools in which the early research was carried out has been eroded by the changes brought about by the introduction of market forces into education. This is a feature which has reshaped educational systems across the western world. The primary and elementary schools of today are far more like their secondary/high school equivalents with their emphasis on achievement in public examinations. Partly as a consequence of this reconfiguring of educational systems to accommodate neoliberalism and partly as a shift in feminist thinking, greater attention has been given to the assessment of pupils' learning than in the past.

Gender and assessment

One area which involves aspects of both the official, and hidden, curricula is the assessment of pupils' work. The assessment of pupils' achievement is of more importance today in the accountability of schools than at any other time in the past. However, issues raised by educational assessment have concerned feminists even prior to this period. For example, in 1987 the Fawcett Society examined all the GCE papers administered that year. The findings bore similarities to those of studies concerning reading schemes and curriculum material, in that they revealed that the questions took no account of girls' interests. For example, maths questions were placed in the context of football games or car engines. Girls were largely absent from maths papers and when they did appear it was largely in stereotypical or frivolous contexts. Only one woman was referred to in the science papers (Marie Curie). The male bias detected by the investigation of the Fawcett Society was as prevalent in 'feminine' curriculum areas as in the 'masculine' maths and sciences. An English paper that concentrated on the work of Emily Bronte asked questions about the male characters in the book whilst history papers focused on military and diplomatic history. The invisibility of females was reversed in home economics papers, a situation which had been identified at other junctures. For example, imagine being a 16-year-old boy in 1979 studying home economics and turning over your O-level exam paper to see the questions:

Prepare, cook and serve a breakfast for a hungry young man on a cold morning ….

Your brother is riding in a series of races at the local cycle track. Prepare, cook and pack a lunch for your brother and his friend to eat after the races.

(Wynn, 1983: 204)

Carolyn Gipps and Patricia Murphy's (1994) award winning text *A Fair Test?* examined the findings of the Assessment and Performance Unit (APU) surveys of children aged 11, 13 and 15. Here they identified various ways in which gender impacted on assessment. For example, the experience children had out of school influenced their performance. As such, although girls and boys would score the same grades in maths and science tasks, their ease in handling certain equipment differed. In terms of measuring instruments, girls were more adept at using weighing scales whilst boys demonstrated more proficiency with electrical circuits. Gipps and Murphy put this down to the likelihood of girls having more experience at home with cooking implements and boys possessing more electrical toys and gadgets that would facilitate a basic understanding of how electricity worked. On another level, whilst boys and girls achieved the same marks when it came to compiling graphs, girls were more likely to attempt and score higher marks when the question was couched in terms of 'a day in the life of a secretary', whilst boys would be more attracted to and be successful in a graph about traffic flow through a town.

Teacher-pupil interactions were also found to have an impact on assessment. It was shown earlier how some studies found teachers interpreting boys' more boisterous behaviour as an indication of their greater confidence and ability as learners. When a group of secondary school science teachers were interviewed by Goddard-Spear (1989) the majority of them claimed they could distinguish between the written work of girls and boys. The teachers were then asked to grade samples of children's work on a number of characteristics. The sex of the pupils was altered so that each work sample was given to half of the teachers as 'boys' work' and to the remaining teachers as 'girls' work'. When teachers believed they were marking 'boys' work', higher ratings were given for scientific accuracy, richness and organisation of ideas than to identical work attributed to girls. Whilst both male and female teachers favoured 'boys' work, Goddard-Spear's research also suggested that the sex of the teacher was an influential factor. The most generous marks were awarded by female teachers of 'boys' work whilst the lowest grades were given by male teachers to 'girls' work.

Tackling gender inequalities in the classroom

The aim of feminists in revealing these inequities was not only to ensure such male dominated representations were addressed but also to encourage the development of interventionist strategies which would tackle girls' stereotyped preferences and choices. Here there was a divergence amongst feminists as to the best way of doing this.

As we said in Chapter 2 on Sex Roles and Schooling, it was mainly the Liberal and Radical Feminisms that set out ways of addressing gender inequalities in the curriculum, pedagogy and practices of schools. Liberal Feminists adopted 'girl-friendly' approaches to schooling whereby girls were provided with the same *access* to educational opportunities as boys (Whyld, 1983; Whyte et al., 1985). The alternative approach was referred to as 'girl-centred' (Arnot and Weiner, 1987) which was founded on the basis that girls' unequal *treatment in* and *outcome of* schooling was informed by inequalities in broader social structures (see Table 6.1).

There were few schools that adopted the more politically radical 'girl-centred' approaches to schooling, the exception being a few local authorities in the UK that leaned to the left (Arends and Volman, 1995). Rather, the majority of equal opportunities policies adopted in schools in Britain and elsewhere were based on 'girl-friendly'/multicultural ('weak') conceptions rather than ('strong') 'girl-centred'/anti-racist approaches (Arnot, 1985; Gillborn, 1995; Arnot and Dillabough, 2000). Examples of government sponsored equal opportunity initiatives in the UK were *Girls Into Science and Technology* (GIST) and in Australia, the *Girls in Schools* report (1988). Such initiatives delivered quite disappointing results. GIST, for example, was set up to tackle the lack of girls' participation and interest in science by raising teachers' awareness and making a traditionally male area more 'girl-friendly'. During the four years of the project (1979–1983) a team of researchers worked with teachers who had responsibility

Table 6.1 Equal opportunities vs anti-sexist policy approaches

Equal opportunities/girl-friendly	Anti-sexist/girl-centred
Persuading girls into science and technology	Recognising the importance of girl-centred study; for example, what is 'herstory' or girl- and woman-centred science or technology?
Providing a compulsory common core of subjects, to include 'hard' sciences for girls and humanities for boys.	Providing girls with skills and knowledge to challenge the male system in the workplace and the home.
Rearranging option blocks to reduce stereotyped choices.	Giving girls a sense of solidarity with other members of their sex, and hence greater confidence and motivations.
Analysing sexism in textbooks, readers and resources.	Widening girls' horizons while not denigrating the lives and work of their mothers, female friends and women in the community.
Reviewing school organisation – for example, registers, assemblies uniform, discipline.	Changing the nature of schooling: replacing hierarchy, competitiveness, authoritarianism and selection with cooperation, democracy, egalitarianism and community.
Producing in-service courses and policy guidelines.	Exploring the relationship between sexuality, women's oppression and sexual harassment in school and the workplace.
Establishing mixed-sex working parties to develop and monitor school policy.	Establishing schoolgirls' and women's support groups.
Creating posts for equal opportunities.	Decision-making through wide consultation and collective writing.

Source: Weiner and Arnot (1987) p. 356.

for science and technology in the lower years of ten co-educational comprehensive schools. Their aim was to encourage more girls to opt for science when they had to make their option choices at aged 13. In their final report, Kelly *et al.*, (1984) described how the project had made little impact on pupils' subject choices; how there was only a slight change in girls' attitudes to science and technology, and the teachers, although being generally supportive of GIST, felt that their own practices had not altered much as a result of it.

Whilst feminists were disappointed with the lack of success of such equal opportunities interventions (in that they seemed to do little to shift girls' interests or take-up of 'masculine' subject areas), there are many others who, today, argue these strategies were *too* successful. As we have discussed throughout the book, one of the points raised in relation to present day concerns over boys' underachievement is that the approaches adopted to provide girls with a more equitable experience of schooling has militated against boys (Moir and Moir, 1999; Hoff Sommers, 2000). This is in spite of evidence that shows that only certain groups of boys are substantially under-achieving at school, and that the gender gap is concentrated around literacy. And further, that, in addition to some groups of girls continuing to achieve below the national average, girls' educational experiences continue to be coloured by stereotypical gender discourses which see them as 'hardworkers' rather than 'brilliant' (Younger and Warrington, 1996; Jones and Myhill, 2004).

Furthermore, with the benefit of hindsight, feminists can see why equal opportunity interventionist strategies such as GIST and the GAMMA Project (see later section) failed in attracting more girls to take an interest in science and mathematics (Arnot, 1991; MacNaughton, 2000; Skelton and Francis, 2001). Developments in feminist theorising and understandings, brought about through post-structuralism, enabled a recognition of how gender possibilities and constraints informed all aspects of pupils' engagement with school. If we accept 'gender as relational' (whereby boys and girls see themselves as opposites of each other) then something like GIST was bound to fail as its basic premise – to make science more 'girl-friendly' – exacerbated the alienation girls already experienced towards science. If science is presented as a 'boys subject' (and in trying to make it 'girl-friendly' suggests that it was 'girl-unfriendly') then girls will withdraw from it in order to present themselves as 'properly feminine'.[4]

So what programmes are schools adopting to tackle these gendered ways of engaging with the curriculum? At the time of writing, the dominant 'equal opportunities' pursuit is not that of breaking down gender stereotypes but remains that of addressing 'boys' underachievement'. Schools have moved increasingly away from interventionist strategies which target equal opportunities at boys and girls and towards those that focus specifically on boys. One survey stated that, in 1995, 52 per cent of schools had equal opportunities strategies aimed at boys and girls, with 14 per cent intended solely for boys; by 1997–8 the figure for the 'boys only' programmes had increased to 41 per cent (Sukhnandan, 1999; Sukhnandan *et al.*, 2000). The kinds of measures recommended in these 'boy-focused' strategies include, choosing books and other learning materials that appeal to boys' interests such as sport and adventure (Noble and Bradford, 2000); employing single-sex classes so that teachers can adopt styles that respond to boys' (supposed) preferred learning methods (Gurian, 2002); and building in to the daily management recognition of boys' needs to regularly 'let off steam' (Neall, 2002). We have discussed these in more depth in Chapter 7 and are noting them here in order to show how, far from breaking down gender stereotypes, such tactics reinforce them and place constraints on how boys and girls can envisage themselves in school sites.

In contrast, 'deconstructionist' approaches to tackling gender stereotyping in UK schools are largely unknown, although the value of addressing these through more holistic attempts have been recognised (Younger *et al.*, 2005; Warrington *et al.*, 2006; Skelton *et al.*, 2007). In Australia, there has been a history of work seeking to put these theories into practice; such work includes that of Bronwyn Davies (1993, 1997); Lingard *et al.* (2003); Keddie and Mills (2007). Work such as the 'Productive Pedagogies' framework (see Lingard *et al.* [2003]) does not centralise gender difference. Herein is a critical point. Because boys and girls are seen as oppositional (i.e. being a boy means not being a girl and vice versa) then there needs to be *less* attention given to differences between 'boys' and 'girls'. This is for the reason that any teaching practices based on assumptions of different preferences due to gender (or social class, or ethnicity, or sexuality, or culture and so forth) will ultimately build on stereotypes and help to channel pupils down different routes of learning. The themes identified with Productive Pedagogies that enable pupils' positive learning experiences are: connectedness (where the content is linked to young people's interests and concerns); intellectual engagement (where there are high expectations of pupils to critically reflect on the ideas); social support; and recognition and valuing of diversity and difference (see Lingard *et al.*, 2003; Keddie and Mills, 2007). Importantly, as references to 'social support' suggests, Productive Pedagogies can only be effective within a whole-school ethos. Three key elements have been identified by Younger *et al.* (2005) and Warrington *et al.* (2006) which, together, create a culture in which pupils and teachers are supported and through which all pupils have their opportunities raised. These are: leadership provided by the headteacher, partnership (with parents, other schools, the local community, etc.) and teaching practices.

In practice, what this means for teachers in their work with children – and it is also important to remember, these kinds of strategies are not going to be effective if not undertaken within the holistic framework just discussed – involves reflecting on investment into gendered (and classed, 'raced') identities. There is not the space here to provide the detailed discussion necessary to appreciate how such an approach 'works' in entirety (for this see Younger *et al.*, 2005; Warrington *et al.*, 2006; Keddie and Mills, 2007). An example of how a curriculum subject can be interrogated for implicit assumptions is provided by Murphy and Whitelegg (2006) in their discussion on girls and physics. They state very clearly that 'girl-centred' approaches are ineffectual as, 'replacing a "masculine" version of physics with a "feminised" version without challenging the purposes for learning physics can be equally restrictive of girls' experiences by limiting them to what they are believed to consider relevant' (p. 293). They go on to observe that a consensus is emerging in the literature about the characteristics of the curriculum that address girls' motivations to learn physics.

- Social situations that organise and determine the content studied and assessed.
- The situation and the problems within it provide the purpose for learning.
- Situations vary between those of relevance to students' daily lives and concerns and wider social issues of concern to societies generally.
- Physics is represented as a social practice, physics knowledge as a social construction open to change and influenced by social, political, historical and cultural factors.
- The values implicit in physics' practices and knowledge are matters for examination.

(Murphy and Whitelegg, 2006: 294)

The intention is for all pupils to come to see themselves as part of a community in which they are users, 'knowers' and producers of scientific knowledge, rather than relating to science as a male domain. This entails investigative work involving application-based projects (hence problem-solving), recourse to personal and subjective responses through group discussions (which helps to move away from the idea that science knowledge is elevated, fixed and distant and towards one that sees it as situated, conditional and relative). It is by teachers reworking conventional subject knowledges with pupils in ways such as these that enables the breaking down of stereotypes.

This chapter has considered various aspects of gender and curriculum, from the way in which subjects are gendered to the ways in which gendered identities are perpetuated via both the official and hidden curriculum. Crucial to the discussion is the way in which the gendered curriculum reproduces power inequalities and hence unequal pupil trajectories.

7   Schools and boys

From the mid-1990s the 'problems of educating boys' have dominated government agendas on educational policy and grabbed media headlines in the UK, Australia and, more recently, the USA, Canada and Continental Europe. The general public and teachers are told that boys are underachieving in examinations when compared to girls. Nor, so we are told, are boys as interested in education (Biddulph, 1998; Hoff Sommers, 2000; Neall, 2002). There are acres of print and numerous websites that discuss 'boys' underachievement', some questioning the extent to which all boys are failing and how ethnicity and social class interact to contribute to success and failure, but, for the most part, offering (stereotypical) solutions as to how to encourage boys' engagement in education. It is not our intention in this chapter to do more than acknowledge and draw out from the current debates on boys' underachievement because deliberations are already so well rehearsed in the literature (including our own writing, e.g. Francis, 2000; Skelton, 2001; Francis and Skelton, 2005; Skelton *et al.*, 2007). Rather, we intend to explore the conceptualisations of boys, men and masculinities within education and how these have been, and are, considered by feminists and pro-feminists. However, to begin with we want to raise the issue of feminist engagement with research and writing on men and masculinities. In these days of 'third-wave feminism' (see Chapter 2) where gender is sometimes seen as potentially disembodied then not to acknowledge the interplay of masculinities and femininities would be regarded as naïve or essentialist research. Yet, second-wave feminists began their work at a time when gender theory was in its infancy and masculinity and femininity were regarded as properties of, respectively, male and female bodies. As such, the first section sets out the struggles feminists had in negotiating and reconciling investigations of boys, men and masculinities. We then look at the perspectives male researchers adopted as they began to explore masculinities and how this work fitted with feminist theorising. The chapter then moves on to provide an overview of the development of research into boys, men and masculinities in schooling and feminist engagement with these.

Feminism and research/writing on boys, men and masculinities

For many, the idea of feminists researching and writing about the ways in which masculinity/masculinities are constructed, was (and, for some, remains) a thorny issue. Early second-wave educational feminism sought to illustrate and then redress the ways in which girls' and women's experiences were subsumed within, or positioned as inferior to, those of boys; how the curriculum was gender stereotyped and women's contribution to knowledge was ignored; how girls were channelled towards lower paid and stereotyped jobs in the caring and service professions; how the teaching profession was segregated, with men occupying the senior posts, and the sectors in which women predominated (primary and early years) being seen as lower status. The conundrum was whether any focus on the ways in which 'masculinity' was constructed either in personal relationships or through structural inequalities, added to analyses of girls' and women's educational experiences or, rather, detracted attention from this intended focus. From the outset, second-wave feminism embraced a range of differing perspectives and this meant support could be found for either argument, with some researchers opting to study masculinities, and others rejecting the idea. For example, some Radical Feminists who were studying men's violence towards women (Hanmer and Maynard, 1987) and the attitudes of those in authority such as the police and the law (Radford, 1987) made the case that the 'doing' of masculinity affects all women and that it was necessary to 'demystify power and its components, one of which is the production of "masculinity" and "masculine" behaviour' (Layland, 1990: 129). However, a more radical version of Radical Feminism, Separatist Feminism, adopted the stance that the focus should be exclusively on women/girls (for example, Natasha Walter, 1999, cites an example of Separatist Feminist lecturers refusing to take questions from men). Many feminists felt that research should be firmly 'girl-centred' in order to redress the balance of historic attention to the needs and behaviours of boys (see e.g. Skeggs, 1994).

Today, there are many feminists who do not see masculinity and femininity as necessarily tied to the bodies of men and women (Butler, 1990; Halberstam, 1998). That is, women can 'do' masculinity as well as femininity (with the same applying to men). However, prior to the emergence of theories that recognised the fluidity of gender concepts, masculinity was taken to be the preserve of those with male bodies and femininity was something that related solely and specifically to women. Also, as we have just argued, some early second-wave feminists (specifically Separatist Feminists) did not want to engage with men, which meant that 'masculinities' were also not open for discussion. Whilst Separatist Feminism attracted relatively few adherents (although larger numbers were *influenced* by this position, including many Radical Feminists), it was this stance that was identified and pilloried by the press, and used as representative of feminism generally in media disparagement.

For feminists working in education, there had to be some consideration of the actions of men and boys. However, whilst feminists in some areas did begin to problematise masculinity (e.g. Hamblin, 1982; Stanko, 1985), for the most part, a majority of feminist writers on education in the early days of second-wave feminism used the concepts and experiences of boys/men/masculinities as a foil against which the inferior and unequal experiences of girls and women could be illustrated. Indeed, analyses of gender relations in schools, which tended to consider gender *as* difference rather than gender differences (Griffin and Lees, 1997), were relatively few. We explore some examples of such contributions later in this chapter.

Men and feminism

Prior to the studies by pro-feminist writers which emerged in the 1980s (e.g. Connell *et al.*, 1982; Walker, 1988; Connell, 1989), there were investigations of masculinity/masculinities in schools carried out by researchers working in radical youth cultural studies who set out to challenge popularist notions of working-class young men as violent, 'work-shy' and destructive, looking to social class positioning as a means of explaining the ways in which these male youths challenged dominant sources of social power (e.g. *Adolescent Boys in the East End of London,* Wilmott 1969; *View from the Boys,* Parker, 1974; *Knuckle Sandwich: Growing Up in the Working-class City,* Robins and Cohen, 1978). As we saw in Chapter 3, included here are those studies by male academics influenced by neo-Marxist ideology who investigated the educational experiences of working-class boys. For example, Paul Willis's (1970) *Learning to Labour: How Working-class Kids Get Working-class Jobs* likened boys' counter-school culture to that of the factory shop-floor. In a similar way, Paul Corrigan's (1979) study of a group of working-class boys in a co-educational school in the North East of England, *Schooling the Smash Street Kids*, drew attention to their truancy and 'mucking about in class' as challenges to the repressive authority of the school and society.

Feminists reflecting on some of the studies carried out by male researchers in schools pointed out two major problems which this research generated. First, that several of these studies drew conclusions about 'school pupils' when they were actually studies of boys' subcultures (McRobbie, 1978; Llewellyn, 1980; Fuller, 1980; Acker, 1981). The famous Manchester studies by Hargreaves (1967) and Lacey (1970) demonstrated how academically successful 'pupils' (sic) were most likely to hold positive attitudes to education and schooling whilst less successful 'pupils' (sic) were liable to reject or sabotage the system in which they found themselves. However, these studies were not set in co-educational schools nor did the conclusions acknowledge that the pupil sample was, in both cases, all boys. Thus, the assumption was either that the behaviours and attitudes found in studies of all-male pupil samples were equally as applicable to girls, or that girls were not of sufficient import to warrant concern. Sandra Acker (1981, 1994) suggested that researchers were drawn towards groups regarded as potential control problems and male researchers have tended towards exploring the ways in which boys manifest these.

A second concern for feminist educationalists was how some male researchers when investigating boys' attitudes and behaviour at school liked to associate themselves with the 'laddish' performances of the boys. There did not appear to be any self-reflection on the part of these male researchers of how they were upholding particular exaggerated, dominant, forms of masculinity. For example, in *View from the Boys*, Parker (1974: 223) observed 'If I hadn't been young, hairy, boozy, etc., willing to keep long hours and accept "permissive" standards the liaison would have failed'. It was for glamorising traditional, dominant, performances of working-class masculinities in his influential study of boys in a secondary school in the Midlands that Paul Willis (1977) was criticised by feminists (McRobbie, 1978; Llewellyn, 1980). Indeed, Walkerdine (1990) maintains that Willis is guilty of a rather swooning admiration for the 'lads' in his study, and suggests that his apparent gratification from his identification with them is based on his own desires for his (re)construction of masculinity from academic 'ear'ole' to being 'one of the lads'. Females were positioned negatively in Willis' text, such as his description of girls as 'giggling sex objects, peripheral to the lads' culture and initiatives' (Willis, 1977: 87) and another example identified by Lynn Davies (1985: 88) who observed:

> ... I am also interested in the need to deepen claims about the male world. Here is Willis once more: 'Despite the increasing numbers of women employed, the most fundamental ethos of the factory is still profoundly masculine'. Not content with the tautology of 'most fundamental', there comes his favourite 'profoundly masculine.' What I wonder is shallowly masculine? Have I any chance of becoming 'profoundly feminine'?

An important point to note is that men who opted to look more closely at boys, men and masculinities were writing from a range of perspectives. Those discussed above were studies on and of boys in schools by male researchers but these made no attempt to problematise masculinity. Rather, explorations on masculinity/ties emerged as a consequence of the Women's Liberation Movement especially from the 'consciousness-raising' aspect of Radical Feminism. As Connell (1987) recalls:

> A historic moment was reached on the American Left when one of the authors of *Unbecoming Men* saw his girlfriend head off for one of the early feminist conferences and realised he was no longer where the action was. The resulting essay, 'Women Together and Me Alone', is a classic of mixed emotions. After some early experiments with mixed CR (consciousness raising) groups, feminism more or less told the men to get their own house in order. (p. 234)

These men were, unsurprisingly, influenced in different ways and adopted different stances. For some, the men's movement was a 'therapeutic project' which was conceived of as an alternative to feminism and required men to recognise, come to terms with and celebrate, their maleness.

Whilst there was little sign of this particular stance on boys and masculinity in the education literature in the 1970s and 1980s, it is one which has been very much in evidence in the debates on 'boys' underachievement' in the 1990s and into the twenty-first century. The strategies based on the idea that 'boys will be boys' advocate competitive testing and sports; using boys' (presumed) interests in football, cars, and adventure stories to stimulate them to read and do homework; sessions with boys in single-sex groups that require boys to talk about their relationships with each other, are all informed by this stance. These kinds of programmes adopted by schools are what Lingard and Douglas (1999) refer to as 'recuperative masculinity' or 'male repair agendas'. The problems posed by such an approach whereby boys are positioned as 'victims' and where no attempt is made to tackle male privilege and power have been widely critiqued (Epstein *et al.*, 1998; Kenway and Fitzclarence, 1997; Skelton, 2001; Weaver-Hightower, 2003; Younger *et al.*, 2005).

Another branch of the men's movement took greater account of feminist concerns around masculinity and male power and has drawn more widely on its literature. Men writers using feminism to debate and discuss the construction of male power and masculinities often self-refer as 'pro-feminists' (Haywood and Mac an Ghaill, 2003). It is fair to say that it was Australian pro-feminists who were amongst the first to begin to analyse the production of masculinities with education and schooling. In *Making the Difference: Schools, Families and Social Division,* Connell *et al.* (1982) introduced concepts of 'emphasised femininity', 'hegemonic masculinity' and 'gender regime' to a consideration of education and schooling whereby they demonstrated how gender relations were historical, linked to wider social structures (for example, ethnicity and social class) and always in a process of transformation. Connell went on to develop ideas around gender construction in relation to schooling in 'Cool guys, swots and wimps' (1989), whilst Jim Walker (1988), using Connell's theoretical approach, considered the interplay between Australian male youth culture and ethnicity in schools in his book *Louts and Legends*. It was the late 1980s/early 1990s when the research studies by pro-feminists into gender/masculinities and schooling began to flourish (Mac an Ghaill, 1988, 1994; Seifert, 1988; Allan, 1993; Connell, 1995).

Having said at the beginning of this section that the majority of feminists in the early period of second-wave feminism did not engage discussions around masculinity does not mean that there were not any pieces problematising 'boys' identities' by feminist educationalists. Whilst fewer in number, such deliberations were not absent from feminist debates.

Second-wave feminist writing on masculinities: boys, men teachers and schooling

The international journal *Gender and Education* was first published in 1989. Its all-female – and feminist – editorial board was a marked contrast to the composition of those of other educational journals, which were dominated by male academics (Ferber and Teiman, 1980). Whilst the majority of articles which appeared in the first few volumes were by feminists on girls and women there were also those addressing issues around masculinities, boys and men. Some of these were authored by men pro-feminists (e.g. Halstead, 1991; Mac an Ghaill, 1991) but others were by women feminists, providing a fairly good indication that, at least as far as education is concerned, boys/men/masculinities have always featured in feminist debates and discussions. For example, in 1991, the journal published an article by one of us which considered whether and how the views of men primary teachers on masculinity and femininity were influenced by them entering a non-traditional career (Skelton, 1991). This interest in men teachers was prompted through explorations of women and teaching which had shown that it was an occupation associated with 'mothering', few men chose it as a career, and those that did tended to teach older pupils and were more likely to be found in senior management posts. As such, feminists, drawing mainly on Liberal and Radical Feminist perspectives, were raising questions about how men were socialised into the profession in order to compare these with women teachers' experiences (Aspinwall and Drummond, 1989; Thornton, 1997).

Other examples of early feminist work which focused on boys and schooling in the early days of second-wave feminism were studies by Arnot (1984b), Paley (1984) and Mahony (1985). Madeleine Arnot's (1984b) chapter on 'How shall we educate our sons?' discussed how boys' stereotypical subject choices, and the processes by which schools channelled them into science/technology careers, were classed as well as gendered but, importantly, she went on to analyse how the institutionalisation and privileging of male power required particularly great effort from individual men. That is, how boys 'have to try to achieve manhood through the dual process of distancing women and femininity from themselves *and* maintaining the hierarchy and social superiority of masculinity by devaluing the female world' (Arnot, 1984b: 47–8). In a similar manner, Vivian Gussin Paley's (1984) book, although not conceptualising how masculinities and femininities 'work', provided early examples of how 'being a boy' was constructed as diametrically opposite to 'being a girl'. At the same time, the ways in which education and schooling interrelated with boys' social/academic development has been approached from a number of different perspectives.

Pat Mahony (1985) in her groundbreaking book *Schools for the Boys?* utilised Radical Feminism in her investigation of girls in three schools. The three co-educational schools in which the study was undertaken were very different: one was a purpose-built comprehensive with a mainly White, middle-class school population; one was an ex-grammar school attended by pupils from a range of minority ethnic and social class groups; the third had been changed from an all-girls to a co-educational school within the recent past. Mahony made it clear in her discussion that the data drew widely on illustrative, corroborative material sent to her by teachers across the UK and from other countries and on which she based her arguments. These findings showed how, for a majority of girls, sexual harassment was encountered on a daily basis. However, rather than argue the case for the implementation of (or, in some cases a return to) single-sex classes, Pat Mahony made the point that this would simply be deferring the problem. She argued that boys should be tackling the taken-for-grantedness of male superiority, privilege and power that enabled them to dominate females as well as each other. Askew and Ross (1988), collecting data from a range of primary and secondary schools in the London area, utilised both Radical Feminism and Liberal Feminist perspectives of sex-role socialisation and stereotyping to demonstrate how boys are at great pains to disassociate themselves from the 'other' (that is, Feminine) and align themselves with the most valued aspects of schooling (which were those depicted as masculine).

These texts were written over twenty years ago yet make the same call for the deconstruction of stereotypical masculinities in schools that is being argued for today (Keddie and Mills, 2007; Skelton *et al.*, 2007) as a means of addressing gender-power differences. For example, Arnot (1984) suggested that active intervention by teachers, parents and boys and girls would eliminate traditional gendered and unequal patterns (as opposed to simply providing *access* to the same educational opportunities).

What we are illustrating here is that feminists in education have, from the start of second-wave feminism, maintained a watch on boys/men/masculinities in order to explore the experiences of girls and women; but, as was discussed earlier, the majority of sociological studies of schools did not explore or even recognise that 'boys' are subjective, gendered beings and it is fairly accurate to say that, at least in those early days of second-wave feminism, an emphasis on power *between* males and females in educational settings failed to grasp the multiple and complex ways in which power is manifested. As a result, this body of work helped to generate an image of a 'typical boy' who was dominant, aggressive and defined in comparison to girls. An example of this can be seen in the work of Katherine Clarricoates:

> The girls condemned boys for being rough and aggressive whilst the boys condemned girls for appearing to be the 'good pupils' since it is through the display of reverse qualities of what girls do that boys gain and reward status. (1987: 199)

The stance adopted by radical feminists in their accounts of schooling has been criticised for its positioning of 'female as victim' and 'male as victimiser' (Measor and Sikes, 1992; Jones, 1993; Hey, 1997b). This is not to undermine the significance of these studies as they reflect the concerns and theoretical tools available at the time in which they were written. Indeed, such discussions stimulated debate around the notion of gender as relationally constructed, and consequent arguments that the study of femininity necessitated attention to masculinity as its relational construction (Stanley and Wise, 1993). These theoretical debates ensured that by the early 1990s more feminist studies were exploring the gender constructions of girls *and* boys, and women *and* men teachers, in educational contexts. Hence, by the time 'boys' underachievement' became '*the* gender problem' in the mid-1990s, feminists had already developed theoretical understandings of boys/masculinities and education. The key difference between the theorising by feminists on masculinities and schooling and those writings prompted more recently by the concerns over boys' underachievement is that the latter tends to focus on boys and boyhood as if gendered behaviours were exclusive, unified and coherent.

The rise of 'men and masculinity in crisis': the early–mid-1990s

These studies, and the ensuing contribution of pro-feminist work on masculinity and education, also coincided with (and in some cases were representative of) a new interest in masculinity in the social sciences more broadly. Where, historically, masculinity and male perspectives had been the norm in the social sciences, and hence tended to be 'taken-as-read' rather than closely analysed, a moral panic concerning a 'crisis of masculinity' positioned masculinity itself as a topic of exploration and conjecture. During the early to mid-1990s various discourses intertwined to posit that traditional forms of masculinity were under threat, challenged by social, economic and political changes in society, leaving the men apparently bearing such masculinities feeling vulnerable, confused, and even useless. The causes cited and blamed for this 'crisis' varied, from those citing the restructuring of economies in 'the Global North' away from manufacturing to service-sector work; to the impact of feminism on women's expectations and roles (see Arnot *et al.*, 1999, for discussion). However, what these explanations held in common was a tendency to blame women for masculinity's 'crisis': the economic explanation was that, as a consequence of restructuring, traditional 'masculine' heavy labour jobs and skilled industrial jobs were being replaced by 'feminised' service sector positions involving 'feminine' communication skills. We have elaborated elsewhere how the very concept of 'feminisation' is not only an inaccurate fallacy, but also insidiously implicates women as responsible for modern evils such as job insecurity, low pay, workplace alienation, and so on (Francis and Skelton, 2005). The other, often more overtly hostile explanation, is that changed social roles and expectations – as a result of the impact of second-wave feminism, and of social changes in the latter part of the twentieth century – have led to a radical shift in women's roles, leaving women financially, ideologically and emotionally independent of men. This, so the popular argument went, left men bereft of their 'male breadwinner role' and uncertain what their new role was, harangued and henpecked on all sides by newly assertive and demanding women!

It was these kinds of perspectives that underpinned the recuperative Men's Movement that we alluded to earlier, as well as the many 'Why-oh-Why' pieces in the popular press. Talk of an 'anti-feminist backlash' emerged, and it is no coincidence that at this time a backlash developed against the notion of 'PC' ('political correctness') which was seen as having taken hold during the 1980s and early 1990s, often as a direct result of feminist, anti-racist and anti-homophobic movements. A raft of 'non-PC' media products emerged in the UK including the 'lad's mag' *Loaded* (which re-introduced the staple of soft-porn and 'ironic' sexist comment that had not been seen in mainstream men's magazines for several years previously – but which has been re-institutionalised in the subsequent explosion of men's magazine titles), and television programmes in the UK such as the popular sitcom shown in the 1990s, 'Men Behaving Badly'.

The academic literature at this time represented various different seams in this debate: there were those in cultural studies and sociology who maintained that a critical, rather than overtly ideological, engagement might be made with some of the new 'post-feminist' or 'non-PC' products. (An example would be Gauntlett's [2002] engagement with men's magazines where he illustrates how non-traditional, even feminine, themes and discourses have invaded these ostensibly hyper-masculine vehicles.) Conversely, many feminist and pro-feminist researchers responded to the 'crisis of masculinity' discourse by angrily critiquing the lack of reflexivity and recognition of continuing power inequalities along gender lines by those perpetuating this discourse. What the debates did positively produce was the speedy development of a large body of work analysing the notion of masculinity and its manifestations. In the mid-1990s there were a flurry of academic books on masculinity (or 'masculinities' as the various productions of masculinity were popularly referred to in this period, following Connell, 1987; 1995): these ranged from those theorising masculinity (e.g. Connell, 1995), to Readers providing overviews of different explanations and theoretical accounts of masculinity (e.g. Edley and Wetherell, 1995), to those charting the changing constructions of masculinity across the ages (e.g. Whitehead, 2002); to MacInnes' book proclaiming *The End of Masculinity* (1998).

Developments in the literature on masculinity and education

Included in this valuable body of new work were several substantive studies of masculinity as produced within educational settings. Mac an Ghaill's ethnographic study of schoolboys, *The Making of Men* (1994), was highly influential, and was followed by a number of others, some sharing Mac an Ghaill's explicit focus on the intersection of 'race' with masculinity (e.g. Sewell, 1997; Connolly, 1998). Many male researchers were engaged in this field, but also feminists increasingly undertook ethnographic studies of boys and their experiences of schooling (see e.g. Heward, 1991; Jordan, 1995; Parry, 1996; Skelton, 1996, 2001; Renold, 1997; Marsh, 2000).

A key achievement of these works was to show how, far from being the 'normal', taken-for-granted, position that masculinist traditional research paradigms have suggested masculinity to be in their Othering and pathologisation of the feminine, in fact boys (and men) tend to have to work hard at their masculinity. As Connell illustrated, many men fail to achieve, or do not seek to achieve, 'hegemonic masculinity'. The studies of boys in educational sites illustrate how many boys attempt to stifle signs of emotional frailty or any sign of 'weakness' (Mahony, 1985; Jackson, 1990; Salisbury and Jackson, 1996; Skelton, 2001). These ethnographic studies of constructions of masculinity began to document the extreme and rampant homophobia used by boys to police and delineate masculinities (Mac an Ghaill, 1994; Epstein, 1994; Martino, 1999). Boys identified as 'insufficiently masculine' by their peers are at risk of homophobic abuse and bullying, as arguably they challenge the gender binary with its clear distinction between masculine and feminine. Via such homophobic practices, boys can police to maintain dominant forms of masculinity, and the subjugation of the feminine; and also can demonstrate their own masculinity (i.e. in their 'macho' subjugation of others) (Epstein and Johnston, 1998; Martino, 2000; Kehily, 2002; Martino and Pallotta-Chiarolli, 2003; Dalley-Trim, 2007).

While much of the work on boys observes and analyses homophobic bullying in schools, relatively little has specifically investigated the experiences of boys with minoritised sexualities (who are of course notoriously hard to identify/contact, often due to the homophobic practices noted). The work of Wayne Martino (e.g. 2000; Martino and Pallotta-Chiarolli, 2003) has made a substantial contribution in exploring the experience of gay boys and those that disrupt the 'heterosexual matrix' (see Butler, 1990) in schools. His articulation of these boys' experiences provides documentation of the effects of homophobia in schools, as well as testimony to the resistance and defiance of some boys who determine not to conform to the heterosexist and misogynist regimes practiced by and within schooling.

Other writers have documented the practices of violence (both serious and 'playful') and bullying that are maintained more generally among boys as a group to perform masculinity in the classroom, part of which involves competing in what Skelton (2001) calls a 'hard man' hierarchy (see also Salisbury and Jackson, 1996; Mills, 2001). Smaller and less physically able boys (often measured in levels of sporting prowess, see e.g. Connolly, 1998; Martino, 1999) are often subject to belittlement and ridicule; and some studies have identified how these constructions of 'effeminacy' in relation to bodies not fitting the Western masculine ideal (large, agile, powerful) are inflected by 'race' (Connolly, 1998; Martino and Pallotta-Chiarolli, 2003). Such practices, along with the homophobia, misogyny, bullying and aggression observed above, suggested that being a schoolboy was not necessarily easy: constructions of masculinity were shown in many ways to be as debilitating as those of femininity – albeit, as Connell (1989, 1995) analysed so carefully, power remained skewed towards males. Even those males bearing what Connell identifies and conceives as subjugated masculinities benefit from a gender order that privileges the male and masculine (Connell, 1989, 1995). Analysing the interaction of male and female pre-school children, Davies (1989) argued further that in a binary dichotomy underpinning gender discourse, power is inevitably located with the male – she maintains that within this discursive configuration girls and women are able only to construct themselves powerfully as helpmeets to males.

Possibly a reminder that, as Reay (2001) observes, boys overwhelmingly consider it better to be a boy than a girl (whereas girls do not overwhelmingly consider it better to be a girl than a boy), boys as a group have been consistently shown to have higher self-esteem/confidence in their abilities than girls. Second-wave feminist studies (e.g. Stanworth, 1983; Clarricoates, 1987) documented this phenomenon, showing how girls and boys as groups rated their abilities differently: even high-achieving girls did not rate their abilities highly, and when girls received high marks they responded that they must have been 'just lucky'. Boys, on the other hand, rated their abilities highly, and when they received low marks blamed this on external factors (such as an unfair test) rather than on themselves. Such patterns have been documented in various different countries over the years (see e.g. Kenway and Willis, 1990; Sadker and Sadker, 1994), and OECD figures drawn from across 'the Global North' illustrate continuity in contemporary times. Even in the face of an international panic around boys' achievement, OECD figures (2007) show that boys tend to think significantly more highly of their own scientific abilities than do girls. Of course, there are a range of possible explanations for such phenomena: it may be that boys tend to adopt strong self-belief and confidence as an aspect of their construction of masculinity, or it may be that such social expectations of masculinity as competitive and self-assured constrains boys from articulating vulnerability or lack of self-confidence. However, whatever the explanation, the outcome remains striking and reflects a remarkable consistency in constructions of masculinity as self-confident.

A further feature of the body of work on masculinity and schooling, already hinted at, was the analysis of differences among boys. It was shown that boys did not all behave in the same ways on the basis of their shared gender, and that 'boyness' alone was not enough to secure the acceptance, let alone admiration of peers. Some forms of behaviour (or versions of masculinity, as it tended to be conceived in these studies) among boys were more able to secure status among their male (and often female) peers, than were others. This recognition of diversity, and the influence of Connell's conception of different forms of masculinity/ masculinities – that might be argued to have facilitated this recognition, led to a tendency among researchers in the 1990s to provide typologies, or at least 'brands', of boys. So in the secondary school studies there were Mac an Ghaill's (1994) identified range of masculinities, including the 'Macho Lads' and the 'Real Englishmen', and Sewell's (1997) 'conformists', 'innovators', 'retreatists' and 'rebels', as well as Martino's (1999) 'cool boys', 'party animals', 'squids' and 'poofters' (Martino himself drawing on a previous range labelled by Connell). 'Macho' forms of masculinity were particularly likely to be identified and branded (examples include Jordan's [1995] 'Fighting Boys', Warren's [1997] 'Working-class Kings', and Connolly's [1998] 'Bad Boys'). Elsewhere we have critiqued this tendency to typologies for a range of reasons, including evocation of a false stability and fixity in gender production, and the implicit conflation of gender (masculinity) with sex (maleness/boys) (see e.g. Francis, 2000, 2006; Francis and Skelton, 2008, for discussion). Yet these theoretical issues aside, these studies were extremely important in their analysis of how among certain groups of boys – and in the educational institutions in which they are taught – domineering and violent behaviours are regarded as acceptable, even desirable. Moreover, tensions between the expectation of the school with regard to educational achievement, and with regard to the behaviours involved with being 'a proper boy', were increasingly identified. Ellen Jordan (1995) suggested that the development of 'school resistant' masculinities is partly a result of the contrasting demands of being a 'boy' and being a conformist pupil. The latter is expected to speak quietly, not seek attention or use domineering behaviour, work diligently and not to express frustration or anger, whilst the opposite is expected of 'real' boys (Alloway and Gilbert, 1997).

Not all boys adopt these more extreme modes of masculinity (and this body of work on masculinities was highly effective in establishing that not all boys behave in similar ways). However, this range of research illustrates the pressure for boys to conform to productions of ostentatious masculinity in school. Connell's (1987, 1995) notion of a masculinity hierarchy (with 'hegemonic masculinity' at the top) was drawn on to analyse both the patterns of interaction between boys in school, and the seductive and coercive power of hegemonic masculine positions (both for those boys able to adopt them, and those unable to).

As we saw above, the *relationality* of gender construction was a strong parallel area of exploration at this time. Hence, while some studies were focusing either primarily or exclusively on masculinity in education, others explored the ways in which masculinity and femininity are expressed by relational behaviours. Empirical work by researchers such as Davies (1989, 1997; Davies and Banks, 1992), Thorne (1993); and later by Epstein (1998) and Francis (1998) provided micro analyses of the multiple, continuous ways in which gender is produced and performed in classroom interaction, via interaction between pupils, between pupils and teachers, and in pupils' interface with materials and practices of the school. Fundamentally, the work showed how constructions of masculinity are produced in their opposition to femininity (and vice versa). Such work, which has been added to from more recent contributions by these authors as well as by powerful work from authors such as MacNaughton (2000, 2006), Reay (2001, 2002), Skelton (2001), Blaise (2005) and Renold (2005) has provided a nuanced account of the interactive mechanisms via which gender work is done, and gender difference produced, in the classroom environment.

The accounts of different 'types' of masculinity in educational settings tended to be attuned to the fact that structural factors could explain some of the differences in production of gender by various groups of boys. Hence there was attention to issues of social class and ethnicity, and to some extent, sexuality. Mac an Ghaill's (1994) ethnography set a standard here in attending to the ways in which social class and ethnicity impacted on productions of masculinity and on the readings of these productions by others. Hence, for example, he showed how the working class 'Macho Lads' in his study were invested in physical, 'macho' demonstrations of masculinity, whereas the White middle-class 'Real Englishmen' distained such physicality and rather invested in intellectual productions of masculinity which reified enlightenment conceptions of rational knowledge and traditional (classed and 'raced') notions of English nationhood.

Researchers of masculinity such as Connolly (1995, 1998), Martino (1999, 2000, 2008), Archer (2003) and Martino and Pallotta-Chiarolli (2003) have similarly been highly attuned to the interaction of different facets of identity in productions of masculinity, identifying the ways in which certain racial discourses both advantage and disadvantage boys in terms of socially acceptable constructions of masculinity. For example, the ways in which associations between Black boys, (hetero)sexuality and 'urban cool' in Western discourses position some Black boys powerfully within masculine peer relations, but conversely work against these boys in terms of their positionings by teachers (and some of these studies offer powerful accounts of the racist stereotypes and consequent low expectations to which these boys are subject). These practices are conceptualised by Majors and Bilson (1992) in relation to some Black boys' 'cool pose'. Connolly (1998) and Martino and Pallotta-Chiarolli (2003) have observed how groups of Asian pupils – South Asian in Connolly's study and East Asian in Martino and Pallotta-Chiarolli's – tend to be constructed as effeminate by other groups of boys within Western educational contexts. As in Connolly's study, even very young boys recognise and negotiate power relations that will enable them to draw on hegemonic identities. For example, Skattebol's (2006) study of a group of four-year-old children showed how Kyle (an Indian boy) at first drew on his knowledge of Indian culture in response to staff interest but then distanced himself from it, choosing instead to utilise aspects of Western hegemonic masculinity so that he could attract his chosen playmates.

Such observations have been pursued further by Archer and Francis (2007), who show how British-Chinese boys are subject to similar discourses applied by both fellow students and teachers to construct their engagements with education as 'not properly masculine'. They discuss how British-Chinese boys are subject to an applied binary of 'boffin/Triad' (Francis and Archer, 2005), wherein the majority are Othered as adopting 'feminised' ways of learning, and the few that are seen not to 'fit' the diligent stereotype are further pathologised as 'bad apples'. Such stereotypical constructions by educationalists (as well as other pupils) and their consequence for boys' experiences and their consequent (re)productions of masculinity, are discussed further in relation to Black boys by Sewell (1997) and in relation to British Muslim boys by Archer (2003).

Some studies of masculinity identified the impact of the practices of educational institutions for the construction of gender difference. For example, researchers observed how those practices centring around discipline, such as school uniform, class registers, school assemblies and different forms of punishment, all involve shaping the pupil population into what Wolpe, citing Foucault (1977), terms a coherent 'normative order' (Wolpe 1988: 23). These authority regimes bear particular implications for modes of masculinity (and femininity). For example, in primary schools the notion of authority has been associated with male teachers (Byrne, 1978; Askew and Ross, 1988; Evetts, 1990). Men teachers are traditionally seen as 'tougher', more disciplinarian and less emotionally connected than women teachers, due to a gender binary that positions the masculine as rational and objective, and the feminine as emotional and nurturing (see e.g. Walkerdine, 1990). The manifestation of such assumptions in educational practice is that men teachers are more likely to:

- be placed in charge of older classes in primary schools in order to 'control' them; and to generally maintain discipline and punishment within schools;
- have responsibility for traditionally masculine – and consequently high status – areas of the curriculum (such as maths, science and ICT);

• occupy central roles in the school requiring leadership and decision making (senior management and management positions).

The idea that discipline and punishment is part of the role of being a male primary school teacher is one that has been raised in many studies of teachers (Sheppard, 1989; Skelton, 1991; Smedley, 1991; Sargent, 2001; Mills *et al.*, 2008). At the same time, there is also evidence to suggest that aggressive forms of discipline are related to the development of particularly 'tough' forms of masculinity in pupils. Research has shown how, when teachers (of either gender) adopt more authoritarian types of discipline with male pupils who are not academically successful, they are helping to create the 'macho' modes of masculinity identified in practically all studies of masculinities and schooling (see e.g. Willis, 1977; Corrigan, 1979; Walker, 1988; Connell, 1989; Stanley, 1989; Mac an Ghaill, 1994; Mills, 2001; Martiona and Pallotta-Chiarolli, 2003). These writers argue that a violent discipline regime, particularly one locked into an educational system of academic success or failure, invites competition in 'machismo' amongst the boys and, sometimes, between the boys and male teachers. These findings initially emerged from studies of masculinities in secondary schooling, but increasingly work in the primary sector also identified authority structures in primary schools as integral to the construction of differentiated gender identities (Jordan, 1995; Warren, 1997; Connolly, 1998; Francis, 1998; Skelton, 2001; Renold, 2005).

The oppositional positions identified by Francis (1998) among primary pupils of 'silly-selfish' (boys) and 'sensible-selfless' (girls) also emerged in Connolly's (1998) ethnography of a multi-ethnic, inner-city primary school. Connolly observed teachers' constructions in this regard, showing how teachers read behaviours differently according to pupil ethnicity. There were several examples of teachers describing boys as 'silly', but clearly there were different constructions of 'silliness' depending on the gender and ethnicity of pupils. The 'silly' behaviours of a group of 5–6-year-old African-Caribbean boys were seen by teachers as serious threats to their control and the social order of the classroom. In contrast, the 'silly' behaviours of South Asian boys were downplayed by teachers and seen as associated with their 'immaturity'. This was related to teachers' perceptions of South Asian children as 'hardworking and helpful' (Connolly, 1998: 119). Such descriptions echo Francis's (1998) feminine construction of 'sensible selflessness' and, indeed, Connolly (1998: 121) observed that teachers' discussion of South Asian boys as being 'quiet and "little", and therefore needing to be befriended and looked after' served to actively feminise them. We discuss how work on the positioning of certain groups of minority ethnic boys as 'not properly masculine' by other pupils and teachers has been taken forward in contemporary work.

Connolly (1998) found that the stereotypical construction of pupils according to 'race' held significance for the teachers' disciplinary strategies. He found that it was the 'hard'/macho group he terms the 'Bad Boys' (including some African-Caribbean boys) that were most likely to receive confrontational/disciplinary teacher attention, and that teachers utilised a similar form of language and posturing in their disciplining of the boys as the ones they saw the boys themselves using; thereby perpetuating the high status accorded to dominant, aggressive actions, and the aggressive actions themselves as teachers and boys became locked into a cycle of conflict.

Hence the research on interaction between dominant, more 'macho' modes of masculinity and classroom disciplinary practices showed that, far from acting to inhibit boys' rule-breaking and anti-authority behaviours, drawing attention to them in public arenas provides individuals with kudos within their peer group (Measor and Woods, 1984; Campbell, 1993). This body of research illustrates how the recognition of gendered identities as a factor in approaches to classroom management is crucial to the design and instigation of control strategies.

What about 'boys' underachievement'?

We said at the beginning of this chapter that there has been a great deal of academic and policy writing debating the notion of boys' achievement, and policy work seeking educational strategies (not usually successfully!) to 'close the gender gap', and that we do not intend to revisit those debates here. However, it would be negligent of us if we did not offer some discussion of how 'boys' underachievement', which might have been seen as a product or illustration of wider issues relating to a 'crisis of masculinity', was a specific issue that policy-makers reacted to and demanded educationalists address.

What does demand mention in any chapter on the development of work on boys in educational contexts is the associated interest in 'laddish' constructions of masculinity. It has been argued by many researchers that a particular construction of masculinity is invested with high peer-group status in the secondary school (and even primary schooling). This construction is what has commonly been referred to as the 'laddish' construction of masculinity. The notion of the 'lad', and 'laddish behaviour', may require some explanation for those outside the UK. The term was traditionally applied to young men and boys, and has gradually taken on a particular meaning around being 'one of the lads' (Francis, 1999). This term evokes a group of young males engaged in hedonistic practices (including 'having a laugh'; alcohol consumption, objectifying women, disruptive behaviour; and an interest in pastimes and subjects constructed as masculine, such as football, etc.). The concept tended in the past to be applied to White working-class youths (see Willis, 1977), but as Francis (1999) explains, the backlash against 'political correctness' in the 1990s led to a defiant resurgence of traditional 'laddish' values in the media (as discussed earlier).

> Thus, the values of 'lads' were appropriated by and popularised for middle-class (and often middle-aged) men, and the term has gained a new prominence in popular and media culture.
>
> (Francis, 1999: 357)

'Laddish' behaviours in the classroom are disruptive (and as such, impede formal learning), but even more than this, laddish values are the antithesis of those required for classroom-based learning. For example, laddish values of rebelliousness, 'having a laugh', non-compliance with authority, and the elevation of sport and other hyper-masculine interests over academic learning, are in direct opposition to the obedience, diligence and valuing of academic learning required for academic achievement in school. Such constructions are inflected by social class and ethnicity. However, Wayne Martino (1999) maintains that where previously it had been particularly working class boys who saw academic application as feminine and consequently sought to disassociate themselves from learning, these attitudes are now increasingly being adopted by middle-class boys. Other studies have shown how these dominant constructions play out across different ethnic groups, with particular racialised productions of popular masculinity emerging within different groups (e.g. Sewell, 1997; Archer, 2003). The construction of 'laddism' itself may subtly differ according to pupils' 'race' and social class (Francis and Archer, 2005).

Some researchers have argued that 'laddish' behaviours are for some boys produced as a result of their negative schooling experiences and subsequent disenchantment (Jackson, 2002a,b; Bleach, 1998). In this view, boys take up 'laddish' expressions of masculinity as an alternative method of building their self-worth or self-esteem, which has been damaged by their experiences of schooling.[1] A slightly different view is the argument that some boys take up disruptive behaviours if they are not doing well in their schoolwork as a result of their competitive behaviours (e.g. Salisbury and Jackson, 1996; Epstein, 1998; Jackson, 2002). In other words, such boys adopt the attitude that 'if they can't win then no-one will'; or they find other competitions to excel in (e.g. being the best at sport, or 'the most rebellious', etc.).

There is now a substantial body of work showing how constructions of masculinity which are high-status among secondary school peers are likely to have a negative impact on boys' attainment (their own, and often on that of their classmates).[2] Indeed, findings from such research demonstrate that constructions of gender difference, and the (anti-academic) productions of masculinity resulting from these relational constructions, constitute the primary explanation for a 'gender gap' in achievement.

'Gender match': Boys and male teachers

There have been many 'solutions' suggested to address boys' underachievement, and these have often drawn on anti-feminist and/or uneducated understandings of boys and girls as distinct and inherently different groups. One of the most prominent of these has been a view apparently popular with both policy and media commentators, that an injection of male teachers to the profession (particularly to primary schooling) would counter the 'feminisation' of schooling and re-engage boys with education. Specifically, it was maintained that such male teachers would provide 'role models' with whom boys might relate, facilitating their academic application and engagement. These arguments have been forwarded by policy-makers in Australia (see e.g. Martino, 2008; Mills *et al.*, 2008), and New Zealand (see Cushman, 2008), as well as in Britain – where recruitment drives were launched by the Training and Development Agency (now Teacher Development Agency) to entice more men into teaching.

This notion of male teachers as 'role models' for boys was fascinating to some of us, due to its lack of theorisation (let alone empirical evidence). Discussion of the form of 'acceptable masculinity' that male teachers are expected to represent to boys is absent from the policy literature (Skelton, 2002; Martino, 2008). Often the sorts of teachers envisaged appear to rest on stereotypes of male teachers as disciplinarian and 'robust' (documented by King, 2000 and Sargent, 2001). Yet on occasion 'fun' male teachers who can engage with 'boys' interests' are evoked (see e.g. Cushman, 2008), and at other times the vision conjured is one of a sensitive and caring male teacher who will challenge boys' views of what it is to be a man. In any case, the form of masculinity which male teachers are envisaged to represent, and the reasons that boys should apparently identify with this, are never articulated in the policy material (Francis and Skelton, 2005). Further, the assumption that a gender 'match' between pupils (boys) and teachers (men) is beneficial to boys' achievement rests upon social learning and sex-role theories (on which the notion of role modelling is predicated). This reliance is intriguing given that social learning theory has been extensively critiqued in the social sciences, as based on essentialised conceptions of identity as fixed, unitary and replicable. Social constructionist and post-structuralist theoretical lenses reveal the notion of identification and emulation between pupil and teacher purely on the basis of gender as hopelessly simplistic. Given this level of conceptual naïveté, it is perhaps not surprising that a large and growing body of international literature based on both quantitative and qualitative work is showing that gender match does not impact positively on boys' motivation or achievement.[3]

These policy initiatives premised on notions of 'gender match' have, however, opened a rich seam of theorising within gender and education. Researchers seeking to investigate and/or critique the ideas underpinning the policy drives concerning notions of male teacher role models have embarked on various studies examining the ways in which male (and female) teachers produce their gendered subjectivities. Our own work in the late 1990s (e.g. Skelton, 2001; Francis and Skelton, 2001), along with contributions by researchers such as Connolly (1998), showed how male teachers sometimes drew on hyper-masculine, misogynist and heterosexist discourses to construct their own (masculine) gender identities, and to bond with certain groups of boys in their classrooms. Such findings have been built on recently in light of the policy drives towards recruitment of more male teachers as a strategy to address 'boys' underachievement'. Male teacher's complicity with hegemonic masculine practices and their perpetuation are analysed by Jo Warin (2006) and Martino and Frank (2006). Indeed, such is the power of the perceived significance utilising dominant, heterosexualised versions of masculinities in dealing with 'hard boys' that female teachers as well as male teachers have been found to take on these attributes and becoming 'cultural accomplices' in maintaining hegemonic masculinity (Smith, 2007: 189; see also Skelton, 2001).

These studies draw out the ways in which men teachers learn to police their masculinities, and how their pedagogical practices are often shaped by 'the normalising gaze of their male students' (Martino and Frank, 2006: 17). However, this work has gone further theoretically by seeking to break from the constraints of dominant accounts of gender. For example, Warin's (2006) analysis of a male teacher case identifies the limitations of Connell's (1995) influential conception of 'hegemonic masculinity', given the teacher's oscillation in and out of positions which could be seen to be hegemonically masculine. Hence, Warin illuminates how such 'positions' (if positions at all) are not fixed: she talks of a 'tussle' between 'resistant' and 'complicit' forms of masculinity. Such conclusions lead her to argue that masculinities do not comprise a hierarchy, but rather different versions are in constant tension and competition. Francis (2008) goes further, again using male teacher cases, but drawing on Halberstam (1998) to see beyond bodies in analysing gender performances. Her findings highlight the extent of diversity in male teachers' practice and in their constructions of gendered subjecthood, emphasising the fluidity and complexity of gender, including the identification of 'male femininity' in male teacher performances. This work ties in with a movement towards re-evaluating understandings of gender which may be seen to have become somewhat stagnant in the field. Consequently, analyses are emerging which interrogate conflations of 'sex' and 'gender', conceptions of gender as plural or singular, and the configurations of power and identity (see e.g. Paechter, 2006).

Such theoretical developments can be mapped across the field of gender and educational achievement more broadly, showing how these (often ferocious) debates have mobilised feminist theoretical resources to counter often reactionary movements in educational policy. For feminists in the field of gender and education, some of the main challenges have been to resist what Epstein and colleagues (1998) branded the 'poor boys' discourse – the discourses emerging from media and policy works which presented boys as a homogenous 'underachieving' group, and as victims (often, as we saw above, directly as victims of females). Feminists developed a strong body of analytical work examining the nature and extent of the gender gap. This work demonstrated that it was not the case that all boys were underachieving and all girls were achieving, rather; (a) other factors of identity, such as ethnicity and (particularly) social class, are stronger predictors of educational achievement than is gender; and (b) boys (as a group) do not underperform girls (as a group) at all curriculum subjects – rather, boys' underachievement is concentrated in literacy and language subjects. The modelling, and subsequent analysis of the figures on educational achievement (usually taken from the DCSF) has sometimes been controversial in its own right, as with the debate on statistical methods of measuring gender gap engaged between Gorard *et al.* (1999) and Connolly (2008). Feminists have also drawn on social policy analysis (e.g. Mahony, 1998; Arnot *et al.*, 1999) to show how the 'moral panic' around boys' achievement has been constructed in specific socio-economic conditions; and on post-structuralist discourse analysis in order to illuminate and deconstruct the various discourses producing the 'underachieving boy', and their consequences (Epstein *et al.*, 1998; Francis and Skelton, 2005; Francis, 2006).

As we have shown, feminists were raising issues around men and masculinities for some considerable time before politicians and the media began making boys' underachievement headline news. At the same time, second-wave feminists have held mixed feelings about this – on the one hand there is a recognition that there is a need to interrogate constructs of men and masculinities in order to better understand power relations, but, on the other, there is a concern that attention to this can detract from funding, research and initiatives that focus on girls and women. Third-wave feminists have been less concerned about these kinds of issues, directing energies to constructions of identities. However, whether a 'second-wave' or 'third-wave' feminist, the analyses of gender are more sophisticated than those utilised by policymakers and the media. This chapter has shown how far feminists/pro-feminists have come in exploring, understanding and theorising gender identities in educational sites, yet when it comes to identifying strategies for tackling gendered achievement by the government and media, the appeal of simple and dichotomous explanations for 'sex differences' hold firm.

8 Gender and teaching

One of the questions we debated was whether we should call this chapter 'Women and Teaching' given that it is this that was of key interest to many second-wave feminist educationalists (Grumet, 1988; Weiler, 1988; Acker, 1983, 1989) and the theorisation of which consequently underpins our knowledge and understanding of teacher gender today. However, at the same time, whilst there continues to be writing and research exploring women teachers' identities, especially in relation to the ways in which social class, sexuality and ethnicity shape their career opportunities and experiences (Kehily, 2002; Beauboeuf, 2004; Maguire, 2005), changes in educational policy and the development of feminist theories, have broadened the area of concerns. Contemporary government unease over the shortage of men teachers, together with an increasing recognition of the importance of looking at how masculinities are 'performed' in relation to femininities (Butler, 1990), has meant feminists have been turning their attention to addressing *gendered* aspects of professional practices, policies and identities (Smulyan, 2006; Martino, 2006; Acker and Dillabough, 2007; Mills *et al.*, 2008). Not least because, as the discussion in this chapter will show, inequalities based on gendered beliefs and attitudes continue to influence the professional identities of teachers. For example, the morning we started to write this chapter an item on the breakfast news reported the results of a poll carried out by the Training and Development Agency saying that boys prefer men teachers. The item included an interview with a schoolboy, a male primary teacher, and a spokesperson from the National Literacy Trust. The questions from the presenters were couched in the same language of concern and anxiety about the 'feminisation' of teaching as that used in newspaper reports headlined 'Betraying Boys' (Daily Mail, 15 June, 2006: 56–7) and 'Why boys need to be taught by male teachers' (*The Independent*, 23 March, 2006: 18). The schoolboy responded to a question about why he preferred men teachers by saying he had only ever had one male teacher but he had explained difficult ideas and made schoolwork fun. The adults taking part nodded their heads wisely and one of the presenters commented 'He sounds like a terrific teacher'. A *Times* newspaper report on the same poll entitled 'Schoolboys join recruitment drive for more male teachers' (Blair, 2007) observed

Although male teachers are thought not to have a significant impact on the academic achievement of boys or girls, Graham Holley, of the agency, says it is important that men are recruited to the staffroom.

We pondered the likelihood of there ever being a major news story on primetime television discussing the absence of women teachers in leadership positions, let alone a government agency undertaking a poll on this to ascertain schoolgirls' views. The suggestion in the report, based on one pupil's experience, is that men teachers are especially able to communicate difficult concepts in a lively way – the implication being that women teachers cannot! It seems unlikely that a news story, based on the experience of one pupil, would ever be countenanced that suggested women teachers had such superior abilities! What such news reports demonstrate is that the different, gender-relational positions assigned to men and women teachers, primary teachers in particular, seem to have been untouched by years of feminist research in education.

It is impossible to do justice to all the research on women, teaching and the gendering of the profession in one chapter (for detailed discussions see Biklen, 1995; Coffey and Delamont, 2000). We have chosen instead to review the research on gender and teaching in terms of the major themes pursued throughout this book: achievement and gender experiences. In looking at this question we bring together the literature on two areas of interest: the gendered nature of teachers and teaching; and the implications of new managerialism for gender and teachers' careers.

These foci might be seen to risk marginalising some important work on women teachers' experiences, particularly from the late 1970s and early 1980s; for example on women teachers' sexualities (e.g. Sanders and Spraggs, 1989; Squirrel, 1989) and experiences of sexual harassment (e.g. Whitbread, 1980; Herbert, 1989). However, we hope that consideration of many of these studies has been included in previous chapters of this book.

As a means of an introduction we set out the links between feminism and women teachers. This leads to a consideration of the gendered nature of teaching. It was the major changes to educational systems against a background of globalisation and the introduction of new managerialist principles into schools that shifted feminist research agendas. We discuss how research is highlighting the ways in which the significance accorded to individualisation (Beck and Beck-Gernsheim, 2002) and the redefinition of equity discourses as being about 'performance' (Davies, 2003) distracts and detracts attention from ongoing gender discriminatory practices within the teaching profession.

In addition to the discussion on gender and teachers' careers, there is another dimension to be explored in this chapter on gender and teaching: achievement and gender constructions. That is, the notion of teachers as perpetuating gender distinctions and inequalities in their interactions with pupils. Here we examine the charge that teachers have taken conservative stances in relation to gender, and secondly, we draw on data from a research study on primary children and teachers' understandings of gender and teaching to demonstrate continuing, and reinforced, gender discriminatory perceptions among teachers.

What we set out to show in this chapter is how the consequences of educational policy and its influence on classroom and pedagogic practices contribute an aspect of 'the schooling scandal' of the third feminist epoch – the reinforcement of gender stereotypical discourses with pupils within teaching practices, and of traditional constructions of 'properly gendered' men and women teachers.

Feminism and women teachers

There is a long and strong link between feminism and teaching. Many of those who were active in the push for equality for women from the 1850s onwards were teachers and headteachers, keen to improve the education of girls, for example, Emily Davies (founder of Girton College, Cambridge in 1873) and Frances Buss (head and founder of North London Collegiate School for girls in 1850). Similarly, activists of second-wave feminism included those who began their careers as teachers[1] and who saw their connections with the classroom as crucial in bringing about change in the lives of pupils.

In the period when women teachers and headteachers were campaigning for a better education for those entering teaching (1850–1918), the future for middle-class girls was seen exclusively as becoming wives and mothers (see Introduction). So, the question of why a higher education was seen to be necessary to teach (and, as such, became a key area for reform) has posed something of a puzzle (Purvis, 1991). One explanation has been that it was increasingly the case that middle-class women needed to earn their own living. There were only a handful of jobs middle-class women could enter without compromising their position as 'ladies' (e.g. governess, teaching). However, poorly educated middle-class women were the ones educating middle-class girls, thus it was not surprising that the Schools Inquiry Commission (1868) reported on the woeful state of the education being given to this group of girls. As such, better education and training of teachers would improve the education of middle-class girls as well as making inroads into higher education (Dyhouse, 1981; Delamont, 1989).

Once the quest for women's suffrage had been achieved, women teachers continued to be confronted with struggles for equality within their own profession. For example, it was largely as a result of the efforts of women teachers inside the union that the National Union of Teachers (NUT) made a stand for equal pay in 1919 (Littlewood, 1995). However, there was no real commitment to the idea, as was evident when the Burnham Committee, on which twenty of the twenty-five NUT representatives were men, opted for women to receive just four-fifths the pay of men (Oram, 1987). Tired of the hostility of men teachers inside and outside the NUT, a splinter group set up the National Union of Women Teachers (NUWT) in 1920. A corresponding group of men, who were antagonistic towards the pressure by women teachers for equal pay, whom they regarded as 'the worst group of profiteers that took advantage of the war to extort money',[2] established a further union, the National Association of Schoolmasters (NAS) in 1922. Throughout the 1930s, the NAS were consistent in their devaluing of their female colleagues arguing that, because of their predominance in terms of numbers in elementary schools and their inability to respond to boys' masculinity, they were responsible for the development of homosexuality in young boys or, alternatively, creating 'the gangster and the hooligan' (Littlewood, 1995). The 'dangers' of women teaching boys has emerged again more recently in the debates over boys' underachievement (Skelton, 2002).

Whilst it was women teachers who pushed for equality in the teaching profession it should not be assumed that this means all women teachers did (or do) subscribe to feminism or feminist goals. At various points since the 1970s, research has indicated the reservations many teachers, women and men, have towards the influence of feminism in schools. Daryl Agnew (1989: 79), describing a weekend career development intervention for women teachers, wrote that several of them rejected the term 'feminist' saying that 'it wasn't for them'. In the late 1990s, Jane Kenway and Sue Willis (1998) talked about the resistance of some women teachers to feminist ideas which emerged in their research investigating attitudes to gender reform in schools in Australia. They quote one woman who felt feminist teachers were obtaining teaching posts that 'really should have gone to a man' (p. 176) and another saying 'I'm really anti that feminist-type thing, where the girls are getting all the rides and the boys are just being left behind' (p. 177). However, despite the reservations of many men and women teachers, as Coffey and Delamont (2000: 1) argue in *Feminism and the Classroom Teacher*, 'feminism … has been responsible for shaping the theory and practice of teaching over the course of the twentieth century'; and it has been the work of feminist educationalists that has provided information about the gendered nature of the teaching profession.

The gendered nature of teaching

The obstacles facing women teachers at the start of second-wave feminism were summarised by Lou Buchan (1980: 81) in her chapter entitled 'It's a good job for a girl (but an awful career for a woman)'. The teaching profession itself had always held a relatively low-status position in the hierarchy of professions, often devalued as a 'quasi-profession'. As a consequence, according to Waller (1932, writing of his reflections of American schools,)[3] it was seen as 'the refuge of unsalable men and unmarriageable women'. Teaching was further stratified internally, with women teaching the younger children, and men the older pupils, based on assumptions that men teachers are more effective than women teachers when it comes to discipline (Aspinwall and Drummond, 1989). Teaching younger children was likened to child-minding or 'mothering' (Browne and France, 1986), and thereby a 'natural' area for women to work in.

The relationship between teaching and motherhood has been discussed and debated widely with different positions being taken up. Some have argued that their research has demonstrated women's commitment to teaching is a consequence of its relationship to 'motherhood' (Partington, 1976). Certainly the history of women and primary teaching is linked with familial roles and responsibilities (Clarricoates, 1980; Steedman, 1987) and seen as a 'natural' activity for women to take up, but when the concept of 'motherhood' is defined, it is notions of 'child-centredness', 'nurturing' and 'caring' that are identified (Walkerdine, 1990; Sikes, 1997). Studies of primary teachers' work have shown that 'caring' is an important factor of their professional identities (Nias, 1989; Acker, 1999) and this was found to be as significant to men teachers as to women teachers (Vogt, 2002). However, as those studies carried out in 'pre-new managerialist' times demonstrate, there were gender differences in the ways in which these nurturing and caring characteristics were performed. Woods (1987) refers to the 'family oriented' ethos of primary schools where the school imitates the way in which (traditional, White, middle-class) families operate, highlighting family events like birthdays and encouraging care and concern for others, for example, through donating unwanted toys to less fortunate children. More specifically, Alexander (1984: 167) talked about the 'familial complementarity' of the roles adopted by men and women teachers. Here Alexander (1984) argued that the traditional family set-up of father, mother and children was emulated in the school whereby the male head was the school's 'father figure', acting as 'head of the household', with the female class teachers in charge of their own small domain – the classroom – where they had immediate, daily responsibility for the children. Indeed, Sara Delamont (1983) pointed out that schools were more gender stereotyped than either the homes pupils came from or the wider society children witnessed around them. She identified five areas of schooling where gender stereotyping could be found; the first of these being the 'formal organisation' of schooling in which she included staffing structures (Delamont, 1980). Here she noted that, for the most part, it was men who were the headteachers, heads of department and who occupied most of the senior management positions. Delamont also observed that females in schools were always in a subordinate position to that of men and gave examples of the male caretaker in charge of an all-female cleaning staff and the female school secretary working for the male headmaster (Delamont, 1983).

The association between teaching and motherhood also meant that teaching was seen as a job for married women, a means of earning a second salary, which they could fit in around their (prime) family responsibilities (Reich, 1974). Men teachers were regarded as more adept at teaching the 'hard' (masculine) curriculum subjects such as maths and science (which ignored the fact that it was men who were more likely than women to have studied these subjects at a higher level; Whyld, 1983). The higher status and leadership positions in teaching were occupied by men and the male domination of the management structures meant it was particularly difficult for women to secure senior positions in the hierarchy of schools (Acker, 1989; Ozga, 1993; see next section).

As time has passed the situation has changed somewhat. In the UK teaching continues to be a profession that relies heavily on female staff, and this appears to be the case internationally, particularly as regards primary education. The report *Attracting, Developing and Retaining Teachers* (OECD, 2004a) notes that in Austria, Italy and the Hebrew sector of Israel over 90 per cent of primary teachers are female. The lowest gender gap between men and women teachers is in Greece where 57 per cent of the primary teaching force are women. However, numbers of female teachers are increasing on a year-by-year basis and the fact that the lowest percentage of women teachers is amongst the older age categories is most likely a consequence of legal restrictions in the appointment of females which existed in Greece prior to 1982. In secondary schools, whilst there are more women teachers than men, the gender distribution is more even. The pattern for the UK reflects that of other countries with 56 per cent female teachers and 44 per cent male teachers (DfES, 2005; see also OECD 2004b). During the 1990s, the number of women in leadership positions in schools began to increase but they are still less likely than men to secure such posts. Over the years, men have become proportionately less likely than they were to obtain head teacher posts but statistics released in 2007 show that, whilst there were only 16 per cent male nursery/primary teachers, 34 per cent of primary school headteachers were men. For secondary schools, men represented 44 per cent of the teaching population but 65 per cent of the headships (DfES 2007). Hence, if we apply this book's 'achievement' theme to the issue of teacher careers, we can see that, although progress has been made, career opportunities remain inequitable, with men remaining disproportionately likely to ascend the career ladder and to gain headships. Recent research has demonstrated the complex interplay of reasons for this outcome, with discursive as well as structural factors affecting women's perceptions of their careers, work-life balance, and constructions of value (Osgood *et al.*, 2006; Moreau *et al.*, 2007). Radical positions question whether achieving 'top' career posts are indeed the most important and valuable aspects of teaching work.

The figures on teacher careers also need to be considered in the light of the fact that many countries are recording a decline in numbers of both men and women coming into the profession (OECD, 2004a; DfES, 2007). Ascertaining the situation in other countries is not always easy as many governments do not prioritise the collection of information on the leadership positions occupied by men and women working in schools. For example, the National Center for Education Statistics in the USA published details on the ethnicity, the qualifications, experience and salary of teachers and principals but the only reference to gender was related to the age profile of men and women teachers (NCES, 2007).

In terms of constructions of gender and teaching, primary teaching continues to be seen by most men as an unappealing career (Drudy *et al.*, 2005; Thornton and Bricheno, 2006). However, this is in spite of an enormous policy push in the UK and elsewhere to recruit more men to teaching (particularly to primary teaching). As we discussed in the previous chapter, the concern about 'boys' underachievement' that emerged as a dominant discourse and policy preoccupation in the mid-1990s has spawned a host of (often anti-feminist) theses to explain this apparent phenomenon. One of these has been that education, especially primary education, is 'feminised' (e.g. Pollack, 1998), and that this disengages and disadvantages boys, with a consequent negative effect on their achievement. Proponents of this view argue that more men are needed as teachers to offer 'role models' to boys in order to re-engage them with education.

As we saw in Chapter 7, arguments about the 'feminisation of schooling' and the consequent need for 'male role models' continue to underpin much media commentary as well as policy premises for bringing more men into teaching. As we have pointed out (Francis *et al.*, 2008), the manifestation of masculinity which these male recruits are expected to 'model' to boys are rarely specified in this literature, but assumptions seem to oscillate wildly between those of the 'robust disciplinarian', the 'laddish joker' and the 'sensitive carer'. Of these, it is the 'robust disciplinarian' version of masculinity which seems to be most commonly elevated and expected of male teachers (see Mills *et al.*, 2008; see also Chapter 7); yet this approach contradicts both official policy statements about the appropriate attributes of primary teachers, and the motivations for most teachers – including male teachers – entering the profession. Research with student and practicing teachers indicates there is a 'professional sameness' in terms of their motivations and attitudes for becoming teachers. Both men and women emphasise a 'desire to work with children' (Johnston *et al.*, 1999; Carrington, 2002; Cushman, 2005). Research has indicated that there are few gender differences between men and women teachers in terms of how they view the job of primary teacher: both see it as a career suitable for both sexes, that it is a stressful occupation; that it is as intellectually demanding as secondary education (Carrington, 2002).

Moreover, as we noted earlier, teaching, and primary teaching especially, is associated with 'caring' and has therefore been linked to women and mothering. However, 'caring' is a term both men and women teachers use in describing the importance of this to their professional identities (Vogt, 2002; Forrester, 2005). Indeed, it is 'sensitive' (i.e. caring) people who were and are actively sought to recruit to teaching. References to recruits to primary teaching as being those who show 'sensitivity' has had a recurrent place in government mandates on selecting and training people for a teaching career:

- Good teaching calls upon those aspects of personality and character [such as] sensitivity … have a sensitive understanding of the society in which their pupils are growing up. (DES *Quality in Schools*, 1987)
- And sensitivity is referenced 7 times in *Qualifying to Teach: the Handbook of Guidance* e.g. [Is] the trainee. … sensitive to the needs of different groups? (TTA, 2004)

Furthermore, according to the Training and Development Agency, an appropriate person for primary teaching is one who demonstrates commitment and understanding; good personal, intellectual and communication skills; a positive attitude towards children and working with children, and enthusiasm. This description references both masculine and feminine ascribed characteristics but the emphasis on personal interactions and relationships would, to use a popular axiom, 'require men who can draw on their feminine side'. Indeed, in analysing different performances of gender among male teachers, one of us has illustrated a case where the male teacher concerned might be considered to be performing himself as feminine, rather than masculine (Francis, 2008). This teacher appeared highly effective, making learning fun and affirming, and engaging both boys *and* girls in his class.

New managerialism, gender and teachers' careers

The increase of women in leadership positions in teaching has brought its own challenges (Blackmore, 1999). Up until the early 1990s, liberal feminist discussions on women and leadership centred around the obstacles encountered in 'breaking through the glass ceiling'. The 'glass ceiling' is a term that first appeared in the literature in the 1980s (Morrison *et al.*, 1987) and was a metaphor to summarise the barriers to achievement which operated at a subtle level. For example, men were more likely to benefit from the sponsorship of other men who occupied senior positions (Skelton, 1991); interview panels that assumed women would not be as adept at management and leadership than a man (Grant, 1989); and women teachers themselves who, as some studies showed, were more reticent than men in applying for leadership posts due to a complex interaction of factors such as lack of confidence and prioritisation of 'family' over career (Evetts, 1987; Burgess, 1989). The facilitation of men teachers into the senior hierarchy of schools was neatly summarised by Segerman-Peck (1991: 28) who argued 'It's not so much that these (–) men queue-jump; it's that they are in a different queue'. Alongside the 'glass ceiling', feminists have also argued that women teachers have had to contend with 'glass walls' (where opportunities for securing wider experience and opportunities are restricted; Lopez, 1992). Once in positions of management, further challenges arise such as the 'perspex ceiling' (Still, 1995) and the 'slippery pole' (Carmody, 1992) where women argue that they have to work twice as hard as men in leadership posts in order to prove they are up to the job (Adler *et al.*, 1993; Blackmore, 1999). Whilst studies continue to explore the implications of the 'glass ceiling' for women teachers (Moreau *et al.*, 2007), the effects of globalisation and the subsequent widespread changes to the structuring of education has focused feminists' attention on how gender and leadership is being reworked in the light of these 'new managerialist' approaches.

There is a substantial literature on 'new managerialism' in education (for further reading see Power, 1997; Slaughter and Leslie, 1997; Bottery, 1998; Davies, 2003). Briefly, new managerialism is where the principles associated with ways of working in business and industry have been incorporated into the public sector. These new managerialist processes place emphasis on the three E's – economy, efficiency and effectiveness (Pollitt, 1993). The consequences of new managerialism for teachers is that their work is under constant surveillance and monitoring through the regular inspection of schools, testing of pupils and through the tying in of pay increases to performance (as in threshold payments; see Mahony and Hextall, 2000). In seeking to examine the gendered implications for teachers in the restructuring of educational systems, feminists have interrogated the theoretical backdrop to these; specifically, the idea that we are in a second or reflexive modernity where rights and responsibilities for society rest on the relationship between state and individual.

There are two key points that need to be made here. First, the emphasis in this period of second modernity is on the *individual* who is seen as having choices and opportunities and therefore to make of themselves what they will.

Here the individual is seen as viewing themselves as the centre of their own world, constantly shaping themselves to secure the life they 'choose' to lead. As such, gender (along with social class) is positioned as less significant in today's society than in earlier periods (Beck, 1992). In this second modernity there have been changes to family structures, changes to the work we do and how we do it, and a raft of legislation ostensibly aimed at bringing about social justice for all. Women are often presented as particular beneficiaries of these changes in society in that they have been released from their traditional positions in the home and labour market (see Walkerdine *et al.*, 2001 for a critique). Whilst this view that women have been released from constraining stereotypes has been vigorously contested by feminists (Adkins, 2002; Walkerdine and Ringrose, 2006), it is accurate to say that the significance of structural inequalities including gender are marginalised in individualist perspectives; gender being regarded simply as one feature of a person's identity. What are the implications here for individualised discourses on the professional lives of women (and men) teachers?

Bronwyn Davies (2003; Davies and Saltmarsh, 2007) has written incisively of how the introduction of new managerialist[4] policies and practices has created a situation in which teachers' professional lives are dictated by the 'vagaries of the market' (2007: 2).

> Within this competitive, consumer-oriented system individuals in pursuit of their own freedom must also be persuaded to freely accept responsibility both for themselves as individuals and for the success of their workplace.
>
> (Davies and Saltmarsh, 2007: 3)

One of the consequences of new managerialism is that gender inequities take on a different guise to those identified at the beginning of second-wave feminism. For example, in the research discussed above on women and leadership, one of the central intentions of breaking through the 'glass ceiling' was to gain access to the networks of power that resided with those in senior management positions. However, power can no longer be seen as residing in the authority of professional practitioners in educational hierarchies. With professional autonomy under attack, there has been a shift of power away from professionals towards auditors. As such, new managerialism has been found to affect the working lives of both men and women similarly in the expectations of what is demanded and orientations to work (Currie *et al.*, 2000). Teachers have their work judged by the success of their pupils in public examinations, their performance in Ofsted inspections, their abilities to provide the required evidence that will secure them a pay increase; similarly the work of headteachers and education advisors is subject to constant monitoring and scrutiny (Mahony and Hextall, 2000). Through this individual monitoring and the focus on the 'self' the findings of research focusing on structural inequalities, such as that referred to earlier showing the privileging of male teachers for promotion, has been sidelined if not totally disregarded. A study by Moreau *et al.* (2007) found that women teachers were more likely to question their *personal* confidence and ambition or query their *own* motivation for undertaking further professional development courses to update or develop new skills, rather than look to structural obstacles to promotion. Similarly, women teachers referred to opportunities they had 'missed' or failed to act on. In this way, the 'self' is seen as the epicentre of possibility and responsibility, and failure is seen as due to the personal failure of the individual.

Alternatively, some research has found that whilst men and women both suffer from the impact of greater accountability and surveillance, men teachers actually experience more problems in some areas than female teachers. For example, Mahony *et al.*, 2004, in their study of teachers who applied for a pay increase (referred to as 'performance related' or 'merit' pay),[5] found that women teachers were more likely to be more assiduous at completing the paperwork and collecting and collating the various pieces of 'evidence' required to support the application. Men teachers had a tendency to assume that they would, with little effort in terms of attention to the paperwork, etc., be given the pay increase and then were surprised and annoyed when they were not. Mahony *et al.* (2004: 140) note that:

> with these levels of expectation it is hardly surprising that one of the issues reported as being referred most to trade unions was, 'White male teachers have come to us to complain that they've not got through the *Threshold*'.

Having looked at the impact of neo-liberalism on teachers' gendered careers we shall now turn our attention to the significance of teachers' gendered attitudes, expectations and behaviours in interactions and relationships with pupils. Interestingly, research has suggested that the teaching profession and policy makers have appeared somewhat ambivalent, if not resistant, to implementing gender equality in relation to girls but have shown comparative enthusiasm in relation to boys within the contemporary discourse of 'boys' underachievement' (Acker, 1984; Epstein *et al.*, 1998; Skelton *et al.*, 2008).

Teacher perspectives on gender

There is a useful reminder in these studies on gender, teachers and new managerialism which often gets lost, especially in the focus on the drive for more men teachers (see below): that is, we should look at the similarities between men and women teachers rather than always centring on difference. In so doing this does not, as may be presumed, play down gender inequalities, but can actually serve to highlight them. An example can be provided by a theme that has emerged in numerous feminist educational studies since the arrival of second-wave feminism: teachers' attitudes and willingness to address gender inequalities with their pupils. We shall concentrate especially on primary teachers as it is primary schools that are being targeted in terms of teacher gender imbalances.

In 1988 Sandra Acker published a paper entitled 'Teachers, gender and resistance' which questioned why gender equality initiatives were 'apparently failing to transform teachers' attitudes and actions' (p. 94). She argued that both male and female teachers' resistance was attributable to a number of factors: the ideologies they hold, the conditions in which they work, the characteristics of the equality initiative and, finally, the type of people teachers are. In a similar way, Alexander (1984) has commented on various and historical characteristics of the nature of teaching and those who teach which are resistant to innovation and change including the pull towards individual intuition, the dominance of ideology, the tendency towards the practical over the theoretical and the failure of teacher education courses to encourage a critical perspective amongst intending teachers. Studies by researchers such as Pratt (1985) found that teachers from some disciplines were more likely than those from others to support equal opportunity initiatives, and that female teachers were more likely to support them than were male (see also Younger, 2007 for recent evidence of some of these trends). The early studies by feminists and others in the 1960s, 1970s and 1980s often describe teachers as generally being 'conservative' (Morrison and McIntyre, 1969; Marriot, 1985) and 'conformist' (Hanson and Herrington, 1976). Delamont (1987) observes how, over the years, teachers have been chastised by politicians and the media for undermining traditional teaching approaches and promoting left-wing ideals, yet cites previous research findings to argue that in fact 'the large majority of teachers [have] very conventional ideas' (p. 12).

More recent studies have often included stronger acknowledgement of the way in which policy has both steered and circumscribed teacher interest and commitment to gender equity initiatives. For example, in the 1980s when studies were focusing on girls' underachievement at maths and science subjects, there was no official policy intervention to raise girls' achievement – this endeavour was left to individual committed teachers and to feminist interventions (Arnot *et al.*, 1999). Yet the introduction of school 'league tables' in England stimulated the emergence of a quasi-market in education, with 'consumers' (parents and pupils) supposedly able to choose their school based on information about pupil achievement published in these league tables. It was with their publication that came the initial realisation that boys, as a group, were not performing as well as had apparently been imagined – and of course, any underperformance among boys had material consequences for both individual schools and government policy, all of which were tasked with 'raising standards' (measured by achievement). Not surprisingly then, policy makers took the apparent 'underachievement of boys' extremely seriously, and freed up a plethora of officially sanctioned resources and interventions with the aim of 'raising boys' achievement', which were enthusiastically seized on by many Local Education Authorities and schools. Hence the perceived 'underachievement of boys' has been approached and addressed very differently to the case of 'girls' underachievement' in previous times (and many feminist researchers have argued that sexist prioritisation of males and their concerns also fed this discrepancy, see e.g. Epstein *et al.*, 1998). Consequently, strategies introduced to 'raise boys achievement' and the whole discourse constructing boys' underachievement has had far more of an effect at the chalkface, making a profound impact on teaching practice, as we shall now illustrate.

Teachers' professionalisation and gender equality.

Whilst there is evidence that suggests school leavers and students think there are so few men primary teachers because they see it as a 'woman's job' (Drudy *et al.*, 2005; Thornton, 1998), interviews with men teachers show that some are shocked to find themselves in a minority (Mulholland and Hansen, 2003) whilst others do not see that their gender is a relevant factor in their career as primary teachers (Carrington, 2002; Skelton, 2003). We have touched on the various manifestations of the notion of the 'masculine teacher' in policy articulations, often projecting a disciplinarian. The majority of studies have shown that this stereotype of 'the' male primary teacher is not reflected in the attitudes, beliefs, perceptions, expectations and experiences of actual men teachers and indeed many have felt compromised by these assumptions (King, 2000; Roulston and Mills, 2000; Sumsion, 2000; Sargent, 2001; Skelton, 2003; Warin, 2006; Mills *et al.*, 2008); and, as we have seen in one of our studies of primary men teachers, it was apparent that men teachers do not have 'one way' of relating to and teaching children and take up various gendered positions in the classroom (Francis, 2008). Another of our studies found there were quite different responses between those men teachers who taught older primary children to those who taught the youngest to questions about whether women teachers were more 'caring' or better communicators. The teachers of the younger children dismissed such claims out of hand and were also slightly less concerned about the public wariness of men who work with young children (Skelton, 2003). One explanation for the difference in responses between men teachers of older and younger primary children might be that, because lower primary males are more in the 'firing line' than upper primary males when it comes to being associated with the 'femaleness' of early childhood teaching, they are keen to demonstrate that they possess the necessary skills and dispositions to work effectively in a traditionally female domain. It might also be the case that, having made the decision to enter lower primary (which is seen as a particularly female area of work), they had confronted the fact that their sexuality would be open to question and had decided to continue their chosen course regardless. Thus, it may be that these men were more comfortable with their gender position than their upper primary peers (see also Johnston *et al.*, 1999).

At the same time, there is evidence to suggest that some men teachers actively take up such stereotypical displays of masculinity (Smedley, 1999; Connolly, 1998; Francis and Skelton, 2001). Such performances may be validated by various factors: for example, finding themselves in a female arena, their masculinity is placed under scrutiny and thus they act out ways of being 'properly male' or redefine their contribution by being seen as different to, or better than, female teachers (King, 2000; Oyler *et al.*, 2001). Another, complementary explanation is that the emphasis given in government guidance to schools on the need to pay attention to boys' underachievement and for men teachers to act as 'role models' legitimates the performance of gender stereotypical behaviours. Added to this, teachers have been told that boys and girls have different learning styles and require different, 'boy-centred' curriculum content and forms of assessment (DfES, 2003). Thus, in terms of accountability they need to be seen to be responding to this aspect of policy.

Whatever the context or the explanations, the point remains that gender relational stereotypes are frequently invoked by teachers themselves. In a study of 300 primary, 7–8 year old, pupils and 51 of their teachers, we found that a majority of teachers rebutted any notion that men teachers taught differently or better than women teachers (Skelton *et al.*, 2008). All argued that a gender balance of staff in primary schools was a positive step forward, with the main reason being given that it was better for children to see men and women doing the same job. However, there were several examples where gender relational stereotypes of men and women teachers were voiced, evoking constructions of (male) paternalistic authority versus (female) maternalistic nurturer. Although there were almost equal numbers of men and women in the study (26 women, 25 men) it was only women teachers who voiced the view that simply being male commanded more respect from children and for the profession:

> *Brenda Upton* (White, female): Typical would be, 'oh it's just a woman's job' and perhaps that's not how the teaching profession is getting the respect that it should have, so perhaps with more male teachers … I know this sounds really sexist, but you know being a realist as well, perhaps attracting more men into the [profession would] up the status for boys you know, perhaps pursuing a career in education.

> *Ruvini Kumari* (South Asian, female): I think there should be a mixture, at the moment I think it is very good children have a kind of role model and also for behaviour as well. For some of the children, men have that authority that females don't have somehow.

> *Megan Baker* (White, female): I think men have the voice, you know, they can project their voice better and they have a better presence.

> *Luisa Perez* (White, female): Now they have got a man teacher and I have just noticed that his presence has caused them [pupils] to be different, maybe behaviour-wise similar, but a little bit more respect, sitting up or listen(ing) more.

In a related way, some of the men and women teachers supported the traditional idea that children responded more to men as disciplinarians than women. The following are examples of such comments but these need to be seen in the context that, at other points in the interviews, the teachers would argue that, from their own observations and experiences of men teachers, there were no differences between how effective male and female teachers are. What such comments illustrate is the powerful influence of a discourse of 'male-female teacher dualism' which many teachers articulate:

> *Dominic Parker* (White, male): There are particular female teachers that are quite strong, quite domineering, in that respect and the kids will respect them as much as what they respect a male teacher. I just think it's a different approach because they're used to that maternal upbringing and especially throughout infants [unclear] in this school have always been female teachers … in terms of the teaching thing it's been a different thing because a lot of the children have gone home and said, 'Dominic's a lot stricter' and things like that which they haven't had before – so it's different.

> *Louise Fletcher* (White, female): I think it's important for children to see both genders in action, because I think both genders are completely different. I think, as I say, women are probably more tolerant … I think because of their genetics more than anything, motherhood and everything else, and obviously father figures have always been seen as a figure that is looked up to and adhered to more. The mother can be negotiated with … whereas males are not negotiable usually once their decision is made.

> *Lee Martin* (White, male): This sounds really terrible but ehm, I mean one of the main reasons I've been put in that class is because there's about eight very unruly boys who have spent the last two years fighting every playtime and dinner time and the idea was that maybe they might settle down a bit for me which is very stereotypical and terrible but it does seem to be having quite a positive effect on their behaviour at the moment.

There are more examples of this 'male-female teacher' dualism than we have the space for here but which provide further illustrations relating to the concept of men teachers being keen on sport whilst women are not interested, men using their 'sense of humour' as a management device, and supplying a compensatory male figure to children who live in a world of single mothers and female teachers. One woman teacher, when discussing the absence of men teachers in schools, went as far as to say:

> *Louise Fletcher* (White, female): I wonder if that's where this, ehm, lesbianism and everything is going to come from? If you haven't got both roles? It would be interesting to track them, wouldn't it? What percentage of children will end up being gay or lesbian?

These notions of male-female teacher dualism are exacerbated by the policy drive to increase the number of men teachers in expectation that they will act as 'role models' for boys. As we have seen, this drive stems from the worries over boys' underachievement which, in itself, has spawned a host of recommended strategies for teachers to follow, ostensibly in order to raise boys' achievement; such recommended strategies have included attention to children's 'gendered learning styles' (despite the research that shows learning styles are not gendered: Coffield *et al.*, 2004; Younger *et al.*, 2005). In a climate where teachers are put under pressure to improve all children's performance in tests (and particularly that of boys), and at a time where teacher training pays little attention to critical reflection on gender inequities (Younger, 2007; Skelton, 2008), it is not then surprising to find that teachers are actively using gender as a means of informing their chosen curriculum and management practices approaches (Skelton and Read, 2006). Of the 51 teachers that took part in the research study cited above, 36 of them said they differentiated by gender for some of their teaching practices. For example, in relation to the (misleading) idea that all boys have different learning styles to all girls:

> *John Fines* (White, male): Well a lot of the boys tend to … learn by the more practical activities … kinaesthetic learning, so … [I] probably build a lot more of those activities in, but it tends to be the boys that go down that avenue.

> *Andy Monaghan* (White, male): And because the boys in my class and the class I [unclear] for are very kinaesthetic learners I've adapted my teaching to that. But I've also used visual and other preferred learning styles in my teaching but with a large number of boys I do adapt my teaching to them.

> *James Hedley* (White, male): I think boys need more specific targets … do this and this, three things done … ehm, I want three differences and girls think of as many as you can. They're happy with that.

Also, several teachers referred to boys liking competitive activities, which comprise another strategy endorsed by government educational policy on boys' underachievement (Ofsted, 2003a, b):

> *Julie Miles* (White, female): I think I do vary it a little bit but I wouldn't say it was one of my main focuses because I don't ehm, see a huge difference between the way the boys and the girls perform in this class. But there are certain things that I know, I know that in maths the boys are very competitive and so any kind of mathematical quiz or competition … ehm, really gets them going and the enthusiasm is there and they like that kind of setup.

> *Kate Cross* (White, female): I try and put in a bit of competition into classrooms, getting team points, if there's a team point on offer the boys sit up and are really desperately keen and we have house teams … so they get achievement for their team, and you'll very often see the boys, going '*yes*', if they get a team point, much more so than the girls.

It may well be the case that the emphasis and interest by government and media on boys' underachievement has served to encourage teachers to focus particularly on gender differences and, in so doing, encourages teachers to replicate 'taken-for-granted' conventional interests in their curriculum planning and reward systems

(Skelton and Francis, 2003; Browne, 2004; Connolly, 2004). We were privy to examples of using gender as a classroom management strategy, and of interventions based on constructed gender divisions, which were worked against and broadly eradicated in the late 1980s and early '90s, but which now seem to be making a comeback. A couple of indicative examples include the way in which in one class, observed prior to Christmas, teachers provided separate 'girls' advent calendars and 'boys' advent calendars; and another teacher Luisa Perez' stated,

> I mean, every half term we have a gift I give out, you know, for working hard – an award system – and I would buy a present for a girl and a present for a boy. A girl would probably get something like Barbie clothes or boys something like to do with football. So I would use gender in that certain time but not for teaching them.

The problem here is that, as well as affirming dominant gender discourses and potentially exacerbating such constructions as a consequence, teachers may fail to recognise the significance for assessment and pupil learning of encouraging particular approaches or framing the content in specifically gendered ways. It appears from our research that some of the gains of second-wave feminist work in schools have actually been lost, with concerns for challenge to gender difference and to the dominant gender order submerged by policy drives to engage boys, the recommended strategies for which are often based on retrograde, stereotypical assumptions (such as that generalisations can be applied to 'the girls' as a group and 'the boys' as a group, and that playing on any differences, real or imagined, is legitimate in the endeavour to raise boys' achievement). As such, 'the schooling scandal' of today is the unreflected and apparently uncontested re-emergence of gender stereotyping and discrimination as an aspect of pedagogy. It remains to be seen whether the Gender Equality Duty (2007) will be interpreted as in conflict with this situation, or will have any impact in turning the tide.

Conclusion

What we have done in this book is to trace six of the key themes identified by second-wave feminists, to the present day: these are, gender theory; social class; ethnicity; sexuality; curriculum; and teacher gender. We also included a chapter on boys, in order to highlight how feminists have always had a concern with boys as well as girls, and to reflect developments in research and government policy since the 1990s.

We have written this book at a point at which feminism is now seen to be in its 'third-wave', largely representing post-structuralism and queer theory perspectives, in which the very notion of gender, and the validity of analysing according to 'gender differences' in education and elsewhere, is being questioned. In reviewing the contemporary research in the field we have attempted to draw out some of the theoretical tensions emerging between what may be characterised as 'second-wave' and 'third-wave' interests and positions. Key to this are the ongoing binaries between structure and post-structure, determinism and agency, that have historically challenged feminist thinking and continue to do so today. Whereas second-wave feminists were often accused of generalising too broadly about 'all girls' and their 'oppression', third-wave feminist positions have been accused of being insufficiently attuned to the on going role of social structure (gender, 'race' and social class) and institutions in perpetuating power differences and social inequalities. As such, these positions may also risk being seen as esoteric and not of practical use to teachers and policy makers in the educational field (or in addressing the many continued and entrenched inequalities we have discussed in this book).

It will be fascinating to see whether these dualisms can be addressed by on-going feminist work in education, and what a book like this might be reporting on a possible 'fourth-wave' feminism in twenty years' time. What is obvious is that the strength of feminist work is undiminished, and highlights how many of the same patterns of inequality, in relation to the key issues of educational achievement and gendered experience, remain as important as ever.

Notes

1 Introduction

1 There were many key feminist thinkers based in the UK writing in this early period and we are anxious not to miss anyone out. At the same time, one of the key aims of this book was to acknowledge the work of the individuals who made up the field of gender and education in the UK. With our apologies to those we have inadvertently overlooked, key UK books produced in the period 1978–1986 include: Sandra Acker (*World Yearbook of Education*, 1984); Madeleine Arnot (nee Macdonald) *Education and the State*, 1984a, see under ref for *Schooling and the Reproduction of Class and Gender Relations*); Leonie Burton (*Girls into Maths Can Go*, 1986); Naima Browne and Pauline France (*Untying the Apron Strings*, 1986); Eileen Byrne (*Women and Education*, 1978); Miriam David (*The State, the Family and Education*, 1980); Rosemary Deem (*Women and Schooling*, 1978; *Schooling for Women's Work*, 1980); Sara Delamont *(Sex Roles and the School*, 1980); Mary Fuller (*Sex Role Stereotyping and Social Science*, 1978); Sue Lees (*Losing Out*, 1986); Pat Mahony (*Schools For The Boys?*, 1985); Dale Spender and Elizabeth Sarah (*Learning to Lose*, 1980); Michelle Stanworth (*Gender and Schooling*, 1983); Carolyn Steedman (*The Tidy House*, 1982); Margaret Sutherland (*Sex Bias in Education*, 1981); Rosie Walden and Valerie Walkerdine (*Girls and Mathematics*, 1982 and 1985); Gaby Weiner (*Just a Bunch of Girls*, 1985); Janie Whyld (*Sexism in the Secondary Curriculum*, 1983); Judith Whyte, Rosemary Deem, Lesley Kant and Maureen Cruickshank (*Girl Friendly Schooling*, 1985); Anne-Marie Wolpe (*Some Processes in Sexist Education*, 1977). Also, not forgetting feminist historians such as Carol Dyhouse (*Girls Growing Up in Late Victorian and Edwardian England*, 1981); Felicity Hunt (*Lessons for Life: The Schooling of Girls and Women 1850–1950*, 1987); Francis Widdowson (*Going Up into the Next Class*, 1983).

2 The USA published its own equal opportunities legislation, Title IX of the Education Amendments in 1972.

3 Compulsory schooling was introduced in Australia, the USA and England towards the end of the nineteenth century. In Australia legislation was passed for compulsory and secular state schooling in 1875 (Whitehead, 2007); in the USA, the first state to pass a compulsory law was Massachusetts in 1852 and the last was Mississippi in 1918 (Tolley, 2003). In the USA, the development of an education for girls was equally as patchy as in the UK, and legally established on a state by state basis. In the US prior to the introduction of compulsory education, some forms of schooling were available. Sadker and Sadker (1994) recount how a school in Rhode Island, USA, in 1767 offered to teach reading and writing to girls but only outside boys' schooling hours, which meant either from six to seven-thirty in the morning or from four to six-thirty in the afternoon. Parents were expected to pay more for this as teachers were, in effect, working overtime.

4 Continuing inequalities notwithstanding: for example the continuing gender pay gap; continuing domination of directorships and other most senior positions by men, and so on.

2 Sex roles and schooling

1 An excellent and succinct articulation of 'third-wave feminism' is given by Gaby Weiner (2006). Briefly, third-wave feminism emerged around the 1990s and marked a shift away from second-wave feminisms adherence to the notions of shared interests amongst women. It is feminism for a 'new generation' of academics who investigate and theorise gender and includes men as well as women researchers. It is 'more individual, complex and "imperfect" than previous waves. It is not as strictly defined or all-encompassing, … especially about personal choices' (Aapola *et al.*, 2005: 205). Also, third-wave feminism is less concerned about aligning activism with academic engagement, and 'seems more attached to the academy than previous waves' (Weiner, 2006: 82).

2 Psychoanalytic feminist perspectives, developed variously in the United States and France, and the 'difference' feminist theory elaborated in France, were being applied in other disciplines during the 1970s and 80s, but were not largely adopted in feminist educational research at this time.

3 During the 1980s women of colour, working class, gay and disabled feminists drew attention to the dominance of feminist agendas by White, middle-class, heterosexual and able-bodied women and the ways in which these women's practices were often marginalising or silencing the issues faced by women from less advantaged sections of society. Awareness was raised that oppressive power relationships are not only dependent on gender, but can occur due to a host of other factors and can exist between women.

4 An example is provided by the feminist keynote symposium entitled. 'The Return of The Thing', and the content of the papers therein, presented at the British Educational Research Association Conference, 2007, and at the American Educational Research Association, New York, 2008, chaired by Helen Colley.

3 Social class in schooling

1 For discussion of the implications and experiences of such delineations for working-class girls, see Brine (2006).

2 The Education Act of 1944 raised the legal age at which children could leave school to 15 (although this was not implemented until 1947) and this was increased again to 16 years of age in 1973.

3 Third Way theorists (such as Beck and Giddens) are specific in their use of the terms 'individualisation' and 'individualism'. 'Individualisation' is not to be confused with individuation (the process of becoming an autonomous individual), nor emancipation. Furthermore, 'individualisation' is not shorthand for egotism, the development of a 'me-first' generation of people (Giddens, 1998; Field, 2006). However, 'individualisation' does place the ego at the centre of decision making and implies that the individual has to (and can) choose and change social identity whilst taking risks in doing so (Reay, 2003). In defining individualism, Beck (quoted by Giddens, 1998: 36) writes:

> (it) is *not* Thatcherism, not market individualism, not atomisation. On the contrary, it means 'institutionalised individualism'. Most of the rights and entitlements of the welfare state, for example, are designed for individuals rather than for families. In many cases they presuppose employment. Employment in turn implies education and both of these presuppose mobility. By all these requirements people are invited to constitute themselves as individuals: to plan, understand, design themselves as individuals.

Giddens (1998) identifies the rise of 'individualisation' with globalisation processes whereby there has been a retreat in tradition such as the significance of the family, religion and politics. Beck (1992) cites three factors that have facilitated individualisation: first, the demise of social class divisions and distinctions; second, women's liberation from traditional gender roles (with the qualification that people are more 'aware' of women's equality than actually practise it); and third, changes in the nature of work. Both Beck and Giddens see this breakdown of traditional ties in a positive light as a means of providing social cohesion through 'more actively accept[ing] responsibilities for the consequences of what we do and the lifestyle habits we adopt' (Giddens, 1998: 37).

4 Bourdieu's concept of 'cultural capital' has been increasingly drawn on in the work of feminists exploring issues of social class and education. According to a leading proponent, Diane Reay, the concept of 'cultural capital' offers a 'powerful explanatory force in relation to educational inequalities of social class' (2007: 23). She cites the work of Bev Skeggs (1997) to illustrate how the concept can explain how working-class women and girls are subject to judgements of 'taste and distinction', and how these judgements blame them for behaviours that are actually determined by the various capitals (economic, cultural, symbolic and social) to which they have access. However, Reay warns that superficial use of Bourdieu's terminology – especially 'cultural capital' – has become so common in academic writing that it functions 'like intellectual hairspray without doing any intellectual work' (2007: 23). Hence she argues for *rigorous* engagement with, and application of, his ideas.

5 For discussion of the social and economic changes which have facilitated this change in the occupational aspirations of many schoolgirls, see Arnot *et al.*, 1999.

6 We qualify this with the word 'relatively' because the most powerful and senior work positions continue to be overwhelmingly dominated by men (Rees, 1999).

4 Ethnicity, gender and education

1 The difficulties created by paralleling 'gender' and 'race', rather than exploring their interaction was as much a feature of first wave feminism and the enfranchisement of Black men as for the civil rights movements of the 1960s/1970s. Sojurner Truth delivered her 'Ain't I a Woman' speech at an 1851 Women's Convention in Ohio, USA, in response to a male speaker's argument that women were too weak and helpless even to get into a carriage without the assistance of a man so they should not want to be given the opportunity to vote. Truth rolled up her sleeves to show the muscles she had developed as a slave woman saying: 'I have ploughed, and planted, and gathered into barns and no man could head me! And ain't I a woman? I could work as much and eat as much as a man – when I could get it – and bear the lash as well! And ain't I a woman? I have borne thirteen children and seen them most all sold off to slavery, and when I cried out with my mother's grief, none but Jesus heard me! And ain't I a woman?' (Quoted in Davis, 1981).

2 For a fuller account of such movements see, for example, Mirza (ed.) *Black British Feminism* (1997).

3 For an indicative example of such approaches see Ali (2003).

4 Prior to the late 1980s, the term 'Asian' tended to be applied to describe those originating from the Asian sub-continent, now usually referred to as 'South Asian'.

5 See, for example, Blair and Bourne (1998); Cline *et al.* (2002); Ofsted (2002a, b); Demie (2005); Tikly *et al.* (2004); Strand (2007).

6 Certainly as a sizable group: Gypsy/Roma children dramatically underachieve even below groups such as Black boys, but the number within this ethnic category is significantly smaller.

7 Except in the case of girls taking Free School Meals, where Black girls outperform White girls. This pattern seems to support Archer and Francis' (2007) argument that social class has less bearing on achievement for some minority ethnic groups than for the White majority population.

5 Sexualities and sexual harassment in schools

1 A famous British example of separatist practice was Greenham Women's Peace Camp, where men were expelled in the early days of the camps formation, and which became a famous symbol both of the Women's Peace Movement and of separatist feminism.

2 Of course, married women teachers did continue in post but without the additional benefits afforded by their contracts such as holiday pay.

3 Although when discussing pupils it would be more appropriate to use the abbreviations LGB (lesbian, gay, bisexual) we have chosen to use LGBT (lesbian, gay, bisexual and transgender) throughout in order to embrace both pupils and teachers where appropriate and for consistency of terms.

4 Interestingly, this contrasts with home sex education provided in Africa which serve more multiple purposes than formal sex education in the West (the latter of which is overwhelmingly preventative) (Ntseane, 2005; Chilisa, 2006).

5 A substantial project directed by Elizabeth Atkinson, funded by the ESRC and supported by government policy bodies such as the TDA. The project involves a team of primary teachers from three areas of the UK, who are being facilitated to develop ideas and resources to address lesbian, gay, bisexual and transgender equality in their own schools and their communities. The project has significant support from policy groups, including the General Teaching Council for England, the National Union of Teachers and Schools Out. It supports the work of Education For All, Stonewall's initiative to promote lesbian, gay, bisexual and transgendered equality in schools, which is supported by a broad coalition of educational bodies, including the Department for Education and Skills (DfES), the Training and Development Agency (TDA) and the General Teaching Council for England (GTC).

6 Robinson (2005) cites Fitzgerald (1990: 25) in defining sexist harassment as 'generalised sexist remarks and behaviour ... not necessarily designed to elicit sexual cooperation, but rather to convey insulting, degrading, or sexist attitudes ...'

7 Hegemonic masculinity is a term used here to describe the mode of masculinity which, at any one point in time, is 'culturally exalted' (Connell, 1995). It is the form of masculinity that claims the highest status, exercises the greatest influence and authority and dominates all other modes of masculinity. It is not 'fixed', there is no 'one' form, nor is it embodied within individual male persons. Elsewhere, we debate however whether there can be seen to be different 'forms' of masculinity; and whether for example 'subordinated masculinity' does not rather reflect a construction of an absence/lack of masculinity (see e.g. Francis, 2000; Francis, 2008; Francis and Skelton, 2008).

8 Albeit there are tensions raised by the perhaps inevitable loss of complexity that such interventions may entail, as Youdell (2008) has discussed.

9 From Rousseau's *Emile* (1911) through to notions of the child in child-centred learning (e.g. Plowden Report 1960) whereby they 'developed' emotionally, physically, socially and intellectually by progressing through a set sequence of stages.

10 However, as Mellor and Epstein (2006) indicate, these should not be confused or conflated with adults' readings or understandings of sexuality, although these may overlap.

6 Curriculum, knowledge and schooling

1 In the belief that boys developed later than girls.

2 This under-representation of women undergraduates began to change in the later decades of the twentieth century, with women undergraduates outnumbering men by the end of the century.

3 A well-documented digression from traditional patterns has been that women have established numerical dominance in the traditionally male-dominated areas of law, medicine and veterinary science; prestigious subjects the latter of which are related to

the 'hard' sciences (although career routes within law and medicine are shown to remain gendered with more women becoming GPs and more men specialising, and more men becoming barristers).
4 And of course Flis Henwood and Katrina Miller (2001) and colleagues point out that actually girls' decisions to avoid such STEM subjects may be entirely rational, given their male domination and the consequent endemic discrimination and sexism within these fields.

7 Schools and boys

1 As we discuss elsewhere (Francis and Skelton, 2005), there is a contradiction between research showing that boys have *higher* self-confidence and belief in their ability than girls, and the idea that they have low self-esteem and low confidence, and retreat into 'laddism' as a result.
2 See, for example, studies by Salisbury and Jackson, 1996; Pickering, 1997; Epstein, 1998; Francis, 2000; Younger *et al.*, 1999, 2005; Warrington *et al.*, 2000, 2006; Skelton, 2001; Martino, 1999, 2000; Martino and Pallotta-Chiarolli, 2003; Keddie and Mills, 2008).
3 For discussion of the extensive international research evidence that most pupils reject gender as a salient factor in teacher-pupil relations, and that matching teachers and children by gender and ethnicity has little impact on attainment; see e.g. Carrington and Skelton (2003); or Francis *et al.* (2008).

8 Gender and teaching

1 For example, Gaby Weiner and Pat Mahony.
2 Cited by Margaret Littlewood (1995), page 7.
3 Reported in Hargreaves and Woods (1984).
4 Refered to as 'neo-liberalism' in the UK and 'total quality management' in the USA.
5 Officially, the term used for this form of pay increase in the UK is 'Threshold Assessment'.

References

Aapola, S., Gonick, M. and Harris, A. (2005) *Young Femininity*. Basingstoke: Palgrave Macmillan.

Abraham, J. (1989) Teacher Ideology and Sex Roles, *British Journal of Sociology of Education*, 10(1): 33–51.

Acker, S. (1981) No-woman's-land: British sociology of education 1960–1979, *Sociological Review*, 29(1): 77–104.

Acker, S. (1983) Women and teaching: A semi-detached sociology of a semi-profession, in S. Walker and L. Barton (eds) *Gender, Class and Education*. Lewes: Falmer, pp. 123–9.

Acker, S. (1984) Sociology, gender and education, in S. Acker, J. Megarry, S. Nisbet and E. Hoyle (eds) *World Yearbook of Education 1984: Women and Education*. London: Kogan Page.

Acker, S. (1987) Feminist theory and the study of gender and education, *International Review of Education*, 33(4): 419–35.

Acker, S. (1988) Teachers, gender and resistance, *British Journal of Sociology of Education*, 9(3): 307–22.

Acker, S. (ed.) (1989) *Teachers, Gender and Careers*. Lewes: Falmer.

Acker, S. (1994) *Gendered Education*. Buckingham: Open University Press.

Acker, S. (1999) *The Realities of Teachers' Work*. London: Cassell.

Acker, S. and Dillabough, J. (2007) Women 'learning to labour' in the 'male emporium': Exploring gendered work in teacher education, *Gender and Education*, 19(3): 297–316.

Adkins, L. (2002) *Revisions: Gender and Sexuality in Late Modernity*. Buckingham: Open University Press.

Adler, S., Laney, J. and Packer, M. (1993) *Managing Women*. Milton Keynes: Open University Press.

Agnew, D. (1989) 'A world of women': An approach to personal and career development for women teachers in primary schools, in H. De Lyon and F. Migniuolo (eds) *Women Teachers*. Milton Keynes: Open University Press.

Ahmad, F. (2001) Modern Traditions? British Muslim women and academic achievement, *Gender and Education*, 13(2): 137–52.

Aikman, S. and E. Unterhalter (eds) (2005) *Beyond Access: Transforming Policy and Practice for Gender Equality in Education*. Oxford: Oxfam.

Ainley, P. (1998) Towards a learning or certified society? Contradictions in the New Labour modernisation of lifelong learning, *Journal of Education Policy* 13(4): 559–73.

Albelda, R. and Tilly, C. (1997) *Glass Ceilings and Bottomless Pits: Women's Work, Women's Poverty.* Boston, MA: South End Press.

Alexander, R. (1984) *Primary Teachers.* Eastbourne: Holt, Rinehart and Winston.

Ali, S. (2003a) 'To be a girl': Culture and class in schools', *Gender and Education*, 15(3): 269–83.

Ali, S. (2003b) *Mixed-race, Post-race: Gender, New Ethnicities and Cultural Practices.* Oxford: Berg Publishers.

Allan, J. (1993) Male elementary teachers: Experiences and perspectives, in C. Williams (ed.) *Doing Women's Work.* London: Sage.

Alldred, P. and David, M. (2007) *Get Real About Sex: The Politics and Practice of Sex Education.* Maidenhead: Open University Press/McGraw Hill.

Allen, L. (2004) Beyond the birds and bees: constituting a discourse of erotics in sexuality education, *Gender and Education*, 16(2): 151–67.

Alloway, N. and Gilbert, P. (1997) Boys and literacy: Lessons from Australia, *Gender and Education*, 9(1): 49–59.

American Association of University Women (AAUW) (1992) *The AAUW Report: How Schools Shortchange Girls.* Washington, DC: American Association of University Women.

Amos, V. and Parmar, P. (1981) Resistances and responses: The experience of black girls in Britain, in A. McRobbie and T. McCabe (eds) *Feminism for Girls: An Adventure Story.* London: Routledge and Kegan Paul.

Amos, V. and Parmar, P. (1984) Challenging imperial feminism, *Feminist Review*, Special Issue: Many voices one chant, black feminist perspectives, 17, pp. 3–20.

Ang, I. (1998) Can one say no to Chineseness? Pushing the limits of the diasporic paradigm, *Boundary 2*, 25(3): 223–42.

Anthias, F. (1992) Beyond feminism and multiculturalism: Locating difference and the politics of location, *Women's Studies International Forum*, 24(4): 619–41.

Anthias, F. (2001) New hybridities, old concepts: The limits of 'culture', *Ethnic and Racial Studies*, 4(1): 610–41.

Anthias, F. and Yuval-Davis, N. (1992) *Racialized Boundaries: Race, Nation, Gender, Colour and Class and the Anti-racist Struggle.* London: Routledge.

Anyon, J. (1983) Intersections of gender and class: Accommodation and resistance by working-class and affluent females to contradictory sex-role, in S. Walker and L. Barton (eds) *Gender, Class and Education.* Lewes: Falmer.

Archer, L. (2003) *Race, Masculinity and Schooling: Muslim Boys and Education.* Buckingham: Open University Press.

Archer, L. (2006) Masculinities, femininities and resistance to participation in post-compulsory education, in: C. Leathwood and B. Francis (eds) *Gender and Lifelong Learning*, London: Routledge.

Archer, L. and Francis, B. (2007) *Understanding Minority Ethnic Achievement.* London: Routledge.

Archer, L. and Yamashita, H. (2003) Theorising inner-city masculinities: 'Race', class, gender and education, *Gender and Education*, 15(2): 115–32.

Archer, L., Leathwood, C. and Hutchings, M. (2001) Engaging with commonality and difference: Theoretical tensions in the analysis of working class women's educational discourses, *International Studies in Sociology of Education*, 11(1): 41–62.

Archer, L., Hutchings, M. and Ross, A. with Leathwood, C., Gilchrist, R. and Phillips, D. (2003) *Higher Education and Social Class: Issues of Exclusion and Inclusion.* London: Routledge.

Archer, L., Halsall, A. and Hollingworth, S. (2007) Inner-city femininities and education: 'Race', class, gender and schooling in young women's lives, *Gender and Education*, 19 (5): 549–67.

Arends, J. and Volman, M. (1995) Equal opportunities in The Netherlands and the policy of the ILEA, in L. Dawtrey, J. Holland and M. Hammer with S. Sheldon (eds) *Equality and Inequality in Education Policy*. Clevedon: Multilingual Matters.

Arnot (nee Macdonald), M. (1980) Schooling and the reproduction of class and gender relations, in L. Barton, R. Meighan and S. Walker (eds) *Schooling Ideology and the Curriculum*. Lewes: Falmer.

Arnot, M. (1983) A cloud over co-education: An analysis of the forms of transmission of class and gender relations, in S. Walker and L. Barton (eds) *Gender, Class and Education*. Lewes: Falmer.

Arnot (nee Macdonald), M. (1984a) Schooling and the reproduction of class and gender relations, in R. Dale, G. Esland, R. Fergusson and M. Macdonald (eds) *Education and the State: Politics, Patriarchy and Practice*. Lewes: Falmer.

Arnot, M. (1984b) How shall we educate our sons? in R. Deem (ed.) *Co-education Reconsidered*. Milton Keynes: Open University Press.

Arnot, M. (1985) *Race and Gender*. Oxford: Pergamon.

Arnot, M. (1991) Equality and democracy: A decade of struggle over education, *British Journal of Sociology of Education*, 12(4): 447–66.

Arnot, M. (2000) *Reproducing Gender?* London: RoutledgeFalmer.

Arnot, M. and Dillabough, J. (eds) (2000) *Challenging Democracy*. London: Routledge-Falmer.

Arnot, M. and Weiner, G. (1987) Introduction, in M. Arnot and G. Weiner (eds) *Gender and the Politics of Schooling*. London: Unwin Hyman with the Open University.

Arnot, M., David, M. and Weiner, G. (1999) *Closing the Gender Gap?* Cambridge: Polity.

Askew, S. and Ross, C. (1988) *Boys Don't Cry: Boys and Sexism in Education*. Milton Keynes: Open University Press.

Aspinwall, K. and Drummond, M. J. (1989) Socialized into primary teaching, in H. De Lyon and F. Migniuolo (eds) *Women Teachers*. Milton Keynes: Open University Press.

Atkinson, E. (2008) No Outsiders Project (http://www.nooutsiders.sunderland.ac.uk/)

Atkinson, E. and DePalma, R. (2008) Dangerous spaces: Constructing and contexting sexual identities in an online discussion forum, *Gender and Education*, 20(2): 183–94.

Bailey, A. (1988) Sex-stereotyping in primary school mathematics schemes, *Research in Education*, 39: 39–46.

Balbus, I. (1987) Disciplining women: Michel Foucault and the power of feminist discourse, in S. Benhabib and D. Cornell (eds) *Feminism as Critique*. Cambridge: Polity Press.

Balfour, R. (2003) Between the lines: Gender in the reception of texts by schoolchildren in rural KwaZulu-Natal, South Africa, *Gender and Education*, 15(2): 183–99.

Bangar, S. and McDermott, J. (1989) Black women speak, in H. De Lyon and F. Migniuolo (eds) *Women Teachers*. Milton Keynes: Open University Press.

Beauboeuf, T. (2004) Reinventing teaching: Womanist lessons from Black women teachers. Paper presented at the Annual Meeting of the American Educational Research Association, San Diego, California.

Beck, U. (1992) *Risk Society*. London: Sage.

Beck, U. and Beck-Gernsheim, E. (2002) *Individualisation*. London: Sage.

Becker, J. (1981) Differential treatment of females and males in mathematics class, *Journal for Research in Mathematics Education*, 12: 40–53.

Becker, J. (1995) Women's ways of knowing in mathematics, in P. Rogers and G. Kaiser (eds) *Equity in Mathematics Education: Influences of Feminism and Culture*. London: Falmer Press, pp. 163–74.

Belotti, E. (1975) *Little Girls*. London: Writers and Readers Publishing Co-op.

Biggart, A. (2002) Attainment, gender, and minimum-aged school leavers' early routes in the labour market, *Journal of Education and Work*, 15: 145–61.

Berrill, D. and Martino, W. (2002) 'Paedophiles and deviants': Exploring issues of sexuality, masculinity and normalization in the lives of male teacher candidates, in R. Kissen (ed.) *Getting Ready for Benjamin*. Lanham, MD: Rowman and Littlefield.

Best, R. (1983) *We've All Got Scars: What Boys and Girls Learn in Elementary School*. Bloomington: Indiana University Press.

Biddulph, S. (1998) *Manhood*. Stroud: Hawthorn.

Biklen, S. (1995) *School Work: Gender and the Cultural Construction of Teaching*. New York: Teachers College Press.

Blackmore, J. (1999) *Troubling Women*. Buckingham: Open University Press.

Blair, A. (2007) Schoolboys join recruitment drive for more male teachers, 1 August, p. 1 http://www.timesonline.co.uk/tol/news/uk/education/article2169804.ece

Blair, M. and Bourne, J. (1998) *Making the Difference: Teaching and Learning Strategies in Successful Multiethnic Schools*. London: HMSO.

Blair, M. and Maylor, U. (1993) Issues and concerns for black women teachers in training, in I. Siraj Blatchford (ed.) *'Race', Gender and the Education of Teachers*. Buckingham: Open University Press.

Blaise, M. (2005) *Playing it Straight: Uncovering Gender Discourses in the Early Childhood Classroom*. London: Routledge.

Blaise, M. and Andrew, Y. (2005). How bad can it be?: Troubling gender, sexuality, and teaching in early childhood education, in N. Yelland (ed.) *Critical Issues in Early Childhood*. Buckingham: Open University Press, pp. 49–57.

Bleach, K. (ed.) (1998) *Raising Boys' Achievement in Schools*. Stoke-on-Trent: Trentham Books.

Blickenstaff, J. (2005) Women and science careers: leaky pipeline or gender filter? *Gender and Education*, 17(4): 369–85.

Blount, J. (2000) Spinsters, bachelors and other gender transgressors in school employment, 1850–1990, *Review of Educational Research*, 70(1): 83–101.

Blount, J. (2004) *Fit to Teach: Same-sex Desire, Gender and Schoolwork in the Twentieth Century*. Albany, NY: SUNY.

Boaler, J. (1997) *Experiencing School Mathematics: Teaching Styles, Sex and Setting*. Buckingham: Open University Press.

Boaler, J. (2002) Paying the price for 'sugar and spice': shifting the analytical lens in equity research. *Mathematical Thinking and Learning*, 4:127–44.

Boaler, J. and Sengupta-Irving, T. (2006) Nature, neglect and nuance: Changing accounts of sex, gender and mathematics, in C. Skelton, B. Francis and L. Smulyan (eds) *The Sage Handbook of Gender and Education*. London: Sage.

Bonnett, A. (2000) *White Identities: Historical and International Perspectives*. Harlow: Prentice Hall.

Bottery, M. (1998) *Professionals and Policy: Management Strategy in a Competitive World*. London: Cassell.

Bourdieu, P. (1987) What makes a social class? On the theoretical and practical existence of groups. *Berkeley Journal of Sociology*, 32: 1–18.

Bowlby, J. (1953) *Child Care and the Growth of Love*. Harmondsworth: Penguin.

Brah, A. (1994) Difference, diversity and differentiation, in D. James and A. Rattansi (eds) *'Race', Culture and Difference*. London: Sage.

Brah, A. and Minhas, R. (1985) Structural racism or cultural difference: Schooling for Asian girls, in G. Weiner (ed.) *Just a Bunch of Girls*. Milton Keynes: Open University Press.

Brewer, R. M. (1993) Theorizing race, class and gender: The new scholarship of black feminist intellectuals and black women's labour, in S.M. James and A.P.A. Busici (eds) *Theorizing Black Feminisms: The Visionary Pragmatism of Black Women*. London: Routledge.

Brickhouse, N., Lowery, P. and Schultz, K. (2000) What kind of a girl does science? The construction of school science identities, *Journal of Research in Science Teaching*, 38: 282–95.

Brine, J. (2006) Tales of the 50-somethings: Selective schooling, gender and social class, *Gender and Education*, 18(4): 431–46.

Brophy, J. and Good, T. (1974) *Teacher-Student Relationships*. New York: Holt.

Browne, N. (2004) *Gender Equity in the Early Years*. Maidenhead: McGraw-Hill/Open University Press.

Browne, N. and France, P. (eds) (1986) *Untying the Apron Strings*. Milton Keynes: Open University Press.

Bryan, B., Dadzie, S. and Scafe, S. (1985) *The Heart of the Race: Black Women's Lives in Britain*. London: Virago.

Buchan, L. (1980) It's a good job for a girl (but an awful career for a woman!), in D. Spender and E. Sarah (eds) *Learning to Lose*. London: The Women's Press.

Bull, M. (2006) *Priority Review: Exclusion of Black Pupils 'Getting it. Getting it Right'*. EMA Unit, London: DfES.

Burchell, H. and Millman, V. (eds) (1989) *Changing Perspectives on Gender: New Initiatives in Secondary Education*. Milton Keynes: Open University Press.

Burgess, H. (1989) 'A sort of career': Women in primary schools, in C. Skelton (ed.) *Whatever Happens to Little Women?* Milton Keynes: Open University Press.

Burstall, S. (1933) *Retrospect and Prospect: Sixty Years of Women's Education*. London: Longman, Green and Co.

Burton, L. (ed.) (1986) *Girls into Maths Can Go*. Eastbourne: Holt, Rinehart and Winston.

Burton, L. (1995) Moving towards a feminist epistemology of mathematics, in P. Rogers and G. Kaiser (eds) *Equity in Mathematics Education: Influences of Feminism and Culture*. London: Falmer Press, pp. 209–25.

Butler, J. (1990) *Gender Trouble*. New York: Routledge.

Butler, J. (1997) Performative acts and gender constitution, in K. Conboy, N. Medina and S. Stanbury (eds) *Writing on the Body: Female Embodiment and Feminist Theory*. New York: Columbia University Press.

Butler, J. (2004) *Undoing Gender*. London: Routledge.

Byrne, E. (1978) *Women and Education*. London: Tavistock.

Cairns, J. and Inglis, B. (1989) A content analysis of ten popular history textbooks for primary schools with particular emphasis on the role of women, *Educational Review*, 41: 221–6.

Calabrese Barton, A. (1998) *Feminist Science Education*. New York: Teachers College Press.

Calabrese Barton, A. and Brickhouse, N. (2006) Engaging girls in science, in C. Skelton, B. Francis, and L. Smulyan (eds) *The Sage Handbook of Gender and Education*. London: Sage.

Campbell, B. (1993) *Goliath*. London: Methuen.

Carby, H. (1982) White woman listen? Black feminism and the boundaries of sisterhood, in Centre for Contemporary Cultural Studies, *The Empire Strikes Back*. London: Hutchinson.

Carby, H. (1987) Black feminism and the boundaries of sisterhood, in M. Arnot and G. Weiner (eds) *Gender and the Politics of Schooling*. London: Hutchinson.

Carmody, H. (1992) Reported on 'No Job for a Woman', ABC, Four Corners, 12 Nov.

Carrington, B. (2002) A quintessentially feminine domain? Student teachers' constructions of primary teaching as a career, *Educational Studies*, 28(3): 287–303.

Cashmore, E. (1987) *The Logic of Racism*. London: Allen and Unwin.

Cassen, R. and Kingdon, G. (2007) *Tackling Low Educational Achievement*. York: Joseph Rowntree Foundation.

Cealey Harrison, W. and Hood-Williams, J. (1998) 'More varieties than Heinz: social categories and sociality in Humphreys, Hammersley and beyond', *Sociological Research Online*, 3(1). http://www.socresonline.org.uk/socresonline/3/1/8.html.

Chambers, D., Tincknell, E. and Van Loon, J. (2004) Peer regulation of teenage sexual identities, *Gender and Education*, 16(3): 397–415.

Charles, H. (1992) Whiteness – the relevance of politically colouring the 'non', in H. Hinds, A. Phoenix and J. Stacey (eds) *Working Out*. London, Falmer.

Chatton, B. (2001) Picture books for pre-school children: Exploring gender issues with three and four year olds, in S. Lehr (ed.) *Beauty, Brains and Brawn: The Construction of Gender in Children's Literature*. Portsmouth, NH: Heinemann.

Chilisa, B. (2006) 'Sex' education: Subjugated discourses and adolescents' voices, in C. Skelton, B. Francis and L. Smulyan (eds) *Sage Handbook of Gender and Education*. London: Sage.

Chodorow, N. (1978) *The Reproduction of Mothering*. Los Angeles: University of California Press.

Chun, A. (1996) Fuck Chineseness: On the ambiguities of ethnicity as culture as identity, *Boundary 2*, 23(2):111–38.

Clarricoates, K. (1980) All in a day's work, in D. Spender and E. Sarah (eds) *Learning to Lose*. London: The Women's Press.

Clarricoates, K. (1987) Child culture at school: A clash between gendered worlds, in A. Pollard (ed.) *Children and their Primary School*. Lewes: Falmer.

Cline, T., De Abreu, G., Fihosy, C., Gray, H., Lambert, H. and Neale, J. (2002) *Minority Ethnic Pupils in Mainly White Schools*, RR 365. Nottingham: DfES.

Cobbe, F. P. (1894) *Life of Frances Power Cobbe*. London: Richard Bentley and Son. (3rd ed.)

Coffey, A. and Delamont, S. (2000) *Feminism and the Classroom Teacher*. London: RoutledgeFalmer.

Coffield, F, Moseley, D., Hall, E. and Ecclestone, K. (2004) *Should We Be Using Learning Styles? What Research Has to Say to Practice*. London: Learning and Skills Research Centre.

Cohen Shabot, S. (2006) "Grotesque bodies: A response to disembodied cyborgs", *Journal of Gender Studies*, 15(3): 223–35.

Connell, R. W. (1987) *Gender and Power*. Cambridge: Polity.

Connell, R. W. (1989) Cool guys, swots and wimps: The interplay of masculinity and education, *Oxford Review of Education,* 15(3): 291–303.

Connell, R. W. (1995) *Masculinities*. Cambridge: Polity Press.

Connell, R. W., Ashenden, D., Kessler, S. and Dowsett, G. (1982) *Making the Difference: Schools, Families and Social Division*. Sydney: Allen and Unwin.

Connolly, P. (1995b) Racism, masculine peer-group relations and the schooling of African/Caribbean Infant Boys, *British Journal of Sociology of Education*, 16(1): 75–92.

Connolly, P. (1998) *Racism, Gender Identities and Young Children*. London: Routledge.

Connolly, P. (2004) *Boys and Schooling in the Early Years*. London: RoutledgeFalmer.

Corrigan, P. (1979) *Schooling the Smash Street Kids*. London: Macmillan.

Currie, J., Harris, P. and Thiele, B. (2000) Sacrifices in greedy universities: Are they gendered? *Gender and Education*, 20(3): 269–91.

Cushman P. (2005) Let's hear it from the males: Issues facing male primary school teachers, *Teacher and Teacher Education*, 21(3): 227–40.

Cushman, P. (2008) So what exactly do you want? What principals mean when they say 'male role model', *Gender and Education*, 20(2): 123–36.

Dalley-Trim, L. (2007) *'The boys'* present ... hegemonic masculinity: A performance of multiple acts, *Gender and Education*, 19(2): 199–217.

David, M. (1980) *The State, The Family and Education*. London: Routledge and Kegan Paul.

David, M. (1993) *Parents, Gender and Education Reform*. Cambridge: Polity Press.

David, M. (2003) *Personal and Political: Feminisms, Sociology and Family Lives*. Stoke-on-Trent: Trentham.

Davies, B. (1989) *Frogs and Snails and Feminist Tales*. London: Allen and Unwin.

Davies, B. (1993) *Shards of Glass: Children Reading and Writing beyond Gendered Identities*. Sydney: Allen and Unwin.

Davies, B. (1997) Constructing and deconstructing masculinities through critical literacy, *Gender and Education*, 9(1): 9–30.

Davies, B. (2003) Death to critique and dissent? The policies and practices of new managerialism and of 'evidence-based practice', *Gender and Education*, 15(1): 91–103.

Davies, B. and Saltmarsh, S. (2006) Gender and literacy, in C. Skelton, B. Francis and L. Smulyan (eds) *The Sage Handbook of Gender and Education*. London: Sage.

Davies, L. (1984) *Pupil Power, Deviance and Gender in School*. Lewes: Falmer.

Davies, L. (1985) Ethnography and status: Focussing on gender in educational research, in R. Burgess (ed.) *Field Methods in the Study of Education*. Lewes: Falmer.

Davies, L. (2004) *Education and Conflict*. London: RoutledgeFalmer.

Davin, A. (1978) Imperialism and motherhood, *History Workshop Journal*, 5: 9–65.

Davis, A. (1981) *Women, Race and Class*. London: The Women's Press.

Davies, B. and Banks, C. (1992) The Gender Trap: a feminist-poststructuralist analysis of primary school children's talk about gender, *Junior Curriculum Studies*, 24(1): 1–25.

Davies, B. and Saltmarsh, S. (2007) Gender economies: literacy and the gendered production of neo-liberal subjectivities, *Gender and Education*, 19(1): 1–20.

Dean, D. W. (1995) Education for moral improvement, Domesticity and social cohesion: The Labour Government, 1945–1951, in L. Dawtrey, J. Holland and M. Hammer (eds) *Equality and Inequality in Education Policy*. Clevedon, Multilingual Matters.

Deem, R. (1978) *Women and Schooling*. London: Routledge and Kegan Paul.

Deem, R. (ed.) (1980) *Schooling for Women's Work*, London: Routledge and Kegan Paul.

Deem, R. (1981) State policy and ideology in the education of women, 1944–80, *British Journal of Sociology of Education*, 2: 131–43.

Deem, R. (1983) Gender, patriarchy and class in the popular education of women, in S. Walker and L. Barton (eds) *Gender, Class and Education*. Lewes: Falmer.

Delamont, S. (1978) The contradictions in ladies' education and the domestic ideology and women's education, in S. Delamont and L. Duffin (eds) *The Nineteenth Century Woman: Her Cultural and Physical World.* London: Croom Helm.

Delamont, S. (1980) *Sex Roles and the School.* London: Methuen.

Delamont, S. (1983) The conservative school? Sex roles at home, at work and at school, in S. Walker and L. Barton (eds) *Gender, Class and Education.* Lewes: Falmer.

Delamont, S. (ed.) (1987) *The Primary School Teacher.* Lewes: Falmer.

Delamont, S. (1989) *Knowledgeable Women, Structuralism and the Reproduction of Elites.* London: Routledge.

Delamont, S. and Duffin, L. (eds) (1978) *The Nineteenth-Century Woman, Her Cultural and Physical World.* London: Croom Helm.

Deleuze, G. and Guatarri, F. (1987) *A Thousand Plateaus* (trans. B. Massumi). Minneapolis: University of Minnesota Press.

Demie, F. (2005) 'Achievement of black Caribbean pupils: Good practice in Lambeth schools', *British Educational Research Journal*, 31(4): 481–508.

DePalma, R. and Atkinson, E. (2007) Strategic embodiment in virtual spaces: Exploring an online discussion about sexualities equality in schools, *Discourse*, 28(4): 499–514.

Department for Children, Schools and Families (DCSF) (2008) Bullying: Don't suffer in silence (http://www.dfes.gov.uk/bullying/) (last accessed 16 May 2008).

Department for Education (1994) Circular 5/94: Education Act 1993 – Sex Education in Schools. London: HMSO.

Department for Education and Skills (2003) *Aiming High: Raising the Achievement of African-Caribbean Pupils.* London: DfES.

Department for Education and Skills (2005) *Higher Standards, Better Schools for All: More Choice for Parents and Pupils*, Cm 6677. Norwich: HMSO.

Department for Education and Skills (2006) *Ethnicity and Education: The Evidence on Minority Ethnic Pupils aged 5–16.* London: DfES.

Department for Education and Skills (2007) *Gender and Education: The Evidence on Pupils in England.* London: DES.

Department for Trade and Industry (2004) www.set4women.gov.uk

Department of Education and Science (1975) *Curricular Differences for Boys and Girls.* London: HMSO.

Department of Education and Science (1987) *Quality in Schools: the Initial Training of Teachers.* London: HMSO.

Dewan, I. (2008) *Recasting Race: Women of Mixed Heritage in Further Education.* Stoke-on-Trent: Trentham Books.

Dixon, B. (1977) *Catching Them Young: Sex, Race and Class in Children's Fiction, Vol. 1.* London: Pluto.

Douglas, J. W. B. (1964) *The Home and the School.* London: MacGibbon and Kee.

Driver, G. (1980) *Beyond Underachievement.* London: Commission for Racial Equality.

Drudy, S., Martin, M., Woods, J. and O'Flynn, J. (2005) *Men and the Classroom.* London: Routledge.

Duncan (1999) *Sexual Bullying: Gender Conflict and Pupil Culture in Secondary Schools.* London: Routledge.

Dunne, M., Humphreys, S. and Leach, F. (2006) Gender violence in schools in the developing world, *Gender and Education*, 18(1): 75–98.

Dworkin, A. (1987) *Intercourse.* New York: Free Press Paperbacks.

Dworkin, A. and MacKinnon, C. (1985) *The Reasons Why: Essays on the New Civil Rights Law Recognizing Pornography as Sex Discrimination*. Minneapolis: Pornography Resource Centre.

Dyhouse, C. (1981) *Girls Growing Up in Late Victorian and Edwardian England*. London: Routledge and Kegan Paul.

Eagleton, T. (1996) *The Illusions of PostModernism*. Oxford: Blackwell.

Edley, N. and Wetherell, M. (1995) *Men in Perspective: Practice, Power and Identity*. London: Prentice Hall/Harvester Wheatsheaf.

Edwards, R., Hadfield, L., Lucey H. and Mauthner, M. (2006) *Sibling Identities and Relationships: Sisters and Brothers*. London: Routledge, Taylor and Francis.

Eisenstein, H. (1984) *Contemporary Feminist Thought*. London: Unwin Paperbacks.

Employment Equality (Sex Discrimination) Regulations (2005) (http://www.opsi.gov.uk/si/si2005/20052467.htm) (last accessed 16th May 2008).

Epstein, D. (ed.) (1994) *Challenging Lesbian and Gay Inequalities in Education*. Buckingham: Open University Press.

Epstein, D. (1997) Keeping them in their place: Hetero/sexist harassment, gender and the enforcement of heterosexuality, in A. Thomas and C. Kitzinger (eds) *Sexual Harassment*. Buckingham: Open University Press.

Epstein, D. (1998) Stranger in the mirror: Gender, ethnicity, sexuality and nation in schooling. Paper presented at Multiple Marginalities: Gender Citizenship and Nationality in Education Conference. Nordic-Baltic Research Symposium (NORFA) in Helsinki: August.

Epstein, D. and Johnson, R. (1998) *Schooling Sexualities*. Buckingham: Open University Press.

Epstein, D., Elwood, J., Hey, V. and Maw, J. (1998) Schoolboy frictions: Feminism and 'failing boys', in D. Epstein, J. Elwood, V. Hey and J. Maw (eds) *Failing Boys?* Buckingham: Open University Press.

Epstein, D., O'Flynn, S. and Telford, D. (2003) *Silenced Sexualities in Schools and Universities*. Stoke-on-Trent: Trentham Books.

Equal Opportunities Commission (1984) *Do You Provide Equal Educational Opportunities?* Manchester: Equal Opportunities Commission.

Equal Opportunities Commission (2004) *Plugging Britain's Skills Gap: Challenging Gender Segregation in Training and Work*. Manchester: EOC and ESF.

Ethington, C. (1992) Gender differences in a psychological model of mathematics achievement, *Journal for Research in Mathematics Education*, 12: 380–5.

Evans, J., Rich, E. and Holroyd, R. (2004) Disordered eating and disordered schooling: What schools do to middle-class girls, *British Journal of Sociology of Education*, 25(2): 123–42.

Evans, J., Rich, E. and Davies, B. (2008) The rise and rise of the child saving movement: The class and cultural dimensions of fat ethics. Paper presented at the International Sociology of Education Conference, London, 2–4/1/08.

Evans, M. (1991) *A Good School: Life at a Girls' Grammar School in the 1960s*. London: Women's Press.

Evetts, J. (1987) 'Becoming career ambitious': The career strategies of married women who became primary headteachers in the 1960s and 1970s, *Educational Review*, 39(1): 15–29.

Evetts, J. (1990) *Women in Primary Teaching: Career Contexts and Strategies*. London: Unwin Hyman.

Fairclough, N. (2000) *New Labour, New Language?* London: Routledge.

Faraday, A. (1989) Lessoning lesbians: Girls' schools, coeducation and anti-lesbianism between the wars, in C. Jones and P. Mahony (eds) *Learning Our Lines.* London: The Women's Press.

Fennell, S. and Arnot, M. (eds) (2008) *Gender Education and Equality in a Global Context.* London, Routledge.

Fennema, E. and Sherman, J. A. (1977) Sex-related differences in mathematics achievement, spatial visualization and affective factors, *American Educational Research Journal*, 14(1): 51–72.

Fennema, E. and Sherman, J. (1978) Sex-related Differences in Mathematics Achievement, Spatial Visualization and Affective Factors, *American Educational Research Journal*, 14(1): 51–72.

Fennema, E. Wolleat, P., Pedro, J. and Becker, A. (1981) Increasing women's participation in mathematics: An intervention study, *Journal for Research in Mathematics Education*, 12: 107–13.

Ferber, M. and Teiman, M. (1980) Are women economists at a disadvantage in publishing journal articles? *Eastern Economic Journal*, 6: 89–94.

Ferfolja, T. (2007) Teacher negotiations of sexual subjectivities, *Gender and Education*, 19(5): 569–86.

Field, J. (2006) *Lifelong Learning and the New Educational Order.* Stoke-on-Trent: Trentham.

Fine, M. (2003) Sexuality, schooling and adolescent females: The missing discourse of desire, in M. Fine and L. Weis (eds) *Silenced Voices and Extraordinary Conversations.* Amsterdam: Teachers College Press.

Fitzgerald, L. F. (1990) Sexual harassment: The definition and measurement of a construct, in M. A. Paludi (ed.) *Ivory Power: Sexual Harassment on Campus.* Albany: State University of New York Press.

Forrest, S. (2006) Straight talking: Challenges in teaching and learning about sexuality and homophobia in schools, in M. Cole (ed.) *Education, Equality and Human Rights: Issues of Gender, 'Race', Sexuality, Disability and Social Class.* London: Routledge, pp. 111–133.

Forrester, G. (2005) All in a day's work: Primary teachers 'performing' and 'caring', *Gender and Education*, 17(3): 271–87.

Foucault, M. (1980) *Power/Knowledge: Selected Interviews and Other Writings, 1972– 1977.* New York: Pantheon.

Foxman, D., Ruddock, G., McCallum, I. and Schagen, I. (1991) *APU Mathematics Monitoring (Phase 2).* London: SEAC.

Francis, B. (1996) Doctor/nurse, teacher/caretaker: Children's gendered choice of adult occupation in interviews and role play, *British Journal of Education and Work*, 9(3): 47–58.

Francis, B. (1998) *Power Plays*, Stoke-on-Trent: Trentham.

Francis, B. (1999) 'Modernist reductionism or post-modernist relativism: Can we move on?', *Gender and Education*, 11: 381–94.

Francis, B. (2000) *Boys, Girls and Achievement.* London: Routledge/Falmer.

Francis, B. (2001) Commonality *and* difference? Attempts to escape from theoretical dualisms in emancipatory research in education, *International Studies in Sociology of Education*, 11(2): 157–71.

Francis, B. (2002) Is the future really female? The impact and implications of gender for 14–16 year olds' career choices, *Journal of Education and Work*, 15(1): 75–88.

Francis, B. (2006). Heroes or zeroes? The construction of the boys' achievement debate within neo-liberal policy discourse. *Journal of Education Policy*, 21(2): 187–99.

Francis, B. (2007) Postmodern and poststructural theories, in B. Banks (ed.) *Gender and Education: An Encylopedia*, Westport, CT: Praeger.

Francis, B. (2008) 'Teaching Manfully? Exploring gendered subjectivities and power via analysis of men teachers' gender performance, *Gender and Education*, 20(2): 109–22.

Francis, B. and Archer, L. (2005) Negotiating the dichotomy of boffin and triad: British-Chinese pupils' constructions of 'laddism', *The Sociological Review*, 53(3): 495–520.

Francis, B. and Skelton, C. (2001) Men Teachers and the Construction of Heterosexual Masculinity in the Classroom, *Sex Education*, 1(1): 1–17.

Francis, B. and Skelton, C. (2005) *Reassessing Gender and Achievement*. London: Routledge.

Francis, B., Hutchings, M., Archer, L. and Melling, L. (2003) Subject-choice and occupational aspirations among pupils at girls' schools, *Pedagogy, Culture and Society*, 11(3): 425–41.

Francis, B., Osgood, J., Delgety, J. and Archer, L. (2005) *Gender Equality in Work Experience Placements for Young People*. Manchester: Equal Opportunities Commission.

Francis, B., Skelton, C., Carrington, B., Hutchings, M., Read, B. and Hall, I. (2008) A perfect match? Pupils' and teachers' views of the impact of matching educators and learners by gender, *Research Papers in Education*, 23(1): 21–36.

Frankenberg, R. (1993) *White Women, Race Matters: The Social Construction of Whiteness*. London: Routledge.

Frankenberg, R. (1997) *Displacing Whiteness*. Duke: Duke University Press.

Frazier, N. and Sadker, M. (1973) *Sexism in School and Society*. New York: Harper and Row.

Frosh, S., Phoenix, A. and Pattman, R. (2002) *Young Masculinities: Understanding Boys in Contemporary Society*. London: Palgrave.

Fuller, M. (1978) Sex-Role stereotyping and social science, in J. Chetwynd and O. Hartnett (eds) *The Sex-Role System*. London: Routledge and Kegan Paul.

Fuller, M. (1980) Black girls in a London comprehensive school, in R. Deem (ed.) *Schooling for Women's Work*. London: Routledge and Kegan Paul.

Gaine, C. (1995) *Still No Problem Here*. Stoke-on-Trent: Trentham Books.

Gaine, C. and George, R. (1999) *Gender, 'Race' and Class in Schooling*. London: Falmer.

Garfinkel, H. (1967) *Studies in Ethnomethodology*. Englewood Cliffs, NJ: Prentice-Hall.

Gaskell, J. (1992) *Gender Matters From School to Work*. Buckingham: Open University Press.

Gauntlett, D. (2002) *Media, Gender and Identity*. London: Routledge.

Giddens, A. (1998) *The Third Way*. Cambridge: Polity.

Gilbert, P. and Gilbert, R. (1995) *What's Going On? Girls' Experiences of Educational Disadvantage*. Sydney: J. S. McMillan.

Gilbert, R. and Gilbert, P. (1998) *Masculinity Goes To School*. London: Routledge.

Gillborn, D. (1995) *Racism and Anti-racism in Real Schools*. Buckingham: Open University Press.

Gillborn, D. and Gipps, C. (1996) *Recent Research on the Achievements of Ethnic Minority Pupils*. London: HMSO.

Gillborn, D. and Mirza, H. (2000) *Educational Inequality: Mapping Race, Class and Gender*. London, HMI.

Gillies, V. (2006) Working-class mothers and school life: exploring the role of emotional capital, *Gender and Education*, 18(3): 281–93.

Gilligan, C. (1982) *In a Different Voice.* Cambridge, MA: Harvard University Press.

Ginn, J. (2003) *Gender, Pensions and the Lifecourse.* Bristol: Polity Press.

Gipps, C. and Murphy, P. (1994) *A Fair Test? Assessment, Achievement and Equity.* Buckingham: Open University Press.

Goddard-Spear, M. (1989) Differences between the written work of boys and girls, *British Educational Research Journal*, 15: 271–7.

Goldstein, H. (1986) Gender bias and test norms in educational selection, *Research Intelligence*, 23: 2–4, British Educational Research Association.

Gorard, S., Rees, G. and Salisbury, J. (1999) Reappraising the apparent underachievement of boys at school, *Gender and Education*, 11(4): 441–54.

Gordon, R. (1996) Legislation and educational policy in Zimbabwe: The state and reproduction of patriarchy, *Gender and Education*, 8(2): 215–29.

Gorman, T.P., White, J., Brooks, G., Maclure, M. and Kispal., A. (1988) *Language Performance in Schools: Review of APU Language Monitoring 1979–1983.* London: HMSO.

Grant, R. (1989) Women teachers' career pathways: Towards an alternative model of 'career', in S. Acker (ed.) *Teachers, Gender and Careers.* Lewes: Falmer.

Griffin, C. and Lees, S. (1997) Editorial, *Gender and Education*, 9(1): 5–8.

Groves, J. and Mansfield, D. (1981) *Making Sense of Science: Chemistry.* London: Addison-Wesley.

Grumet, M. (1988) *Bitter Milk: Women and Teaching.* Amherst, MA: University of Massachusetts Press.

Gurian, M. (2002) *Boys and Girls Learn Differently!* Jossey Bass: San Francisco.

Guzzetti, B.J., Young, J.P., Gritsavage, M.M., Fyfe, L.M., and Hardenbrook, M. (2002) Reading, writing, and talking gender in literacy learning. Newark, DE: International Reading Association.

Halberstam, J. (1998) *Female Masculinity.* Durham and London: Duke University Press.

Hall, S. (1992) New ethnicities, in J. Donald and A. Rattansi (eds) *'Race', Culture and Difference.* London: Sage.

Halsey, A., Heath, A. and Ridge, J. (1980) *Origins and Destinations: Family, Class and Education in Modern Britain.* Oxford: Clarendon Press.

Halstead, M. (1991) Racial feminism, Islam and the single-sex school debate, *Gender and Education*, 3(3): 263–78.

Hamblin, A. (1982) What can one do with a son? in S. Friedman and E. Sarah (eds) *On the Problem of Men.* London: Women's Press.

Hanmer, J. and Maynard, M. (eds) (1987) *Women, Violence and Social Control.* London: Macmillan.

Hanson, D. and Herrington, M. (1976) *From College to Classroom.* London: Routledge and Kegan Paul.

Hanson, S. (1996) *Lost Talent: Women in the Sciences.* Philadelphia: Temple University Press.

Harding, J. (1980) Sex differences in performance in science examinations, in R. Deem (ed.) *Schooling for Women's Work.* London: Routledge and Kegan Paul.

Harding, S. (1986) *The Science Question in Feminism.* Milton Keynes: Open University Press.

Harding, S. (1990) Feminism, science, and the anti-enlightenment critiques, in L. Nicholson (ed.) *Feminism/Postmodernism.* London: Routledge.

Harding, S. (1991) *Whose Science? Whose Knowledge?* Milton Keynes: Open University Press.

Hargreaves, A. and Woods, P. (eds) (1984) *Classrooms and Staffrooms*. Milton Keynes: Open University Press.

Hargreaves, D. H. (1967) *Social Relations in a Secondary School*. London: Routledge and Kegan Paul.

Hart, L. (1989) Classroom processes, sex of student, and confidence in learning mathematics, *Journal for Research in Mathematics Education*, 20: 242–60.

Hartmann, H. (1981) The unhappy marriage of Marxism and feminism: Toward a more progressive union, in L. Sargent (ed.) *Women and Revolution*. Boston, MA: South End Press.

Hartsock, N. (1986) *Money, Sex, and Power: Toward a Feminist Historical Materialism*. New York: Longman.

Hartsock, N. (1990) Foucault on power: A theory for women, in L. Nicholson (ed.) *Feminism/Postmodernism*. London: Routledge.

Hartsock, N. (1999) *The Feminist Standpoint Revisited*. Boulder, CO: Westview Press.

Hawkesworth, M. (1997) Confounding gender, *Signs*, 22(3): 670–85.

Haywood, C. and Mac an Ghaill, M. (2003) *Men and Masculinities*. Buckingham: Open University Press.

Henwood, F. and Miller, K. (2001) Boxed in or coming out? On the treatment of science, technology and gender in educational research, *Gender and Education*, 13(3): 237–42.

Herbert, C. (1989) *Talking of Silence: The Sexual Harassment of School Girls*. London: Falmer.

Heward, C. (1991) *Public School Masculinities – An Essay in Gender and Power* (Private Correspondence).

Hey, V. (1997a) Northern accent and southern comfort: Subjectivity and social class, in P. Mahony and C. Smroczek (eds) *Class Matters: 'Working-class' Women's Perspectives on Social Class*. London: Taylor and Francis.

Hey, V. (1997b) *The Company She Keeps: An Ethnography of Girls' Friendships*. Buckingham: Open University Press.

Hey, V. (2006) Getting over it? Reflections on the melancholia of reclassified identities, *Gender and Education*, 18(3): 295–308.

Hey, V., Creese, A, Daniels, H., Fielding, S. and Leonard, D. (2001) 'Sad, bad or sexy boys: Girls talk in and out of the classroom' in W. Martino and B. Meyenn (eds) *Teaching Boys: Issues of Masculinity in Schools*. Buckingham: Open University Press, pp. 124–39.

Hill-Collins, P. (1991) *Black Feminist Thought*. New York: Routledge.

Hills, L. (1995) The Senga syndrome: Reflections on twenty-one years in Scottish education, in M. Blair and J. Holland with S. Sheldon (eds) *Identity and Diversity: Gender and the Experience of Education*. Clevedon: Multilingual Matters.

Hingley, P. (1983) Modern Languages, in J. Whyld (ed.) *Sexism in the Secondary Curriculum*. London: Harper and Row.

Hoffer, C. P. (1974) 'Madam Yoko: ruler of the Kpa Mende Confederacy, in M. Z. Rosaldo and L. Lamphere (eds) *Women, Culture and Society*. Stanford: Stanford University Press.

Hoff Sommers, C. (2000) *The War Against Boys*. New York: Simon and Schuster.

Holly, L. (1985) Mary, Jane and Virginia Woolf: Ten-year-old girls talking, in G. Weiner (ed.) *Just a Bunch of Girls*. Milton Keynes: Open University Press.

Hood-Williams, J. (1998) Stories for sexual difference, *British Journal of Sociology of Education*, 18: 81–99.

hooks, b. (1982) *Ain't I a Woman: Black Women and Feminism*. London: Pluto Press.

hooks, b. (1995) Black women shaping feminist theory, in B. Guy-Sheftall (ed.) *Words of Fire: An Anthology of African-American Feminist Thought*. New York: New Press.

Hough, J. (1985) Developing individuals rather than boys and girls, *School Organization*, 5(1): 17–25.

Humphreys, C. and Stanley, N. (eds) (2006) *Domestic Violence and Child Protection*. London: Jessica Kingsley Publishers.

Hunt, F. (ed.) (1987) *Lessons for Life, The Schooling of Girls and Women, 1850–1950*. Oxford: Basil Blackwell.

Ingham, R. (1997) The Development of an Integrated Model of Sexual Conduct Amongst Young People. End of Award Report No. H52427501495. Economic and Social Research Council.

Ivinson, G. and Murphy, P. (2007) *Rethinking Single Sex Teaching*. Maidenhead: Open University Press/McGraw-Hill Education.

Jacklin, C. N. (1983) Boys and girls entering school, in M. Marland (ed.) *Sex Differentiation and Schooling*. London: Heinemann.

Jackson, C. (2002a) Can single-sex classes in co-educational schools enhance the learning experiences of girls and/or boys? an exploration of pupils' perceptions, *British Educational Research Journal*, 28: 37–48.

Jackson, C. (2002b) 'Laddishness' as a self-worth protection strategy, *Gender and Education*, 14(1): 37–51.

Jackson, C. (2006) 'Wild' girls? An exploration of 'ladette' cultures in secondary schools, *Gender and Education*, 18(4): 339–60.

Jackson, D. (1990) *Unmasking Masculinity*. London: Unwin Hyman.

Jackson, M. (1989) Sexuality and Struggle: Feminism, Sexology and the Social Construction of Sexuality, in: C. Jones and P. Mahony (Eds) *Learning our Lines*. London: The Women's Press.

Jackson, S. (2007) She might not have the right tools ... and he does: Children's sense making of gender, work and abilities in early school readers, *Gender and Education*, 19(1): 61–77.

Jackson, S. and Gee, S. (2005) 'Look Janet', 'No you look John': Constructions of gender in early school reader illustrations across 50 years, *Gender and Education*, 17(2): 115–28.

Jeffreys, S. (1986) *The Spinster and Her Enemies: Feminism and Sexuality, 1880–1930*. London: Pandora.

Jeffreys, S. (1987) *The Sexuality Debates*. London: Women's Source Library.

Jeffreys, S. (2005) *Beauty and Misogyny*. London: Routledge.

Johnston, J., McKeown, E. and McEwen, A. (1999) 'Choosing teaching as a career: the perspectives of males and females in training', *Journal of Education for Teaching*, 25(1): 55–64.

Jones, A. (1993) Becoming a 'girl': Post-structuralist suggestions for educational research, *Gender and Education*, 5(2): 157–66.

Jones, A. (1999) Surveillance and student handwriting, in C. O'Farrell (ed.) *Taught Bodies*. New York: Peter Lang, pp. 64–75.

Jones, A. (2001) *Touchy Subject: Teachers Touching Children*. Dunedin: Otago University Press.

Jones, C. (1985) Sexual tyranny: Male violence in a mixed secondary school, in G. Weiner (ed.) *Just a Bunch of Girls*. Milton Keynes: Open University Press.

Jones, C. and Mahony, P. (eds) (1989) *Learning Our Lines*. London: The Women's Press.

Jones, L.G. and Jones, L.P. (1989) Context, confidence and the able girl, *Educational Research*, 31(3): 189–94.

Jones, S. and Myhill, D. (2004) Seeing things differently: Teachers' constructions of underachievement, *Gender and Education*, 16(4): 531–46.

Jordan, E. (1995) Fighting boys and fantasy play: The construction of masculinity in the early years of school, *Gender and Education*, 7(1): 69–86.

Kanaris, A. (1999) Gendered journeys: Children's writing and the construction of gender, *Language and Education*, 13: 254–68.

Kannen, V. and Acker, S. (2008) Identity 'issues' and pedagogical silences: exploring teaching dilemmas in the northern Ontario kindergarten classroom, Special issue: Teacher identities, *Pedagogy, Culture and Society*. 16(1): 25–41.

Keddie, A. and Mills, M. (2007) *Teaching Boys*. Crows Nest, NSW: Allen and Unwin.

Kehily, M. (2002) *Sexuality, Gender and Schooling*. London: RoutledgeFalmer.

Kehily, M. and Nayak, A. (2007) *Gender, Youth and Culture*. London: Palgrave Macmillan.

Kelly, A. (ed.) (1981) *The Missing Half*. Manchester: Manchester University Press.

Kelly, A. (ed.) (1987) *Science for Girls*. Milton Keynes: Open University Press.

Kelly, A., Whyte, J. and Smart, B. (1984) *Girls into Science and Technology: Final Report. GIST*. Department of Sociology, University of Manchester.

Kenway J. and Fitzclarence, L. (1997) Masculinity, violence and schooling: Challenging 'poisonous pedagogies', *Gender and Education*, 9(1): 117–33.

Kenway, J. and Gough, A. (1998) Gender and science education in schools, *Studies in Science Education*, 31: 1–30.

Kenway, J. and Willis, S. (1990) *Hearts and Minds: Self-esteem and the Schooling of Girls*. Lewes: Falmer Press.

Kenway, J. and Willis, S. (1998) *Answering Back*. London: Routledge.

Kenway, J., Kraack, A. and Hickey-Moody, A. (2006) *Masculinity Beyond the Metropolis*. Basingstoke: Palgrave Macmillan.

Kessler, S. J. and Mckenna, W. (1978) *Gender: An Ethnomethodological Approach*. New York: Wiley.

Khayatt, M. D. (1997) 'Sex and the teacher': Should we come out in class? *Harvard Educational Review*, 6(7): 126–43.

King, J. (2000) The problem(s) of men in early education, in N. Lesko (ed.) *Masculinities at School*. Thousand Oaks, CA: Sage.

Lacey, C. (1970) *Hightown Grammar*. Manchester: Manchester University Press.

Lake, A. (1975) Are we born into our sex roles or programmed into them? *Woman's Day*, January, pp. 24–5.

Lambart, A. (1976) The sisterhood, in M. Hammersley and P. Woods (eds) *The Process of Schooling*. London: Routledge and Kegan Paul.

Larkin, J. (1994) Walking through walls: The sexual harassment of high school girls, *Gender and Education*, 6(3): 263–80.

Lavigeur, J. (1980) Co-education and the tradition of separate needs, in D. Spender and E. Sarah (eds) *Learning to Lose: Sexism and Education*. London: The Women's Press.

Layland, J. (1990) On the conflicts of doing feminist research into masculinity, in L. Stanley (ed.) *Feminist Praxis*. London: Routledge.

Leder, G. (1982) Mathematics achievement and fear of success, *Journal for Research in Mathematics Education*, 13: 124–35.

Lee, A. (1980) 'Together we learn to read and write': Sexism and literacy, in D. Spender and E. Sarah (eds) *Learning to Lose: Sexism and Education*. London: The Women's Press.

Lee, D. (1989) 'Chatterboxes', *Child Education*, 67(7): 26–9.

Lee, D. (2000) Hegemonic masculinity and male feminization: The sexual harassment of men at work, *Journal of Gender Studies*, 9(2): 47–65.

Leeds Revolutionary Feminist Group (1981) *Love Your Enemy?: The Debate Between Heterosexual Feminism and Political Lesbianism*. London: Onlywomen Press

Lees, S. (1986) *Losing Out*. London: Hutchinson.

Lees, S. (1993) *Sugar and Spice: Sexuality and Adolescent Girls*. London: Penguin.

Lees, S. (2000) Sexuality and citizenship education, in M. Arnot and J. Dillabough (eds) *Challenging Democracy*. London: RoutledgeFalmer.

Leonard, D. (2006) Single-Sex Schooling, in C. Skelton, B. Francis and L. Smulyan (eds) *Sage Handbook of Gender and Education*. London: Sage.

Lenskyj, H. (1990) Beyond plumbing and prevention, *Gender and Education*, 2(2): 217–31.

Licht, B. and Dweck, C. (1983) Sex differences in achievement orientations: Consequences for academic choices and attainments, in M. Marland (ed.) *Sex Differentiation and Schooling*. London: Heinemann.

Lightbody, P. (1997) A respectable job: factors which infuence young Asians' choice of career, *British Journal of Guidance and Counselling*, 17: 179–200.

Lingard, B. (2003) Where to in gender policy in education after recuperative masculinity politics?, *International Journal of Inclusive Education*, 7: 33–56.

Lingard, B. and Douglas, P. (1999) *Men Engaging Feminisms*. Buckingham: Open University Press.

Lingard, B., Hayes, D., Mills, M. and Christie, P. (2003) *Leading Learning: Making Hope Practical in Schools*. Buckingham: Open University Press.

Littlewood, M. (1995) Makers of men, in L. Dawtrey, J. Holland and M. Hammer with S. Sheldon (eds) *Equality and Inequality in Education Policy*. Clevedon: Multilingual Matters.

Llewellyn, M. (1980) Studying girls at school: The implications of confusion, in R. Deem (ed.) *Schooling for Women's Work*. London: Routledge and Kegan Paul.

Lloyd, B. and Duveen, G. (1992) *Gender Inequalities and Education*. Hemel Hempstead: Harvester Wheatsheaf.

Lobban, G. (1975) Sex roles in reading schemes, *Educational Review*, 27(3): 202–10.

Lobban, G. (1978) The influence of the school on sex-role stereotyping, in J. Chetwynd and O. Hartnett (eds) *The Sex Role System*. London: Routledge and Kegan Paul.

Lopez, J. A. (1992) Studies say women face glass walls as well as ceilings, *Wall Street Journal*, 3rd March, pp. B1–B2.

Lorde, A. (1984) *Sister Outsider*. Berkeley, CA: Crossing Press.

Lown, J. (1995) Feminist perspectives, in M. Blair and J. Holland with S. Sheldon (eds) *Identity and Diversity: Gender and the Experience of Education*. Clevedon: Multilingual Matters.

Lucey, H. (2001) 'Social class, gender and schooling' in Becky Francis and Christine Skelton (eds) *Investigating Gender: Contemporary Perspectives in Education*. Buckingham, Open University Press.

Lucey, H. and Reay, D. (2000) Excitement and anxiety in the move to secondary school, *Oxford Review of Education*, 26: 191–205.

Lucey, H. and Reay, D. (2002) A market in waste: Psychic and structural dimesntions of school-choice policy in the UK and children's narratives on 'demonised' schools, *Discourse*, 23(1): 23–40.

Lucey, H., Brown, M., Denvir, H., Askew, M. and Rhodes, V. (2003) Girls and boys in the primary maths classroom, in C. Skelton and B. Francis (eds) *Boys and Girls in the Primary Classroom*. Maidenhead: Open University Press/McGraw-Hill Education.

Luttrell, W. (1997) *School-smart and Mother-wise: Working-class Women's Identity and Schooling*. New York: Routledge.

Luttrell, W. (2003) *Pregnant Bodies, Fertile Minds: Gender, Race, and the Schooling of Pregnant Teens*. New York: Routledge.

Mac an Ghaill, M. (1988) *Young, Gifted and Black: Student-teacher Relations in the Schooling of Black Youth*. Milton Keynes: Open University Press.

Mac an Ghaill, M. (1991) Schooling, sexuality and male power: Towards an emancipatory curriculum, *Gender and Education*, 3(3): 291–309.

Mac an Ghaill, M. (1994) *The Making of Men: Masculinities, Sexualities and Schooling*. Buckingham: Open University Press.

Maccoby, E. and Jacklin, C. (1974) *The Psychology of Sex Differences*. Stanford, CA: Stanford University Press.

Macdonald, M. (1980) Schooling and the reproduction of class and gender relations, in L. Barton, R. Meighan and S. Walker (eds) *Schooling Ideology and the Curriculum*. Lewes: Falmer.

MacInnes, J. (1998) *The End of Masculinity*. Buckingham: Open University Press.

MacNaughton, G. (2000) *Rethinking Gender in the Early Childhood Education*. London: Paul Chapman.

MacNaughton, G. (2006) *Doing Foucault in Early Childhood Studies*. London: Routledge.

McPherson, A. and Douglas Willms, J. (1997) Equalization and improvement: Some effects of comprehensive reorganization in Scotland, in A. Halsey, H. Lauder, P. Brown and A. Stuart Wells (eds) *Education: Culture, Economy, Society*. Oxford: Oxford University Press.

McRobbie, A. (1978a) Working-class girls and the culture of femininity, in women's studies groups (eds) *Women Take Issue*. London: Hutchinson.

McRobbie, A. (1978b) *Jackie: Ideology of Adolescent Femininity*. Birmingham: University of Birmingham.

McRobbie, A. (2004) Notes on postfeminism and popular culture: Bridget Jones and the new gender regime, in A. Harris (ed.) *All About the Girl: Culture, Power and Identity*. London: Routledge.

Madden, A. (2004) Gendered Subject Choices, in: H. Claire (ed) *Gender in Education 3–19*, London: ATL.

Maguire, M. (1997) Missing links: Working-class women of Irish descent, in P. Mahony and C. Zmroczek (eds) *Class Matters: 'Working-class' Women's Perspectives on Social Class*. London: Taylor and Francis.

Mahony, P. (1998) Girls will be girls and boys will be first, in D. Epstein, J. Elwood, V. Hey and J. Maw (eds) *Failing Boys?* Buckingham: Open University Press.

Maguire, M. (2005) 'Not footprints behind but footsteps forward': Working-Class women who teach, *Gender and Education*, 17(1): 3–18.

Mahony, P. (1985) *Schools For The Boys?* London: Hutchinson.

Mahony, P. and Hextall, I. (2000) *Reconstructing Teaching*. London: RoutledgeFalmer.

Mahony, P. and Zmorczek, C. (eds) (1997) *Class Matters: 'Working-class' Women's Perspectives on Social Class*. London: Taylor and Francis.

Mahony P., Menter, I. and Hextall, I. (2004) The emotional impact of performance-related pay on teachers in England, *British Educational Research Journal*, 30(3): 435–56.

Maier, K. S., Ford, T. G. and Schneider, B. (2008) Are middle-class families advantaging their children?, in L. Weis (ed.) *The Way Class Works*. Abingdon: Routledge.

Majors, R. and Bilson, J. M. (1992) *Cool Pose: The Dilemmas of Black Manhood in America*. New York: Lexington Books.

Marland, M. (ed.) (1983) *Sex Differentiation and Schooling*. London: Heinemann.

Marks, P. (1976) Femininity in the classroom: An account of changing attitudes, in J. Mitchell and A. Oakley (eds) *The Rights and Wrongs of Women*. Harmondsworth: Penguin.

Marriott, S. (1985) *Primary Education and Society*. Lewes: Falmer.

Marsh, J. (2000) 'But I want to fly too!' Girls and superhero play in the infant classroom, *Gender and Education*, 12: 209–20.

Marsh, J. (2003) Superhero Stories, in C. Skelton and B. Francis (eds) *Boys and Girls in the Primary Classroom*. Maidenhead: Open University Press/McGraw Hill.

Martin, J. (1999) *Women and the Politics of Schooling in Victorian and Edwardian England*. Leicester: Leicester University Press.

Martin, J. and Goodman, J. (2004) *Women and Education, 1800–1980: Educational Change and Personal Identities*. London: Palgrave.

Martino, W. (1995) Gendered learning practices: Exploring the costs of hegemonic masculinity for girls and boys at school, MCEETYA, Canberra: Department for Education and Training.

Martino, W. (1999) 'Cool boys', 'party animals','squids' and 'poofters': Interrogating the dynamics and politics of adolescent masculinities in school, *British Journal of Sociology of Education*, 20(2): 239–63.

Martino, W. (2000) Policing masculinities: Investigating the role of homophobia and heteronormativity in the lives of adolescent boys at school, *Journal of Men's Studies*, 8(2): 213–36.

Martino, W. (2006) The 'right' way to educate boys: Interrogating the politics of boys' education in Australia, in C. Skelton, B. Francis and L. Smulyan (eds) *Sage Handbook of Gender and Education*. London: Sage.

Martino, W. (2008) Male teachers as role models: Addressing issues of masculinity, pedagogy and the re-masculinization of schooling, *Curriculum Inquiry*, 38(2): 189–223.

Martino, W. and Frank, B. (2006) The Tyranny of Surveillance: Male teachers and the policing of masculinities in a single-sex school, *Gender and Education*, 18(1): 17–33.

Martino, W. and Pallotta-Chiarolli, M. (eds) (2003) *So What's a Boy?* Maidenhead: Open University/McGraw Hill.

Maylor, U. and Read, B. with Mendick, H., Ross, A. and Rollock, N. (2007) Diversity and citizenship in the curriculum: Research review, Research Report 819 Nottingham: DfES.

Maylor, U., Ross, A., Rollock, N. and Williams, K. (2006) *Black Teachers in London*. London: GLA.

Maylor, U. (forthcoming) They do not relate to black people like us': Black teachers as role models for black pupils, *Journal of Education Policy*.

Maynard, T. (2002) *Boys and Literacy: Exploring the Issues*. London: Routledge.

Measor, L. and Sikes, P. (1992) *Gender and Schooling*. London: Cassell.

Measor, L. and Woods, P. (1984) *Changing Schools*. Milton Keynes: Open University Press.

Meighan, R. (1981) *A Sociology of Educating*. London: Holt, Rinehart and Winston.

Mellor, D. J. and Epstein, D. (2006) Appropriate behaviour? Sexualities, schooling and hetero-gender, in C. Skelton, B. Francis and L. Smulyan (eds) *Sage Handbook of Gender and Education*. London: Sage.

Mendick, H. (2005) A beautiful myth? The gendering of being/doing 'good at maths', *Gender and Education*, 17(2): 205–19.

Mendick, H. (2006) *Masculinities in Mathematics.* Maidenhead: Open University Press/McGraw-Hill.

Middleton, S. (1987) The sociology of women's education as a field of academic study, in M. Arnot and G. Weiner (eds) *Gender and the Politics of Schooling.* London: Unwin Hyman.

Millard, E. (1997) *Differently Literate: Boys, Girls and the Schooling of Literacy.* London: Falmer Press.

Millard, E. (2003) Transformative pedagogy: Towards a literacy of fusion, *Reading, Literacy and Language,* 37(1): 3–9.

Miller, L. and Budd, J. (1999) The development of occupational sex-role stereotypes, occupational presences and academic subject preferences of children ages 8, 12 and 16, *Educational Psychology,* 19: 17–35.

Millman, V. and Weiner, G. (1985) *Sex Differentiation in Schooling.* London: Longmans/Schools Council.

Mills, M. (2001) *Challenging Violence in Schools.* Buckingham: Open University Press.

Mills, M., Haase, M. and Charlton, E. (2008) Being the 'right' kind of male teacher: The disciplining of John, Special issue: Teacher identities, *Pedagogy, Culture and Society.* 16(1): 71–84.

Mirza, H. (1992) *Young, Female and Black.* London: Routledge.

Mirza, H. (1997) Introduction, in H. Mirza (ed.) *Black British Feminism.* London: Routledge.

Mitchell, J. (1974) *Psychoanalysis and Feminism.* London: Allen Lane.

Modood (1994) The end of a hegemony: The concept of 'black' and British Asians, in J. Rex and B. Drury (eds) *Ethnic Mobilisation in a Multicultural Europe.* Aldershot: Avebury Press.

Moir, A. and Moir, B. (1999) *Why Men Don't Iron.* London: Harper Collins.

Mojab, S. (2006) War and diaspora as lifelong learning contexts for immigrant women, in C. Leathwood and B. Francis (eds) *Gender and Lifelong Learning: Critical Feminist Engagements.* London: Routledge.

Moreau, M.-P., Osgood, J. and Halsall, A. (2007) Making sense of the glass ceiling in schools: An exploration of women teachers' discourses, *Gender and Education,* 19(2): 237–53.

Morrell, F. (1989) *Children of the Future.* London: Hogarth Press.

Morrell, F. (2000) An episode in the thirty years war: Race, sex and class in the ILEA 1981–90, in K. Myers (ed.) *Whatever Happened to Equal Opportunities in Schools?* Buckingham: Open University Press.

Morrison, A. and McIntyre, D. (1969) *Teachers and Teaching.* Harmondsworth: Penguin.

Morrison, A. M., White, R. P. and Van Velsor, E. (1987) *Breaking the Glass Ceiling.* Reading, MA: Addison Wesley.

Mulholland, J. and Hansen, P. (2003) Men who become primary school teachers: An early portrait, *Asia-Pacific Journal of Teacher Education,* 31(3): 213–24.

Murphy, P. and Whitelegg, E. (2006) 'Girls and physics: Continuing barriers to 'belonging', *The Curriculum Journal,* 17(3): 281–305.

Musgrave, P. W. (1968) *Society and Education in England since 1800.* London: Methuen.

Myers, K. (ed.) (2000) *Whatever Happened to Equal Opportunities in schools?* Buckingham: Open University Press.

National Center for Education Statistics (NCES) (2007) *Characteristics of Schools, Districts, Teachers, Principals, and School Libraries in the United States 2003–04.* Washington: Department for Education.

Nayak, A. (2001) 'Ice white and ordinary': New perspectives on ethnicity, gender and youth cultural identities, in B. Francis and C. Skelton (eds) *Investigating Gender.* Buckingham: Open University Press.

Nayak, A. and Kehily, M. (2006) *Gender, Youth and Culture: Young Masculinities and Femininities.* Basingstoke: Palgrave MacMillan.

Neall, L. (2002) *Bringing Out The Best in Boys.* Gloucester: Hawthorn Press.

Nias, J. (1989) *Primary teachers talking: A study of teaching as work.* London: Routledge.

Nilsen, A. P. (1975) Women in children's literature, in E.S. Maccia *et al.* (eds) *Women and Education.* New York: C. C. Thomas.

Noble, C. and Bradford, W. (2000) *Getting it right for boys . . . and girls.* London: Routledge.

Northam, J. (1982) Girls and boys in primary maths books, *Education 3–13*, 10(1): 11–14.

Ntseane, P. (2005) Cultural dimensions of sexuality: empowerment challenges for HIV/AIDS prevention in Botswana. UNESCO Special Issue on HIV/AIDS.

Oakley, A. (1972) *Sex, Gender and Society.* London: Temple Smith.

Oakley, A. (1981a) *25. The Division of Labour by Gender.* Block 6, E200 Contemporary Issues in Education. Milton Keynes: The Open University Press.

Oakley, A. (1981b) *Subject Women.* London: Fontana.

O'Brien, M. (2003) Girls and transition to secondary-level schooling in Ireland: 'Moving on' and 'moving out', *Gender and Education*, 15: 249–67.

Ofsted (2002a) *Achievement of Black Caribbean Pupils: Three Successful Primary Schools.* London: HMSO.

Ofsted (2002b) *Achievement of Black Caribbean Pupils: Good Practice in Secondary Schools.* London: HMSO.

Ofsted (2005) *Managing Challenging Behaviour.* London: Ofsted, HMI 2363.

Oram, A. (1987) 'Sex antagonism' in the teaching profession: Equal pay and the marriage bar, 1910–39, in M. Arnot, and G. Weiner (eds) *Gender and the Politics of Schooling.* London: Unwin Hyman.

Oram, A. (1999) 'To cook dinners with love in them?' Sexuality, marital status and women teachers in England and Wales, 1920–39, in K. Weiler and S. Middleton (eds) *Telling Women's Lives.* Buckingham: Open University Press.

Organisation for Economic Co-operation and Development (2004a) *Attracting, Developing and Retaining Effective Teachers.* (www.oecd.org/edu/teacherpolicy)

Organisation for Economic Co-operation and Development (2004b) Individual Country Reports, *Attracting, Developing and Retaining Effective Teachers* (see those for Austria, Germany, Italy, Norway). (www.oecd.org/edu/teacherpolicy)

Organisation for Economic Co-operation and Development (2007) PISA 2006: Science Competencies for Tomorrow's World Executive Summary. (www.pisa.oecd.org.)

Osgood, J. (2005) Who cares? The classes nature of childcare, *Gender and Education*, 17(3): 289–303.

Osgood, J., Francis, B. and Archer, L. (2006) Gendered identities and work placement: Why don't boys care?, *Journal of Education Policy*, 21(3): 305–21.

Osler, A. (1989) *Speaking Out: Black Girls in Britain.* London: Virago.

Osler, A. (2006) Excluded girls: Interpersonal, institutional and structural violence in schools, *Gender and Education*, 18(6): 571–90.

Osler, A. and Hill, J. (1999) Exclusion from school and racial equality: an examination of government proposals in the light of recent research evidence, *Cambridge Journal of Education*, 29(1): 33–62.

Osler, A. and Vincent, K. (2003) *Girls and Exclusion: Rethinking the Agenda.* London: RoutledgeFalmer.

Osler, A., Street, C., Liall, M. and Vincent, K. (2002) *Not a Problem? Girls and School Exclusion*. London: National Children's Bureau and Joseph Rowntree Foundation.

Oyler, C., Jennings, G. T. and Lozada, P. (2001) Silenced gender: the Construction of a male primary educator, *Teaching and Teacher Education*, 17: 367–79.

Ozga, J. (ed.) (1993) *Women in Educational Management*. Buckingham: Open University Press.

Paechter, C. (2000) *Changing School Subjects: Power, Gender and Curriculum*. Buckingham: Open University Press.

Paechter, C. (2004) The gendered curriculum, in H. Claire (ed.) *Gender in Education 3–19: A Fresh Approach*. London: ATL.

Paechter, C. (2006) Masculine/femininities/feminine masculinities: Power, identities and gender, *Gender and Education*, 18(3): 253–63.

Paechter, C. (2007) *Being Boys, Being Girls*. Maidenhead: Open University Press/ McGraw-Hill.

Paley, V. G. (1984) *Boys and Girls*. Chicago: University of Chicago Press.

Pang, M. (1999) The employment situation of young Chinese adults in the British labour market, *Personnel Review*, 28: 41–57.

Parker, H. J. (1974) *View from the Boys*. Newton Abbot: David and Charles.

Parry, O. (1996) 'Schooling is Fooling': Why do Jamaican boys underachieve in school? *Gender and Education*, 9(2): 223–31.

Parsons, C. G., Godfrey, R., Annan, G., Cornwall, J., Dussart, M., Hepburn, S., Howlett, K. and Wennerstrom, V. (2005) *Minority Ethnic Exclusions and the Race Relations (Amendment) Act 2000*, RR 616. Nottingham: DfES

Partington, G. (1976) *Women Teachers in the 20th Century*. Windsor: NFER.

Pateman, C. (1988) *The Sexual Contract*. Oxford: Polity.

Phoenix, A. (1987) Theories of gender and black families, in G. Weiner and M. Arnot (eds) *Gender Under Scrutiny*. London: Hutchinson.

Phoenix, A. (1991) *Young Mothers?* Cambridge: Polity Press.

Phoenix, A. (1997) 'I'm white! So what? The construction of whiteness for young Londoners', in M. Fine (ed.) *Off White: Readings on Race, Power and Society*. London: Routledge.

Phoenix, A., Woolett, A. and Lloyd, E. (eds) (1991) *Motherhood: Meanings, Practices and Ideologies*. London: Sage.

Phoenix, A., Frosh, S. and Pattman, R. (2003) Producing contradictory masculine subject positions: Narratives of threat, homophobia and bullying in 11–14-year-old boys, *Journal of Social Issues*, 59(1): 179–95.

Picard, L. (2006) *Victorian London: The Life of a City 1840–1870*. London: Phoenix.

Pickering, J. (1997) *Raising Boys' Achievement*. London: Network Educational Press.

Pipher, M. (1994) *Reviving Ophelia*. New York: Penguin.

Platt, A. and Whyld, J. (1983) Introduction, in J. Whyld (ed.) *Sexism in the Secondary Curriculum*. London: Harper and Rowe.

Plummer, G. (2000) *Failing Working-Class Girls*. Stoke-on-Trent: Trentham

Pollack, W. (1998) *Real Boys*. New York: Owl Books.

Pollitt, C. (1993) *Managerialism and the Public Service: Cuts or Cultural Change in the 1990s*, 2nd edn. Oxford: Blackwell.

Power, M. (1997) *The Audit Society*. Oxford: Oxford University Press.

Power, S., Edwards, T., Whitty, G. and Wigfall, V. (2003) *Education and the Middle Class*. Buckingham: Open University Press.

Pratt, J. (1985) The attitudes of teachers, in J. Whyte, R. Deem, L. Kant and M. Cruickshank (eds) *Girl Friendly Schooling.* London: Methuen and Co.

Purvis, J. (1987) Social class, education and ideals of femininity in the nineteenth century, in M. Arnot and G. Weiner (eds) *Gender and the Politics of Schooling.* London, Unwin Hyman.

Purvis, J. (1991) *A History of Women's Education in England.* Buckingham: Open University Press.

Purvis, J. (1995) Women and education: A historical account 1800–1914, in L. Dawtrey, J. Holland and M. Hammer with S. Sheldon (eds) *Equality and Inequality in Education Policy.* Clevedon: Multilingual Matters.

Radford, J. (1987) Policing male violence – policing women, in J. Hanmer and M. Maynard (eds.) *Women, Violence and Social Control.* London: Macmillan.

Ramazanoglu, C. (1987) Sex and violence in academic life or you can keep a good woman down, in J. Hanmer and M. Maynard (eds) *Women, Violence and Social Control.* London: Routledge and Kegan Paul.

Raphael-Reed, L. (1998) 'Zero tolerance': Gender performance and school failure, in D. Epstein, J. Elwood, V. Hey and J. Maw (eds) *Failing Boys?* Buckingham: Open University Press.

Reay, D. (1990) Working with boys, *Gender and Education*, 2(3): 269–81.

Reay, D. (1998) *Class Work.* London: UCL Press.

Reay, D. (1998) Rethinking social class: Qualitative perspectives on class and gender, *Sociology*, 32(2): 259–75.

Reay, D. (2001) 'Spice girls', 'nice girls', 'girlies' and 'tomboys': Gender discourses, girls' cultures and femininities in the primary classroom, *Gender and Education*, 13(2): 153–66.

Reay, D. (2002) 'Shaun's story: Troubling discourses of white working-class masculinities, *Gender and Education*, 14(3): 221–33.

Reay, D. (2003) A risky business? Mature working-class women students and access to higher education, *Gender and Education*, 15(3): 301–17.

Reay, D. (2006) Gender and class in education, in C. Skelton, B. Francis and L. Smulyan (eds) *The Sage Handbook of Gender and Education.* London and New York: Sage.

Reay, D. (2007) Cultural capital theories, in B. Bank (ed.) *Gender and Education: An Encylopedia.* Conneticut: Praegar.

Reay, D. and Ball, S. (1998) 'Making up their minds': Family dynamics of school choice, *British Educational Research Journal*, 14(4): 431–48.

Reay, D. and Lucey, H. (2003) The limits of choice: Children and inner-city schooling, *Sociology*, 37: 121–43.

Reay, D., David, M. and Ball, S. (2005) *Degrees of Choice: Social Class, Race and Gender in Higher Education.* Stoke-on-Trent: Trentham Books.

Reay, D., Hollingsworth, S., Williams, K., Crozier, J., Jamieson, F., James, D. and Beedell, P. (2007) 'A darker shade of pale?' Whiteness, the middle classes and multi-ethnic inner city schooling, *Sociology*, 41(6): 1041–60.

Reay, D., Crozier, G., James, D., Hollingsworth, S., Williams, K., Jamieson, F. and Beedell, P. (2008) Re-invigorating democracy?: White middle class identities and comprehensive schooling, *Sociological Review*, 56(2): 238–56.

Redman, P. (1996) Curtis loves Ranjit: Heterosexual masculinities, schooling and pupils sexual cultures, *Educational Review*, 48(2): 175–82.

Rees, T. (1999) *Mainstreaming Equality in the European Union.* London: Routledge.

Reich, A. (1974) Teaching is a good profession … for a woman, in J. Stacey, S. Bereraud, J. Daniels (eds) *And Jill Came Tumbling After: Sexism in American Education*. New York: Dell.

Renold, E. (1997) 'All they've got on their brains is football: Sport, masculinity and the gendered practices of playground relations, *Sport, Education and Society*, 2(1): 5–23.

Renold, E. (2000) 'Coming out': Gender, (hetero)sexuality and the primary school, *Gender and Education*, 12(3): 309–26.

Renold, E. (2001) 'Square-girls', femininity and the negotiation of academic success in the primary school, *British Educational Research Journal*, 27(5): 577–88.

Renold, E. (2005) *Girls, Boys and Junior Sexualities*. London: Routledge.

Renold, E. (2006a) 'They won't let us play unless you're going out with one of them': Girls, boys and Butler's 'heterosexual matrix' in the primary years, Special issue: Troubling identities: Reflections on Judith Butler's philosophy for the sociology of education, *British Journal of Sociology of Education*, 27(4): 489–509.

Renold, E. (2006b) Gendered classroom experiences, in C. Skelton, B. Francis and L. Smulyan (eds) *The Sage Handbook of Gender and Education*. London: Sage.

Renold, E. (2007) Primary school 'studs': (de)Constructing young boys' heterosexual masculinities, *Men and Masculinities*, 9(3): 275–98.

Renold, E. (2008) Tomboys and 'female masculinity': (dis)Embodying hegemonic masculinity, queering gender identities and relations, in W. Martino, M. Kehler and M. Weaver-Hightower (eds) *The Problem with Boys: Beyond Recuperative Masculinity Politics in Boys' Education*. London: Sage.

Reynolds, T. (1997) Class matter, 'race' matters, gender matters, in P. Mahony and C. Zmroczek (eds.) *Class Matters: 'Working-class' Women's Perspectives on Social Class*. London: Taylor and Francis.

Rich, A. (1980) Compulsory heterosexuality and lesbian existence, *Signs*, 5(4): 631–60.

Riddell, S. (1989) Pupils, resistance and gender codes: A study of classroom encounters, *Gender and Education*, 1(2): 183–97.

Riddell, S. (1992) *Politics and the Gender of the Curriculum*. London: Routledge.

Riley, K. (1985) Black girls speak for themselves, in G. Weiner (ed.) *Just a Bunch of Girls*. Milton Keynes: Open University Press.

Ringrose, J. and Renold, E. (2007) Presumed guilty: The gendered, sexualized, racialized and classed effects of bully discourses for boys and girls. Paper presented at Gender and Education Association conference, Trinity College Dublin, 28–30/3/07.

Robins, D. and Cohen, P. (1978) *Knuckle-sandwich: Growing Up in the Working-class City*. Harmondsworth: Penguin.

Robinson, K. (2005) Reinforcing hegemonic masculinities through sexual harassment: Issues of identity, power and popularity in secondary schools, *Gender and Education*, 17(1): 19–37.

Robinson-Pant, A. (2004) *Women, Literacy and Development*. London: Routledge.

Rolfe, H. (1999) *Gender Equality and the Careers Service*. Manchester: Equal Opportunities Commission.

Rollock, N. (2007) *Failure by Any Other Name?: Educational Policy and the Continuing Struggle for Black Academic Success*. London: The Runnymede Trust.

Rosser, S. (1997) *Re-engineering female friendly science*. New York: Teachers College Press.

Roulston, K. and Mills, M. (2000) Male teachers in feminised teaching areas: Marching to the beat of the men's movement drums?, *Oxford Review of Education*, 26(2): 221–37.

Rousseau, J-J. (1762) *Emile* (Publisher unknown). Recent edition (2007) Translated by Barbara Foxley, Charleston, S.C.: BiblioBazaar, LLC.

Rowan, L., Knobel, M., Bigum, C. and Lankshear, C. (2002) *Boys, Literacies and Schooling*. Buckingham: Open University Press.

Sadker, M. and Sadker, D. (1994) *Failing at Fairness: How Our Schools Cheat Girls*. New York: Touchstone.

Said, E. (1978) *Orientalism*. New York: Pantheon.

Salisbury, J. and Jackson, D. (1996) *Challenging Macho Values*. London: Falmer.

Sanders, S. and Spraggs, G. (1989) Section 28 and education, in C. Jones and P. Mahony (eds) *Learning Our Lines: Sexuality and Social Control in Education*. London: Women's Press.

Sargent, P. (2001) *Real Men or Real Teachers?* Harriman, TN: Men's Studies Press.

Scharff, C. (2007) Perspectives on feminist (dis-)identification in the British and German contexts: A performative approach. Paper presented at 'New Femininities – An International Conference', British Library, London, 26th January (http://www.lse.ac.uk/collections/newFemininities/finalprogramme.htm)

Scott, M. (1980) Teach her a Lesson: Sexist Curriculum in Patriarchal Education, in D. Spender and E. Sarah (eds) *Learning to Lose*. London: The Women's Press.

Segerman-Peck, L. M. (1991) *Networking and Mentoring: A Woman's Guide*. London: Piatkus.

Seidler, V. (1989) *Rediscovering Masculinity*. London: Routledge.

Seifert, K. (1988) The culture of early education and the preparation of male teachers, *Early Child Development and Care*, 38: 69–80.

Serbin, L. (1983) The hidden curriculum: Academic consequences of teacher expectations, in M. Marland (ed.) *Sex Differentiation and Schooling*. London: Heinemann.

Sewell, T. (1997) *Black Masculinities and Schooling: How Black Boys Survive Modern Schooling*. Stoke-on-Trent: Trentham Books.

Shain, F. (2003) *The Schooling and Identity of Asian Girls*. Stoke-on-Trent: Trentham Books.

Sharpe, S. (1976) *Just Like a Girl*. Harmondsworth: Penguin.

Sharpe, S. (1994) *Just Like a Girl*, 2nd edn. London: Penguin.

Sheppard, N. (1989) *Equal Opportunity in the Nursery: An Investigative Study*. North Tyneside: North Tyneside Education Authority.

Short, G. and Carrington, B. (1989) Discourse on gender: The perceptions of children aged between six and eleven, in C. Skelton (ed.) *Whatever Happens to Little Women? Gender and Primary Schooling*. Milton Keynes: Open University Press.

Sikes, P. (1997) *Parents Who Teach. Stories from Home and from School*. London: Cassell.

Siraj Blatchford, I. (ed.) (1993) *'Race', Gender and the Education of Teachers*. Buckingham: Open University Press.

Skattebol, J. (2006) Playing boys: The body, identity and belonging in the early years, *Gender and Education*, 18(5): 507–22.

Skeggs, B. (1994) Situating the production of feminist ethnography, in M. Maynard and J. Purvis (eds) *Researching Women's Lives from a Feminist Perspective*. London: Taylor and Francis.

Skeggs, B. (1997) *Formations of Class and Gender*. London: Sage.

Skeggs, B. (2004) *Class, Self, Culture*. London: Routledge.

Skelton, C. (1988) Demolishing 'the house that jack built': Anti-Sexist initiatives in the primary school, in B. Carrington and B. Troyna (eds) *Children and Controversial Issues*. Lewes: Falmer.

Skelton, C. (ed.) (1989) *Whatever Happens to Little Women?: Gender and Schooling.* Milton Keynes: Open University Press.

Skelton, C. (1991) A study of the career perspectives of male teachers of young children, *Gender and Education,* 3(3): 279–89.

Skelton, C. (1996) Learning to be 'tough': The fostering of maleness in one primary school, *Gender and Education,* 8(2): 185–97.

Skelton, C. (1997) Revisiting gender issues in reading schemes, *Education 3–13,* 25(1): 37–43.

Skelton, C. (1998) Feminism and research into masculinities and schooling, *Gender and Education,* 10(2): 217–27.

Skelton, C. (2001) *Schooling the Boys.* Buckingham: Open University Press.

Skelton, C. (2002) The 'feminisation of schooling' or 're-masculinising' primary education?, *International Studies in Sociology of Education,* 12(1): 77–96.

Skelton, C. (2003) Male primary teachers and perceptions of masculinity, *Educational Review,* 55(2):195–209.

Skelton, C. and Francis, B. (2001) Endnotes, in B. Francis and C. Skelton (eds) *Investigating Gender.* Buckingham: Open University Press.

Skelton, C. and Francis, B. (2003) Introduction: Boys and girls in the primary classroom, in C. Skelton and B. Francis (eds) *Boys and Girls in the Primary Classroom.* Buckingham: Open University Press.

Skelton, C. and Francis, B. (eds) (2005) *A Feminist Critique.* Routledge: London.

Skelton, C. and Read, B. (2006) Male and Female Teachers' Evaluative Responses to Gender and the Learning Environments of Primary Age Pupils, *International Studies in Sociology of Education,* 16(2): 105–20.

Skelton, C., Francis, B. and Valkanova, Y. (2007) *Breaking Down the Stereotypes: Gender and Achievement in Schools.* Manchester: Equal Opportunities Commission.

Skelton, C., Carrington, B., Francis, B., Hutchings, M. Read, B. and Hall, I. (2008) Gender 'matters' in the primary classroom: Pupils' and teachers' perspectives, *British Educational Research Journal.* (published on IFirst http://www.informaworld.com/smpp/content~content=a902340012~db=all~order=pubdate)

Slaughter, S., and Leslie, L. (1997) *Academic Capitalism: Politics, Policies and the Entrepreneurial University.* Baltimore, MD: Johns Hopkins University Press.

Smedley, S. (1999) 'Don't rock the boat': Men student teachers' understanding of gender and equality'. Paper presented to the British Educational Research Association Conference, University of Sussex, 2–5 September.

Smith, C. and Lloyd, B. (1978) 'Maternal behavior and perceived sex of infant: revisited', *Child Development,* 49: 1263–5.

Smith, J. (2007) 'Ye've got to 'ave balls to play this game sir!' Boys, peers and fears: The negative influence of school-based 'cultural accomplices' in constructing hegemonic masculinities, *Gender and Education,* 19(2): 179–98.

Smulyan, L. (2006) Constructing teaching identities, in C. Skelton, B. Francis and L. Smulyan (eds) *The Sage Handbook of Gender and Education.* London: Sage.

Soper, K. (1990) *Troubled Pleasures.* London: Verso.

Spender, D. (1982) *Invisible Women: The Schooling Scandal.* London: Writer and Readers Publishing.

Spender, D. (ed.) (1987) *The Education Papers.* London: Routledge and Kegan Paul.

Spender, D. and Sarah, E. (eds) (1980) *Learning to Lose.* London: The Women's Press.

Spraggs, G. (1994) Coming out in the National Union of Teachers, in D. Epstein (ed.) *Challenging Lesbian and Gay Inequalities in Education*. Buckingham: Open University Press.

Squirrell, G. (1989) In passing ... teachers and sexual orientation, in S. Acker (ed.) *Teachers, Gender and Careers*. Lewes: Falmer.

Stables, A. and Stables, S. (1995) Gender differences in students' approaches to A-level subject choices and perceptions of A-level subjects, *Educational Research*, 37(1): 39–51.

Stacey, J., Bereaud, S. and Daniels, J. (eds) (1974) *And Jill Came Tumbling After: Sexism in American Education*. New York: Dell.

Stanko, E. (1985) *Intimate Intrusions: Women's Experience of Male Violence*. London: Routledge and Kegan Paul.

Stanley, J. (1989) *Marks on the Memory*. Milton Keynes: Open University Press.

Stanley, L. and Wise, S. (1993) *Breaking Out: Feminist Consciousness and Feminist Research*, 2nd edn. London: Routledge.

Stanworth, M. (1983) *Gender and Schooling*. London: Hutchinson.

Steedman, C. (1982) *The Tidy House: Little Girls Writing*. London: Virago.

Steedman, C. (1987) Prison houses, in M. Lawn and G. Grace (eds) *Teachers: The Culture and Politics of Work*. Lewes: Falmer.

Still, L. (1995) Women in management: Glass ceiling or slippery poles?, in B. Limerick and B. Lingard (eds) *Gender and Changing Educational Management*. New South Wales: Hodder Education. Rydalmere.

Stones, R. (1983) *'Pour out the cocoa Janet': Sexism in Children's Books*. York: Longman.

Stopes, M. (1926) *Sex and the Young*. London: Gill Publishing Co.

Strand, S. (2007) *Minority Ethnic Pupils in the Longitudinal Study of Young People in England*. London: DCSF.

Stromquist, N. (2000) Voice, harmony and fugue in global feminism, *Gender and Education*, 12(4): 419–33.

Sukhnandan, L. (1999) An Investigation into Gender Differences in Achievement. Phase 1: A Review of Recent Research and LEA Information on Provision. Slough: National Foundation for Educational Research.

Sukhnandan, L., Lee, B. and Kelleher, S. (2000) *An Investigation into Gender Differences in Achievement. Phase 2: School and Classroom Strategies*. Slough: National Foundation for Educational Research.

Sumsion, J. (2000) Rewards, risks and tensions: Perceptions of males enrolled in an early childhood teacher education programme, *Asia-Pacific Journal of Teacher Education*, 28(1): 87–100.

Sutherland, M. (1981) *Sex Bias in Education*. Oxford: Blackwell.

Teacher Training Agency (2004) *Qualifying to teach: handbook of guidance*. London: Teacher Training Agency.

Thomas, K. (1990) Gender and Subject in Higher Education. Buckingham: SRHE/Open University.

Thomas, A. and Kitzinger, C. (eds) (1997) *Sexual Harassment*. Buckingham: Open University Press.

Thorne, B. (1993) *Gender Play: Girls and Boys in School*. Buckingham: Open University Press.

Thorne, B. and Luria, Z. (1986) Sexuality and gender in children's daily worlds, *Social Problems*, 33: 176–90.

Thornton, M. (1997) Gender issues in the recruitment, training and career prospects of early years and primary school teachers. Paper presented to the British Educational Research Association Conference, University of York, 11–14 September.

Thornton, M. (1998) 'Save the whale, sorry – male: Wasted role models in primary ITE. Paper presented to the British Educational Research Association Conference, Queen's University, Belfast, 27–30 August.

Thornton, M. and Bricheno, P. (2006) *Missing Men in Education*. Stoke-on-Trent: Trentham.

Tickly, L., Caballero, C. and Haynes, J. (2004) *Understanding the Educational Needs of Mixed Heritage Pupils*. London: DfES.

Tikly, L., Haynes, J., Caballero, C., Hill, J. and Gillborn, D. (2006) *Evaluation of Aiming High: African Caribbean Achievement Project*, RR 801. Nottingham: DfES.

Tizard, B. and Phoenix, A. (2002) *Black, White or Mixed Race?* London: Routledge.

Tolley, K. (2003) *The Science Education of American Girls*. New York: RoutledgeFalmer.

Trenchard, L. and Warren, H. (1984) *Something to Tell You*. London: Gay Teenagers Project.

Troyna, B. (1984) Fact or artefact? The 'educational underachievement' of black pupils, *British Journal of Sociology of Education*, 5(2): 153–66.

Tsolidis, G. and Dobson, I. (2006) Single-sex schooling: Is it simply a 'class act'?, *Gender and Education*, 18(1): 213–28.

Turnbull, A. M. (1980) Women in the making. South Bank Sociology Occasional Paper No. 2.

Turnbull, A., Pollock, J. and Bruley, S. (1983) History, in J. Whyld (ed.) *Sexism in the Secondary Curriculum*. London: Harper and Row.

Unterhalter, E. (2007) *Gender, Schooling and Global Social Justice*. Abingdon: Routledge.

Vogt, F. (2002) A caring teacher: Explorations into primary school teachers' professional identity and ethic of care, *Gender and Education*, 14(3): 251–64.

Volman, M. and Ten Dam, G. (1998) Equal but different: Contradictions in the development of gender identity, *British Journal of Sociology of Education*, 19: 529–45.

Walden, R. and Walkerdine, V. (1985) *Girls and Mathematics*, Bedford Way Papers, 24. London: University of London, Institute of Education.

Walford, G. (1980) 'Sex bias in physics textbooks', *School Science Review*, 1(62): 224–5.

Walker, J. (1988) *Louts and Legends*. Sydney: Allen and Unwin.

Walkerdine, V. (1983) It's only natural: rethinking child-centred pedagogy, in: A.M. Wolpe and J. Donald (eds.) *Is there anyone here from education?* Pluto: London.

Walkerdine, V. (1984) Dreams for an Ordinary Childhood, in E. Heron (ed.) *Truth, Dare or Promise*. London: Virago.

Walkerdine, V. (1988) *The Mastery of Reason*. Cambridge: Routledge and Kegan Paul.

Walkerdine, V. (1989) *Counting Girls Out*. London: Virago.

Walkerdine, V. (1990) *Schoolgirl Fictions*. London: Verso.

Walkerdine, V. (1997) *Daddy's Girl*. Basingstoke: Macmillan Press.

Walkerdine, V. (2003) Reclassifying upward mobility: femininity and the neoliberal subject, *Gender and Education* 15(3): 237–47.

Walkerdine, V. and Lucey, H. (1989) *Democracy in the Kitchen: Regulating Mothers and Socialising Daughters*. London: Virago.

Walkerdine, V. and Ringrose, J. (2006) Reclassifying upward mobility and the neo-liberal subject, in C. Skelton, B. Francis and L. Smulyan (eds) *The Sage Handbook of Gender and Education*. London and New York: Sage.

Walkerdine, V., Lucey, H. and Melody, H. (2001) *Growing Up Girl. Psychosocial Explorations of Gender and Class*. London: Palgrave.

Wallace, C. (1987) From girls and boys to women and men: The social reproduction of gender, in M. Arnot and G. Weiner (eds) *Gender and the Politics of Schooling*. London: Unwin Hyman with the Open University.

Wallace, M. (1995) 'Anger in Isolation: a Black feminist's search for sisterhood', in B. Guy-Sheftall (ed.) *Words of Fire: An anthology of African-American Feminist Thought*. New York, New Press.

Walter, N. (1999) *The New Feminism*. London: Virago.

Ward, J. V. and Robinson-Wood, T. L. (2006) Room at the table: Racial and gendered realities in the schooling of black children, in C. Skelton, B. Francis and L. Smulyan (eds) *The Sage Handbook of Gender and Education*. London: Sage.

Ware, V. (1992) *Beyond the Pale*. London: Verso.

Warin, J. (2006) Heavy-metal Humpty Dumpty: Dissonant masculinities within the context of the nursery, *Gender and Education*, 18(5): 523–37.

Warren, S. (1997) Who do these boys think they are?: An investigation into the construction of masculinities in a primary classroom, *International Journal of Inclusive Education*, 1(2): 207–22.

Warrington, M. and Younger, M. (2000) The other side of the gender gap, *Gender and Education*, 12: 493–507.

Warrington, M. and Younger, M. (2003) 'We Decided To Give It a Twirl': single-sex teaching in English Comprehensive Schools, *Gender and Education*, 15(4): 339–50.

Warrington, M., Younger, M. and Williams, J. (2000) Student attitudes, image and the gender gap, *British Educational Research Journal*, 26: 393–407.

Warrington, M., Younger, M. and Bearne, E. (2006) *Raising Boys' Achievement in Primary Schools: Towards a Holistic Approach*. Maidenhead: Open University Press/ McGraw-Hill.

Weaver-Hightower, M. (2003) Crossing the divide: Bridging the disjunctures between theoretically oriented and practice-oriented literature about masculinity and boys at school, *Gender and Education*, 15: 407–23.

Weedon, C. (1987) *Feminist Practice and Poststructuralist Theory*. Oxford: Blackwell.

Weiler, K. (1988) *Women Teaching for Change: Gender, Class and Power*. Westport, CT: Bergin and Garvey.

Weiner, G. (1985) *Just a Bunch of Girls*. Milton Keynes: Open University Press.

Weiner, G. (1994) *Feminisms in Education*. Buckingham: Open University Press.

Weiner, G. (2006) Out of the ruins: Feminist pedagogy in recovery, in C. Skelton, B. Francis and L. Smulyan (eds) *The Sage Handbook of Gender and Education*. London: Sage.

Weiner, G. and Arnot, M. (1987) Teachers and gender politics, in M. Arnot and G. Weiner (eds) *Gender and the Politics of Schooling*. London: Unwin Hyman.

Weis, L. (1989) The 1980s: De-industrialization and change in white working-class male and female youth cultural forms, in S. Walker and L. Barton (eds) *Politics and the Processes of Schooling*. Milton Keynes: Open University Press.

Werbner, P. and Modood, T. (eds.) (1997) *Debating Cultural Hybridity*. London: Zed.

Wheeler, E. A. (2007) Black feminism, womanism, and standpoint theories, in E. Banks (ed.) *Gender and Education: An Encylopaedia*. Westport: Praeger.

Whelehan, I. (1995) *Modern Feminist Thought*. Edinburgh: Edinburgh University Press.

Whitbread, A. (1980) Female teachers are women first: Sexual harassment at work, in D. Spender and E. Sarah (eds) *Learning to Lose*. London: The Women's Press.

Whitehead, K. (2007) The teaching family, the state, and new women in nineteenth-century Australia, in K. Tolley (ed.) *Transformations in Schooling*. New York: Palgrave Macmillan.

Whitehead, S. (2002) *Men and Masculinities*. Cambridge: Polity.

Whyld, J. (ed.) (1983) *Sexism in the Secondary Curriculum*. London: Harper and Row.

Whyte, J. (1983) *Beyond the Wendy House: Sex Role Stereotyping in Primary Schools.* York: Longman Press for Schools Council.

Whyte, J., Deem, R., Kant, L. and Cruickshank, M. (eds) (1985) *Girl Friendly Schooling.* London: Methuen.

Wickham, A. (1986) *Women and Training.* Milton Keynes: Open University Press.

Widdowson, F. (1983) *Going Up into the Next Class.* London: Hutchinson.

Wikeley, F. and Stables, A. (1999) Changes in school students' approaches to subject option choices: A study of pupils in the west of England in 1984 and 1996. *Educational Research*, 41: 287–99.

Wilkinson, S. and Mulgan, G. (1995) *Freedom's Children: Work, Relationships and Politics for 18–34-year-olds in Britain Today.* London: Demos.

Williams, J. (1987) The construction of women and black students as educational problems: Re-evaluating policy on gender and 'race', in M. Arnot and G. Weiner (eds) *Gender and the Politics of Schooling.* London: Unwin Hyman.

Willis, P. (1977) *Learning to Labour.* Aldershot: Saxon House.

Wilmott, P. (1969) *Adolescent Boys in the East End of London.* London: Harmondsworth.

Wilson, A. (1978) *Finding a Voice.* London: Virago.

Wilson, M. and Daly, M. (1998) Sexual rivalry and sexual conflict: Recurring themes in fatal conflicts, *Theoretical Criminology*, 2(3): 291–311.

Windass, A. (1989) Classroom Practices and Organisation, in C. Skelton (ed) *Whatever Happens to Little Women.* Milton Keynes: Open University Press.

Wing, A. (1997) How can children be taught to read differently? *Bill's New Frock* and the hidden curriculum, *Gender and Education*, 9(4): 491–504.

Wise, S. and Stanley, L. (1987) *Georgie Porgie: Sexual Harassment in Everyday Life.* London: Pandora.

Wollstonecraft, M. (1972) *Vindication of the Rights of Women* (republished, 1985, London: Penguin).

Wolpe, A. M. (1977) *Some Processes in Sexist Education.* London: Women's Research and Resources Centre.

Wolpe, A. M. (1988) *Within School Walls.* London: Routledge and Kegan Paul.

Wood, J. (1987) Groping towards sexism: Boys' sex talk, in M. Arnot, and G. Weiner (eds) *Gender Under Scrutiny.* London: Hutchinson.

Woods, P. (1987) Managing the primary teacher's role, in S. Delamont (ed.) *The Primary School Teacher.* Lewes: Falmer.

Wright, C., Weekes, D. and McGlaughlin, A. (2000) *'Race', Class and Gender in Exclusion from School.* London: Falmer.

Wright, C. (1987) The relations between teachers and Afro-Caribbean pupils: Observing multiracial classrooms, in G. Weiner and M. Arnot (eds) *Gender Under Scrutiny.* London: Hutchinson.

Wright, N. (1977) *Progress in Education.* London: Croom Helm.

Wynn, B. (1983) Home Economics, in J. Whyld (ed) Sexism and the Secondary Curriculum. London: Harper & Row.

Yates, L. (1987) Australian research on girls and schooling 1975–1985, in J. P. Keeves (ed.) *Australian Education: Review of Recent Research.* Sydney: Allen and Unwin.

Yeoman, E. (1999) 'How does it get into my imagination?' Elementary school children's inter-textual knowledge and gendered storylines, *Gender and Education*, 11(4): 427–40.

Youdell, D. (2003) 'Identity traps or how black students fail: The interactions between biographical, sub-cultural, and learner identities', *British Journal of Sociology of Education*, 24(1): 3–18.

Youdell, D. (2005) Sex-gender-sexuality: How sex, gender and sexuality constellations are constituted in secondary schools, *Gender and Education*, 17(3): 249–70.

Youdell, D. (2006) *Impossible Bodies, Impossible Selves*. Dordrecht: Springer.

Youdell, D. (2008) Intersections, constellations and subjectivations: Making sense of the intelligible and unintelligible subjects of schooling. Paper presented at the International Sociology of Education Conference, London, 3–5/1/08.

Younger, M. (2007) The gender agenda in secondary ITET in England: Forgotten, misconceived or what?, *Gender and Education*, 19(3): 387–414.

Younger, M. and Warrington, M. (1996) Differential achievement of boys and girls at GCSE: Some observations from the perspective of one school, *British Journal of Sociology of Education*, 17(3): 299–313.

Younger, M., Warrington, M. and Williams, J. (1999) The gender gap and classroom interactions: Reality and rhetoric? *British Journal of Sociology of Education*, 20(3): 352–42.

Younger, M., Warrington, M. and McLellan, R. (2005) *Raising Boys' Achievements in Secondary Schools: Issues, Dilemmas and Opportunities*. Maidenhead: Open University Press/McGraw-Hill.

Index

Tables in *italics*